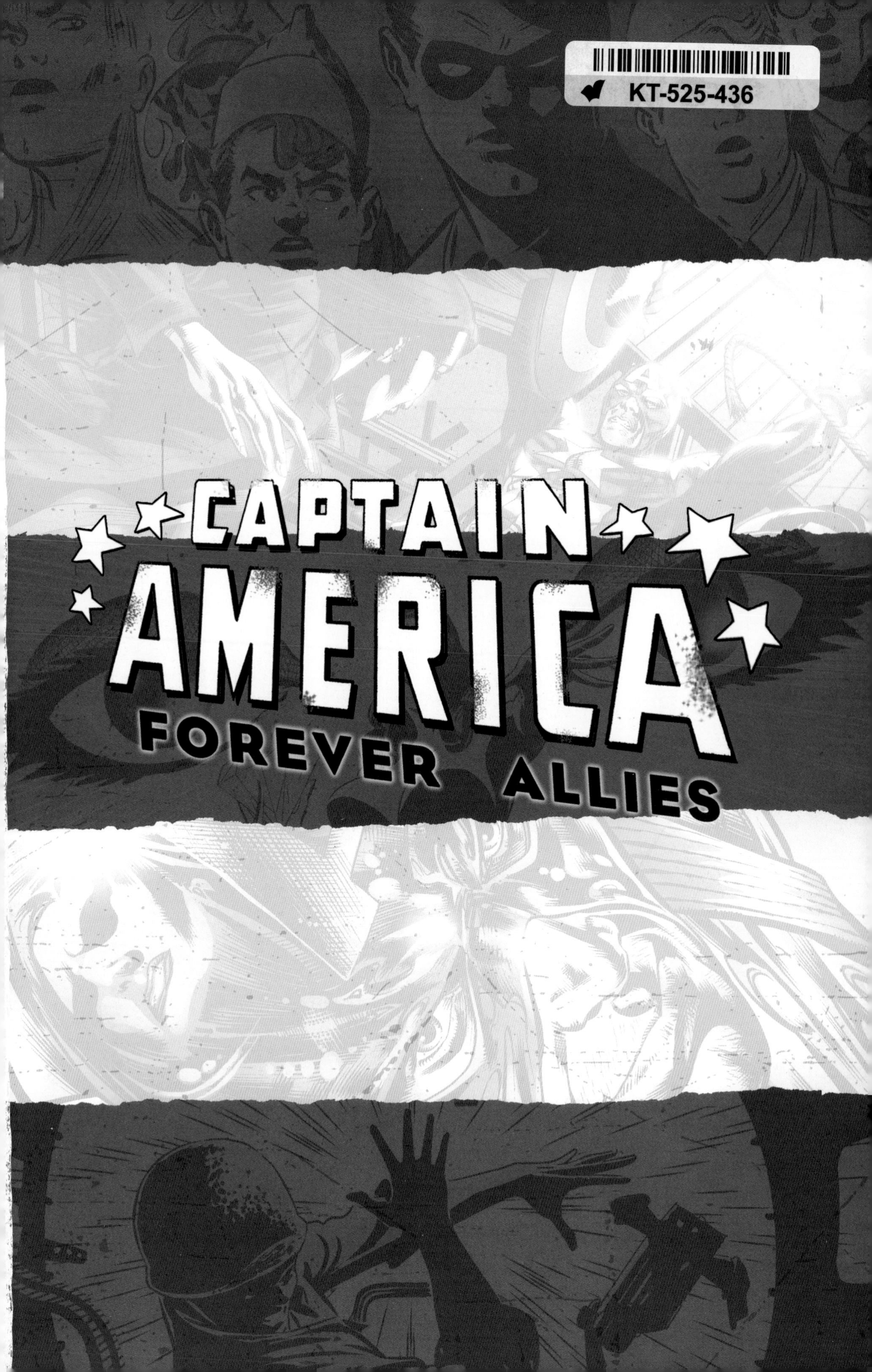
CAPTAIN
AMERICA
FOREVER ALLIES

CAPTAIN ★ AMERICA

FOREVER ALLIES

CAPTAIN AMERICA: FOREVER ALLIES. Contains material originally published in magazine form as CAPTAIN AMERICA: FOREVER ALLIES #1-4, YOUNG ALLIES COMICS 70TH ANNIVERSARY SPECIAL #1 and YOUNG ALLIES #1. First printing 2011. ISBN# 978-0-7851-5324-5. Published by MARVEL WORLDWIDE, INC., a subsidiary of MARVEL ENTERTAINMENT, LLC. OFFICE OF PUBLICATION: 135 West 50th Street, New York, NY 10020.
Copyright © 1941, 2009, 2010 and 2011 Marvel Characters, Inc. All rights reserved. $24.99 per copy in the U.S. and $27.99 in Canada (GST #R127032852); Canadian Agreement #40668537. All characters featured
in this issue and the distinctive names and likenesses thereof, and all related indicia are trademarks of Marvel Characters, Inc. No similarity between any of the names, characters, persons, and/or institutions in this
magazine with those of any living or dead person or institution is intended, and any such similarity which may exist is purely coincidental. **Printed in the U.S.A.** ALAN FINE, EVP - Office of the President, Marvel Worldwide,
Inc. and EVP & CMO Marvel Characters B.V.; DAN BUCKLEY, Publisher & President - Print, Animation & Digital Divisions; JOE QUESADA, Chief Creative Officer; JIM SOKOLOWSKI, Chief Operating Officer; DAVID BOGART,
SVP of Business Affairs & Talent Management; TOM BREVOORT, SVP of Publishing; C.B. CEBULSKI, SVP of Creator & Content Development; DAVID GABRIEL, SVP of Publishing Sales & Circulation; MICHAEL PASCIULLO,
SVP of Brand Planning & Communications; JIM O'KEEFE, VP of Operations & Logistics; DAN CARR, Executive Director of Publishing Technology; JUSTIN F. GABRIE, Director of Publishing & Editorial Operations; SUSAN
CRESPI, Editorial Operations Manager; ALEX MORALES, Publishing Operations Manager; STAN LEE, Chairman Emeritus. For information regarding advertising in Marvel Comics or on Marvel.com, please contact Ron
Stern, VP of Business Development, at rstern@marvel.com. For Marvel subscription inquiries please call 800-217-9158. **Manufactured between 3/21/2011 and 4/18/2011 by R.R. DONNELLEY INC., SALEM, VA, USA.**

YOUNG ALLIES COMICS 70TH ANNIVERSARY SPECIAL #1

WRITER: **ROGER STERN**
ARTIST: **PAOLO RIVERA**
LETTERS: **JARED K. FLETCHER**
COVER ART: **PAOLO RIVERA**
EDITOR: **THOMAS BRENNAN**
CONSULTING EDITOR: **STEPHEN WACKER**
EXECUTIVE EDITOR: **TOM BREVOORT**

CAPTAIN AMERICA: FOREVER ALLIES

WRITER: **ROGER STERN**
ART, 1940S: **NICK DRAGOTTA** WITH BRAD SIMPSON
PENCILS, PRESENT: **MARCO SANTUCCI**
INKS, PRESENT: **MARCO SANTUCCI & PATRICK PIAZZALUNGA**
COLORS, PRESENT: **CHRIS SOTOMAYOR** WITH ANDREW CROSSLEY
LETTERS: **JARED K. FLETCHER**
COVER ART: **LEE WEEKS** WITH MATT HOLLINGSWORTH & DEAN WHITE
EDITOR: **THOMAS BRENNAN**

YOUNG ALLIES #1 [SUMMER 1941]

SCRIPT: **OTTO BINDER**
CHAPTER 1 PENCILS: **CHARLES NICHOLAS WOJTKOWSKI**
CHAPTER 2 TITLE PAGE ART: **JOE SIMON & JACK KIRBY**
CHAPTER 2 PENCILS: **CHARLES NICHOLAS WOJTKOWSKI**
CHAPTER 3 TITLE PAGE ART: **JOE SIMON & JACK KIRBY**
CHAPTER 3 PENCILS: **CHARLES NICHOLAS WOJTKOWSKI**
CHAPTER 4 TITLE PAGE ART: **ERNIE HART**
CHAPTER 4 PENCILS: **CHARLES NICHOLAS WOJTKOWSKI**

CHAPTER 5 TITLE PAGE ART: **JOE SIMON & JACK KIRBY**
CHAPTER 5 PENCILS: **UNKNOWN**
CHAPTER 6 TITLE PAGE ART: **JOE SIMON & JACK KIRBY**
CHAPTER 6 PENCILS: **CHARLES NICHOLAS WOJTKOWSKI & UNKNOWN**
"CROOKS ARE COWARDS" SCRIPT: **UNKNOWN**
"UNSOLVED MYSTERIES" SCRIPT: **STAN LEE**
"UNSOLVED MYSTERIES" ART: **UNKNOWN**

CAPTAIN AMERICA CREATED BY **JOE SIMON & JACK KIRBY**

COLLECTION EDITOR: JENNIFER GRÜNWALD • EDITORIAL ASSISTANTS: JAMES EMMETT & JOE HOCHSTEIN • ASSISTANT EDITORS: ALEX STARBUCK & NELSON RIBEIRO
EDITOR, SPECIAL PROJECTS: MARK D. BEAZLEY • SENIOR EDITOR, SPECIAL PROJECTS: JEFF YOUNGQUIST • SENIOR VICE PRESIDENT OF SALES: DAVID GABRIEL
BOOK DESIGN: JEFF POWELL • EDITOR IN CHIEF: AXEL ALONSO • CHIEF CREATIVE OFFICER: JOE QUESADA • PUBLISHER: DAN BUCKLEY • EXECUTIVE PRODUCER: ALAN FINE

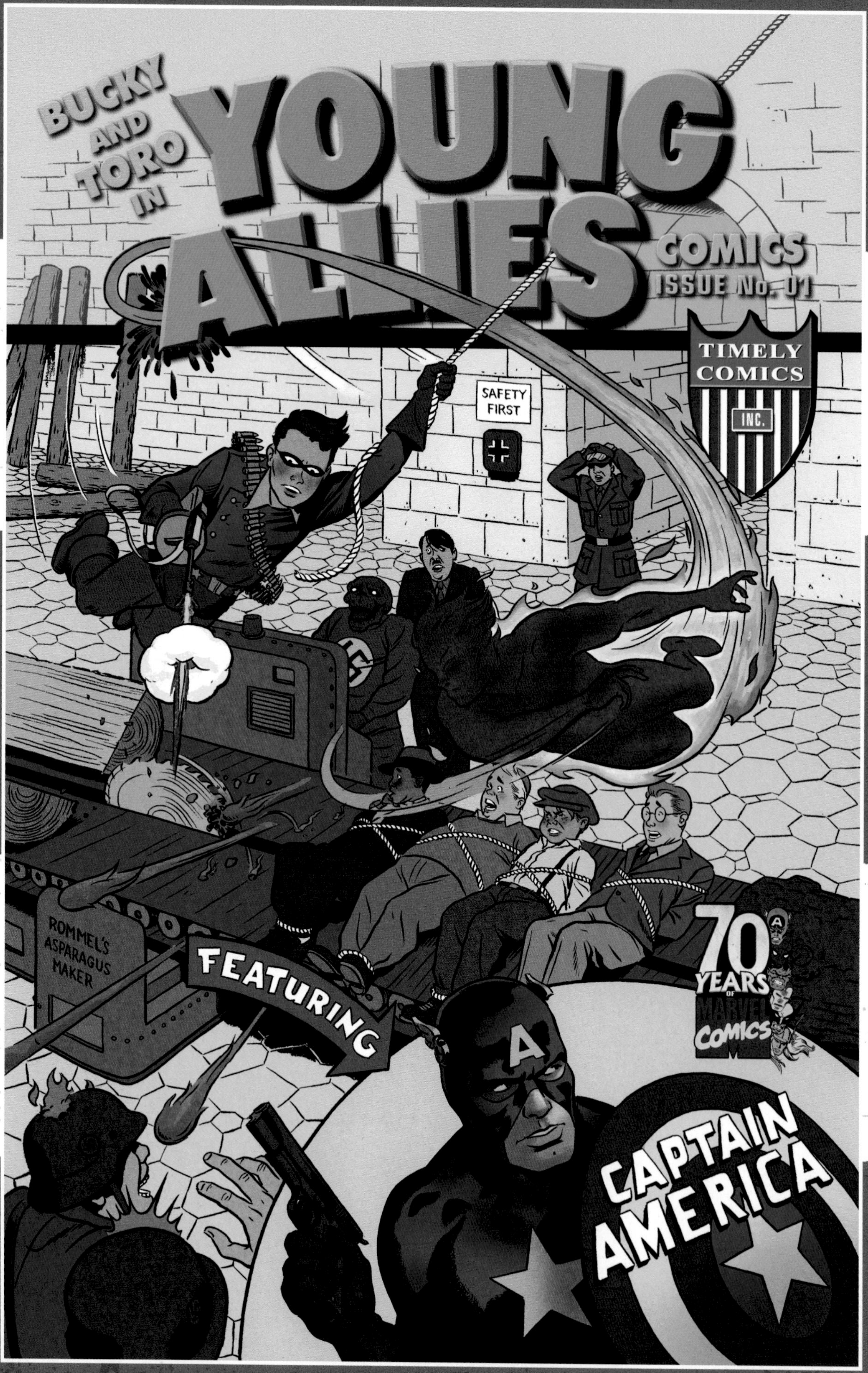
BUCKY AND TORO IN
YOUNG ALLIES
COMICS
ISSUE No. 01
TIMELY COMICS
INC.
SAFETY FIRST
ROMMEL'S ASPARAGUS MAKER
FEATURING
70 YEARS OF MARVEL COMICS
CAPTAIN AMERICA

YOUNG ALLIES COMICS 70TH ANNIVERSARY SPECIAL #1

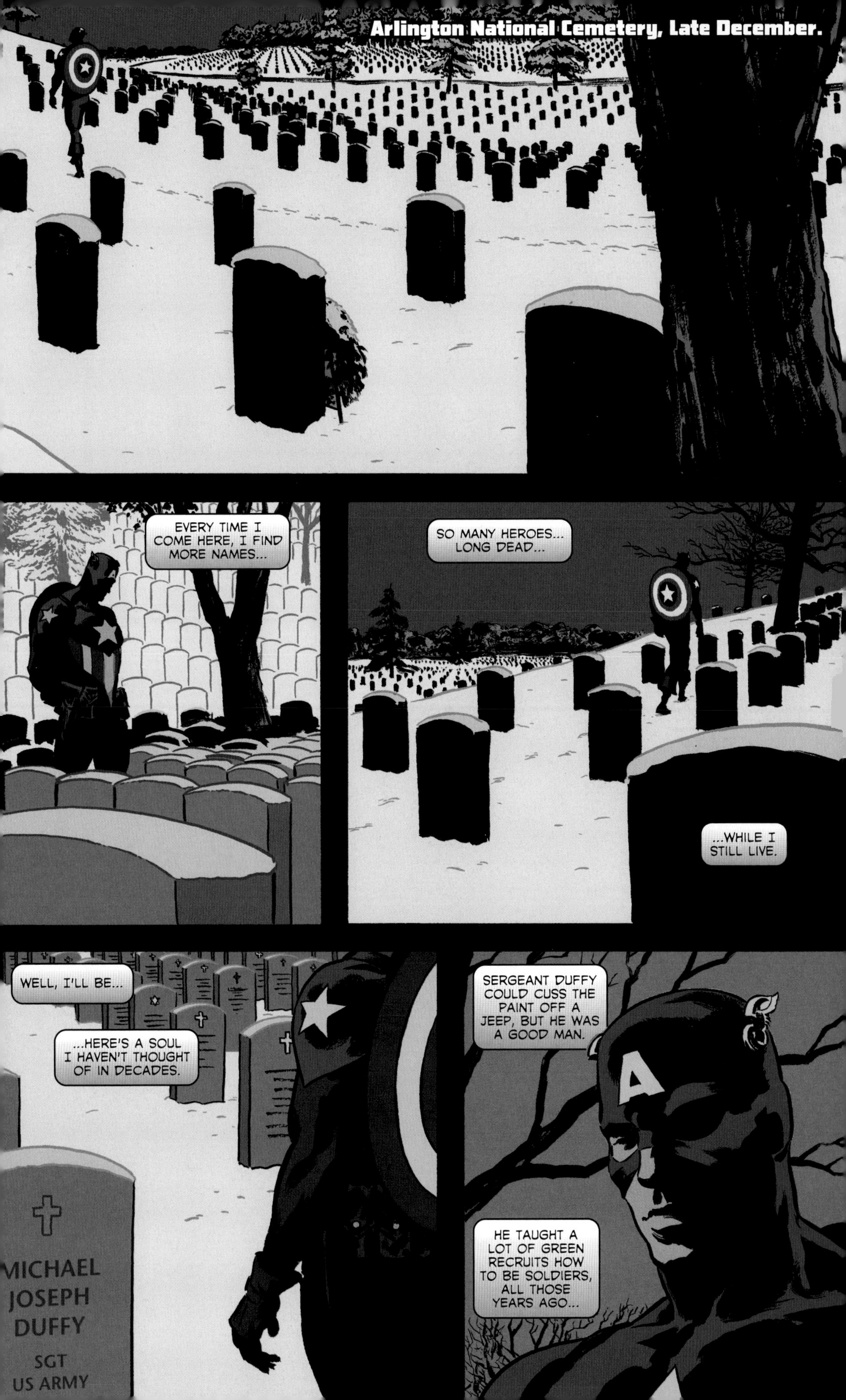
Arlington National Cemetery, Late December.
EVERY TIME I COME HERE, I FIND MORE NAMES...
SO MANY HEROES... LONG DEAD...
...WHILE I STILL LIVE.
WELL, I'LL BE...
...HERE'S A SOUL I HAVEN'T THOUGHT OF IN DECADES.
MICHAEL JOSEPH DUFFY SGT US ARMY
SERGEANT DUFFY COULD CUSS THE PAINT OFF A JEEP, BUT HE WAS A GOOD MAN.
HE TAUGHT A LOT OF GREEN RECRUITS HOW TO BE SOLDIERS, ALL THOSE YEARS AGO...

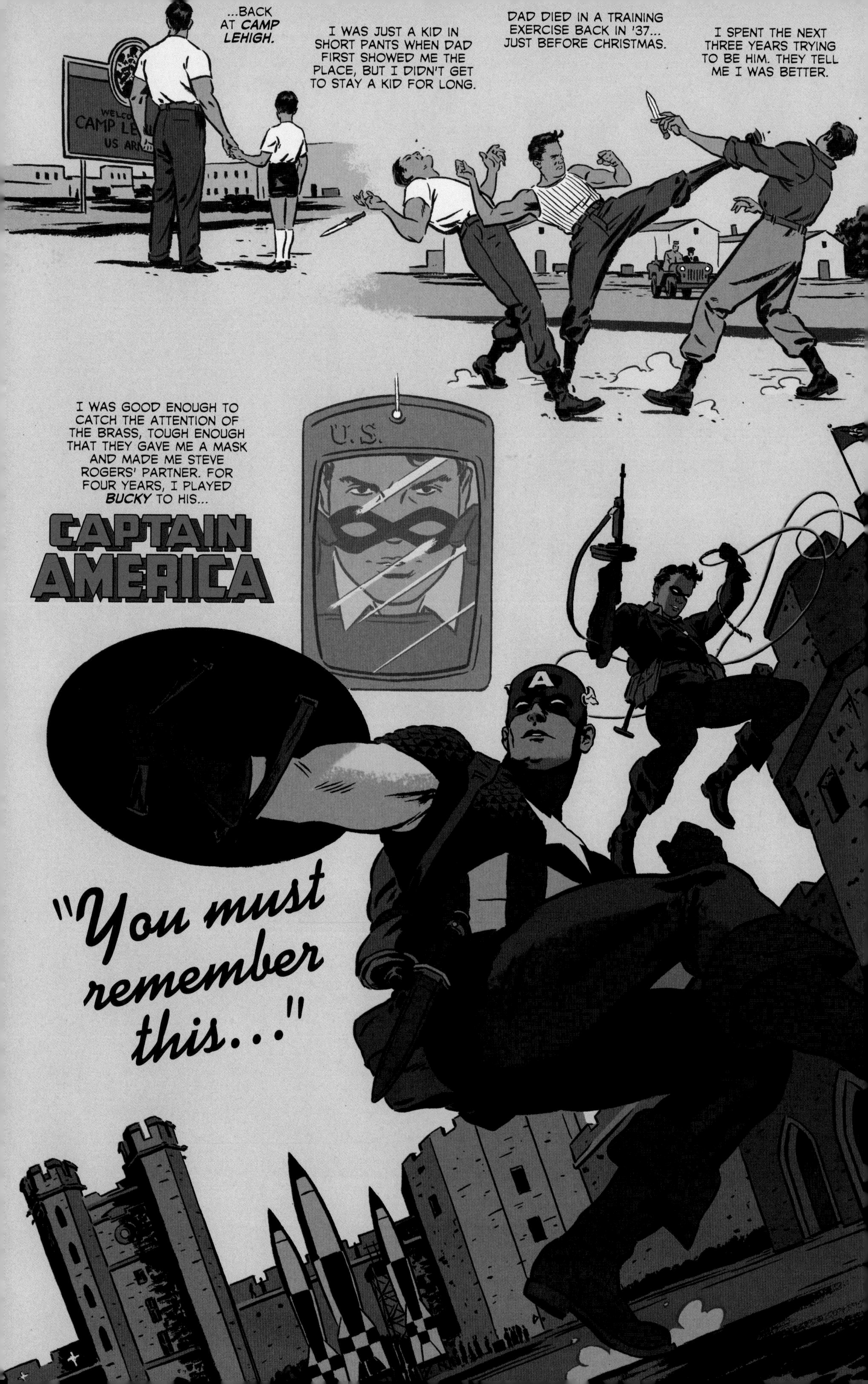

...BACK AT CAMP LEHIGH.
I WAS JUST A KID IN SHORT PANTS WHEN DAD FIRST SHOWED ME THE PLACE, BUT I DIDN'T GET TO STAY A KID FOR LONG.
DAD DIED IN A TRAINING EXERCISE BACK IN '37... JUST BEFORE CHRISTMAS.
I SPENT THE NEXT THREE YEARS TRYING TO BE HIM. THEY TELL ME I WAS BETTER.
I WAS GOOD ENOUGH TO CATCH THE ATTENTION OF THE BRASS, TOUGH ENOUGH THAT THEY GAVE ME A MASK AND MADE ME STEVE ROGERS' PARTNER. FOR FOUR YEARS, I PLAYED BUCKY TO HIS...
CAPTAIN AMERICA
U.S.
"You must remember this..."

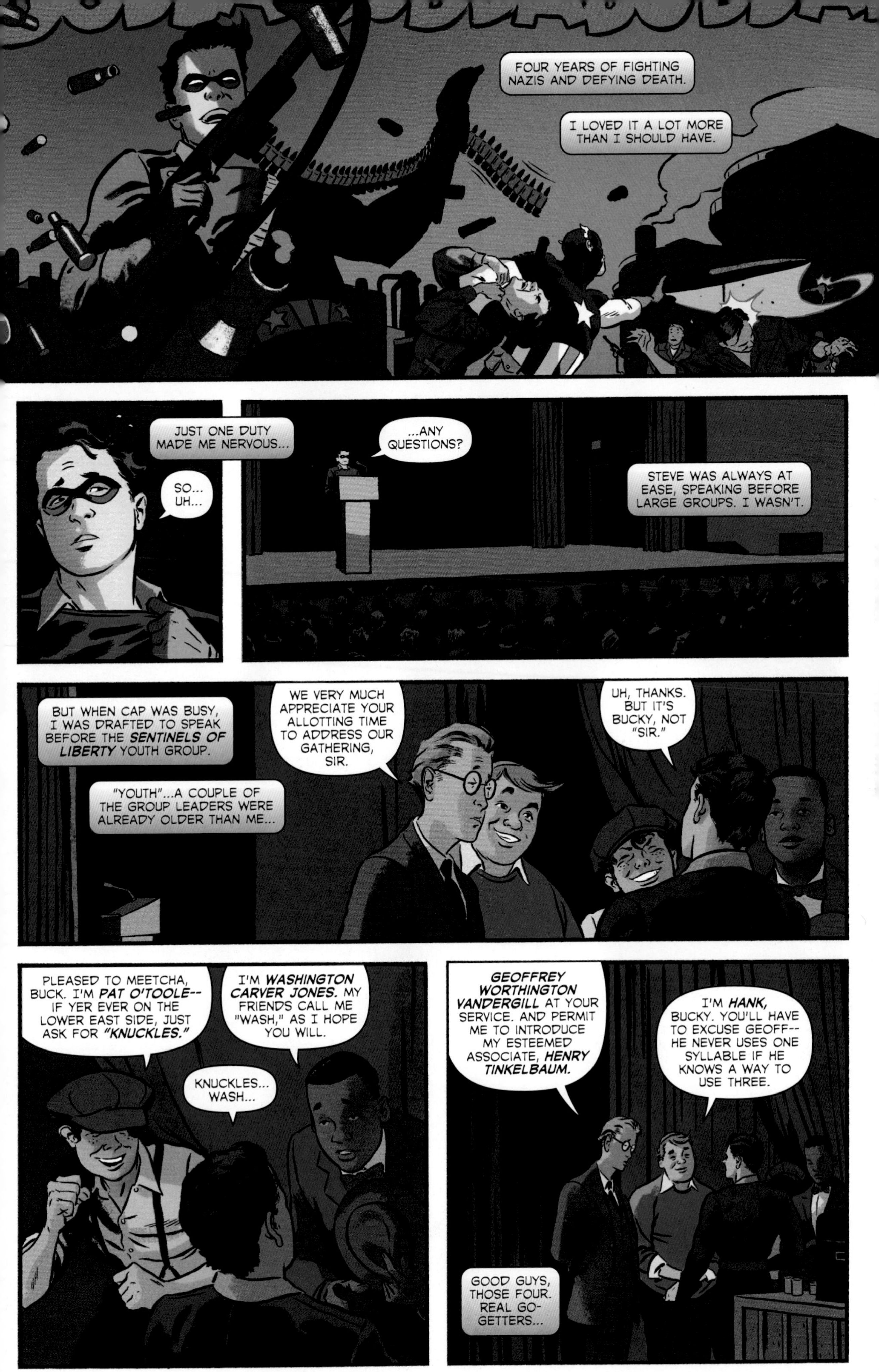
FOUR YEARS OF FIGHTING NAZIS AND DEFYING DEATH.
I LOVED IT A LOT MORE THAN I SHOULD HAVE.
JUST ONE DUTY MADE ME NERVOUS...
SO... UH...
...ANY QUESTIONS?
STEVE WAS ALWAYS AT EASE, SPEAKING BEFORE LARGE GROUPS. I WASN'T.
BUT WHEN CAP WAS BUSY, I WAS DRAFTED TO SPEAK BEFORE THE SENTINELS OF LIBERTY YOUTH GROUP.
"YOUTH"...A COUPLE OF THE GROUP LEADERS WERE ALREADY OLDER THAN ME...
WE VERY MUCH APPRECIATE YOUR ALLOTTING TIME TO ADDRESS OUR GATHERING, SIR.
UH, THANKS. BUT IT'S BUCKY, NOT "SIR."
PLEASED TO MEETCHA, BUCK. I'M PAT O'TOOLE-- IF YER EVER ON THE LOWER EAST SIDE, JUST ASK FOR "KNUCKLES."
I'M WASHINGTON CARVER JONES. MY FRIENDS CALL ME "WASH," AS I HOPE YOU WILL.
KNUCKLES... WASH...
GEOFFREY WORTHINGTON VANDERGILL AT YOUR SERVICE. AND PERMIT ME TO INTRODUCE MY ESTEEMED ASSOCIATE, HENRY TINKELBAUM.
I'M HANK, BUCKY. YOU'LL HAVE TO EXCUSE GEOFF-- HE NEVER USES ONE SYLLABLE IF HE KNOWS A WAY TO USE THREE.
GOOD GUYS, THOSE FOUR. REAL GO-GETTERS...

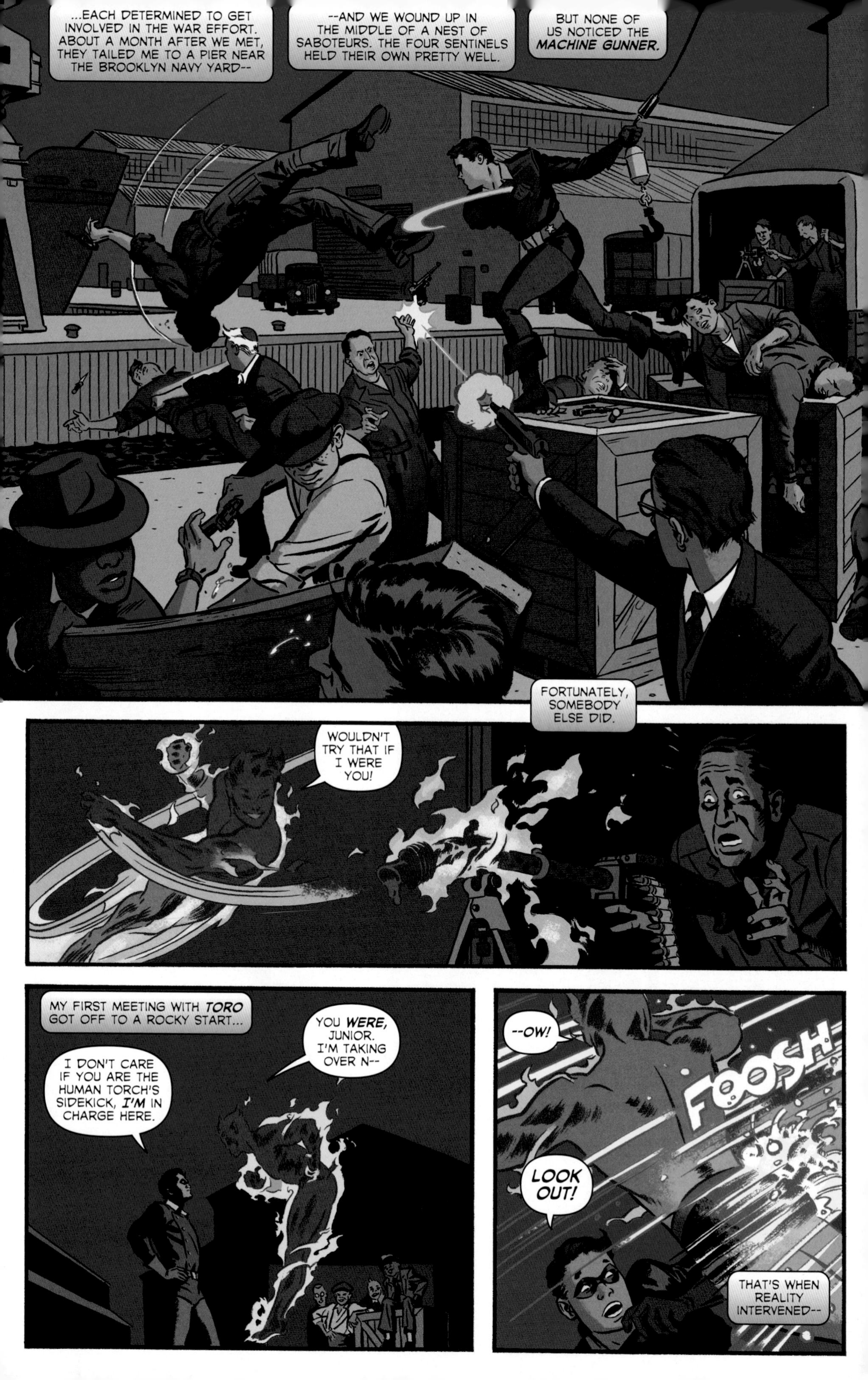
...EACH DETERMINED TO GET INVOLVED IN THE WAR EFFORT. ABOUT A MONTH AFTER WE MET, THEY TAILED ME TO A PIER NEAR THE BROOKLYN NAVY YARD--
--AND WE WOUND UP IN THE MIDDLE OF A NEST OF SABOTEURS. THE FOUR SENTINELS HELD THEIR OWN PRETTY WELL.
BUT NONE OF US NOTICED THE *MACHINE GUNNER.*
FORTUNATELY, SOMEBODY ELSE DID.
WOULDN'T TRY THAT IF I WERE YOU!
MY FIRST MEETING WITH *TORO* GOT OFF TO A ROCKY START...
I DON'T CARE IF YOU ARE THE HUMAN TORCH'S SIDEKICK, *I'M* IN CHARGE HERE.
YOU *WERE,* JUNIOR. I'M TAKING OVER N--
--OW!
FOOSH!
LOOK OUT!
THAT'S WHEN REALITY INTERVENED--

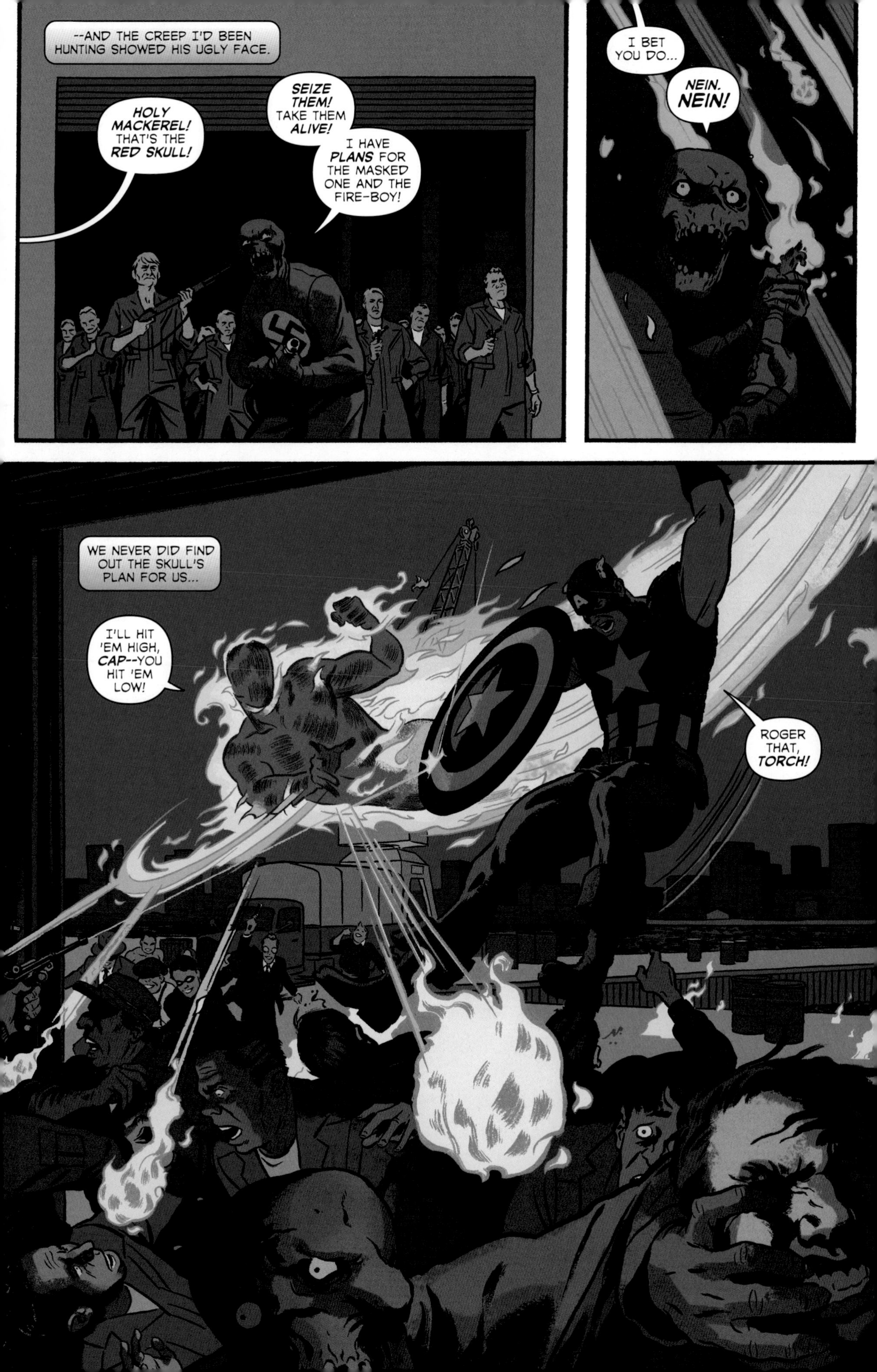
--AND THE CREEP I'D BEEN HUNTING SHOWED HIS UGLY FACE.
HOLY MACKEREL! THAT'S THE RED SKULL!
SEIZE THEM! TAKE THEM ALIVE!
I HAVE PLANS FOR THE MASKED ONE AND THE FIRE-BOY!
I BET YOU DO...
NEIN. NEIN!
WE NEVER DID FIND OUT THE SKULL'S PLAN FOR US...
I'LL HIT 'EM HIGH, CAP--YOU HIT 'EM LOW!
ROGER THAT, TORCH!

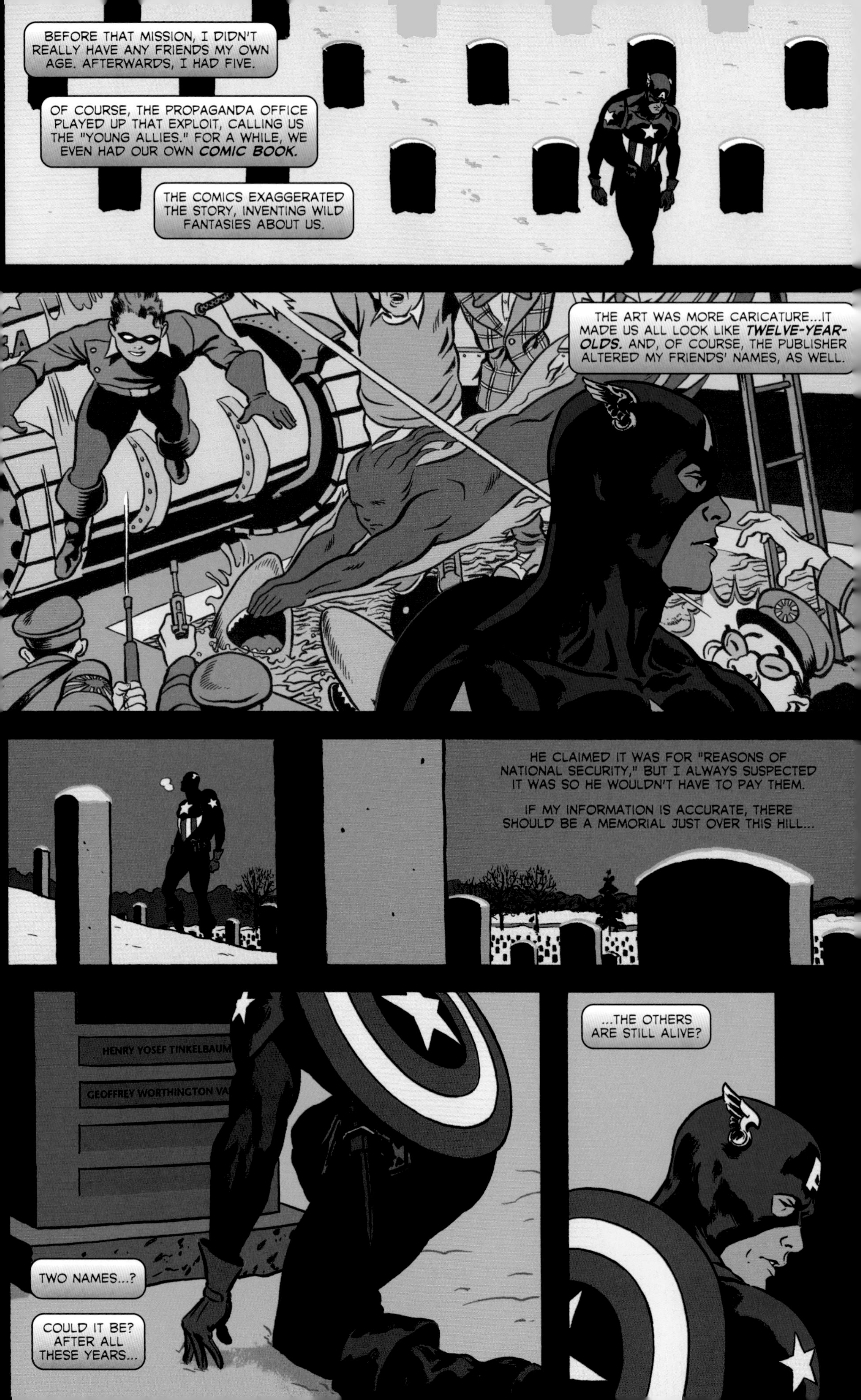
BEFORE THAT MISSION, I DIDN'T REALLY HAVE ANY FRIENDS MY OWN AGE. AFTERWARDS, I HAD FIVE.
OF COURSE, THE PROPAGANDA OFFICE PLAYED UP THAT EXPLOIT, CALLING US THE "YOUNG ALLIES." FOR A WHILE, WE EVEN HAD OUR OWN COMIC BOOK.
THE COMICS EXAGGERATED THE STORY, INVENTING WILD FANTASIES ABOUT US.
THE ART WAS MORE CARICATURE...IT MADE US ALL LOOK LIKE TWELVE-YEAR-OLDS. AND, OF COURSE, THE PUBLISHER ALTERED MY FRIENDS' NAMES, AS WELL.
HE CLAIMED IT WAS FOR "REASONS OF NATIONAL SECURITY," BUT I ALWAYS SUSPECTED IT WAS SO HE WOULDN'T HAVE TO PAY THEM.
IF MY INFORMATION IS ACCURATE, THERE SHOULD BE A MEMORIAL JUST OVER THIS HILL...
HENRY YOSEF TINKELBAUM
GEOFFREY WORTHINGTON VA
TWO NAMES...?
COULD IT BE? AFTER ALL THESE YEARS...
...THE OTHERS ARE STILL ALIVE?

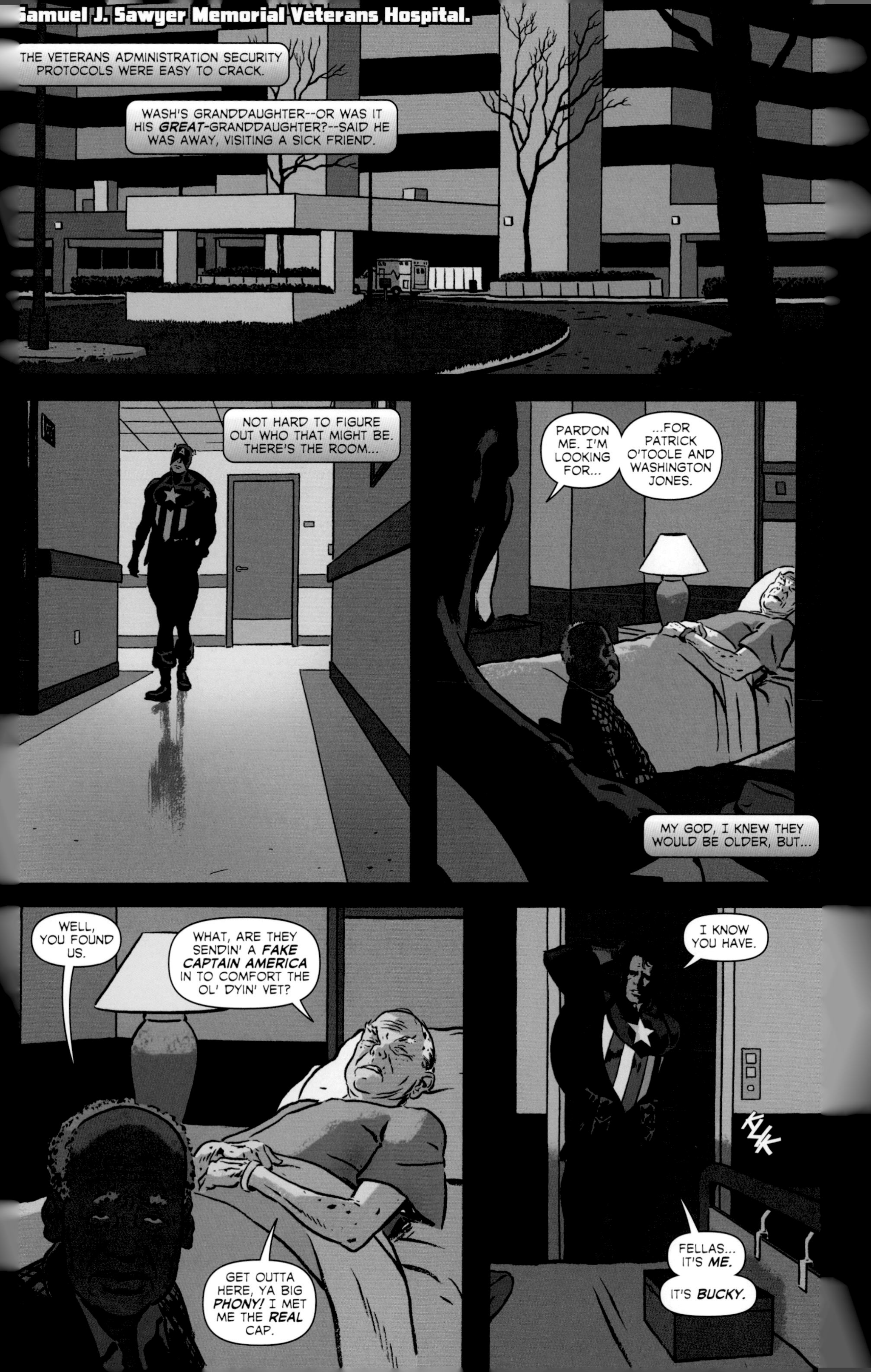
Samuel J. Sawyer Memorial Veterans Hospital.
THE VETERANS ADMINISTRATION SECURITY PROTOCOLS WERE EASY TO CRACK.
WASH'S GRANDDAUGHTER--OR WAS IT HIS GREAT-GRANDDAUGHTER?--SAID HE WAS AWAY, VISITING A SICK FRIEND.
NOT HARD TO FIGURE OUT WHO THAT MIGHT BE. THERE'S THE ROOM...
PARDON ME. I'M LOOKING FOR...
...FOR PATRICK O'TOOLE AND WASHINGTON JONES.
MY GOD, I KNEW THEY WOULD BE OLDER, BUT...
WELL, YOU FOUND US.
WHAT, ARE THEY SENDIN' A FAKE CAPTAIN AMERICA IN TO COMFORT THE OL' DYIN' VET?
GET OUTTA HERE, YA BIG PHONY! I MET ME THE REAL CAP.
I KNOW YOU HAVE.
KLIK
FELLAS... IT'S ME.
IT'S BUCKY.

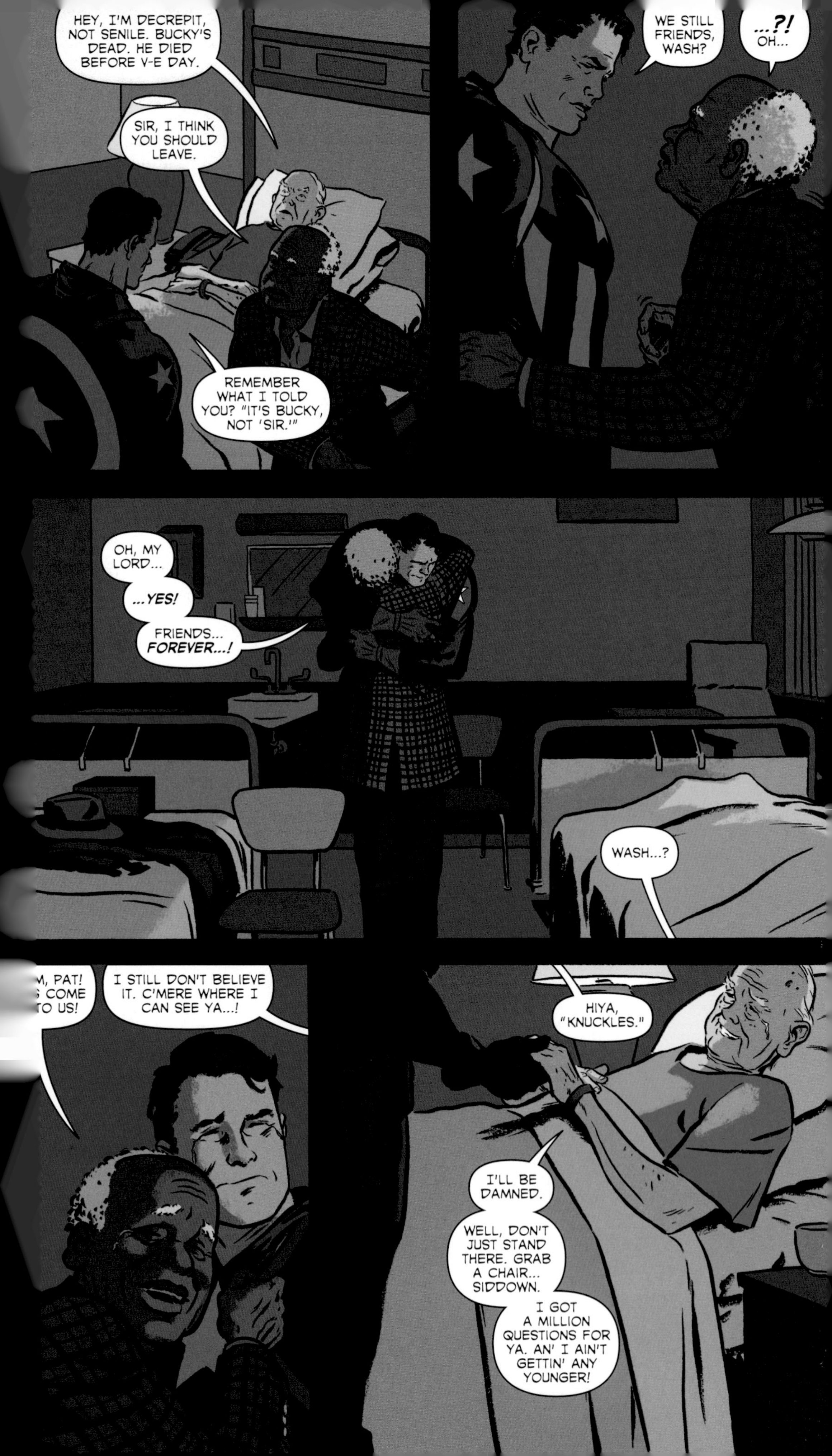
HEY, I'M DECREPIT, NOT SENILE. BUCKY'S DEAD. HE DIED BEFORE V-E DAY.
SIR, I THINK YOU SHOULD LEAVE.
REMEMBER WHAT I TOLD YOU? "IT'S BUCKY, NOT 'SIR.'"
WE STILL FRIENDS, WASH?
...?! OH...
OH, MY LORD...
...YES!
FRIENDS... FOREVER...!
WASH...?
M, PAT! S COME TO US!
I STILL DON'T BELIEVE IT. C'MERE WHERE I CAN SEE YA...!
HIYA, "KNUCKLES."
I'LL BE DAMNED.
WELL, DON'T JUST STAND THERE. GRAB A CHAIR... SIDDOWN.
I GOT A MILLION QUESTIONS FOR YA. AN' I AIN'T GETTIN' ANY YOUNGER!

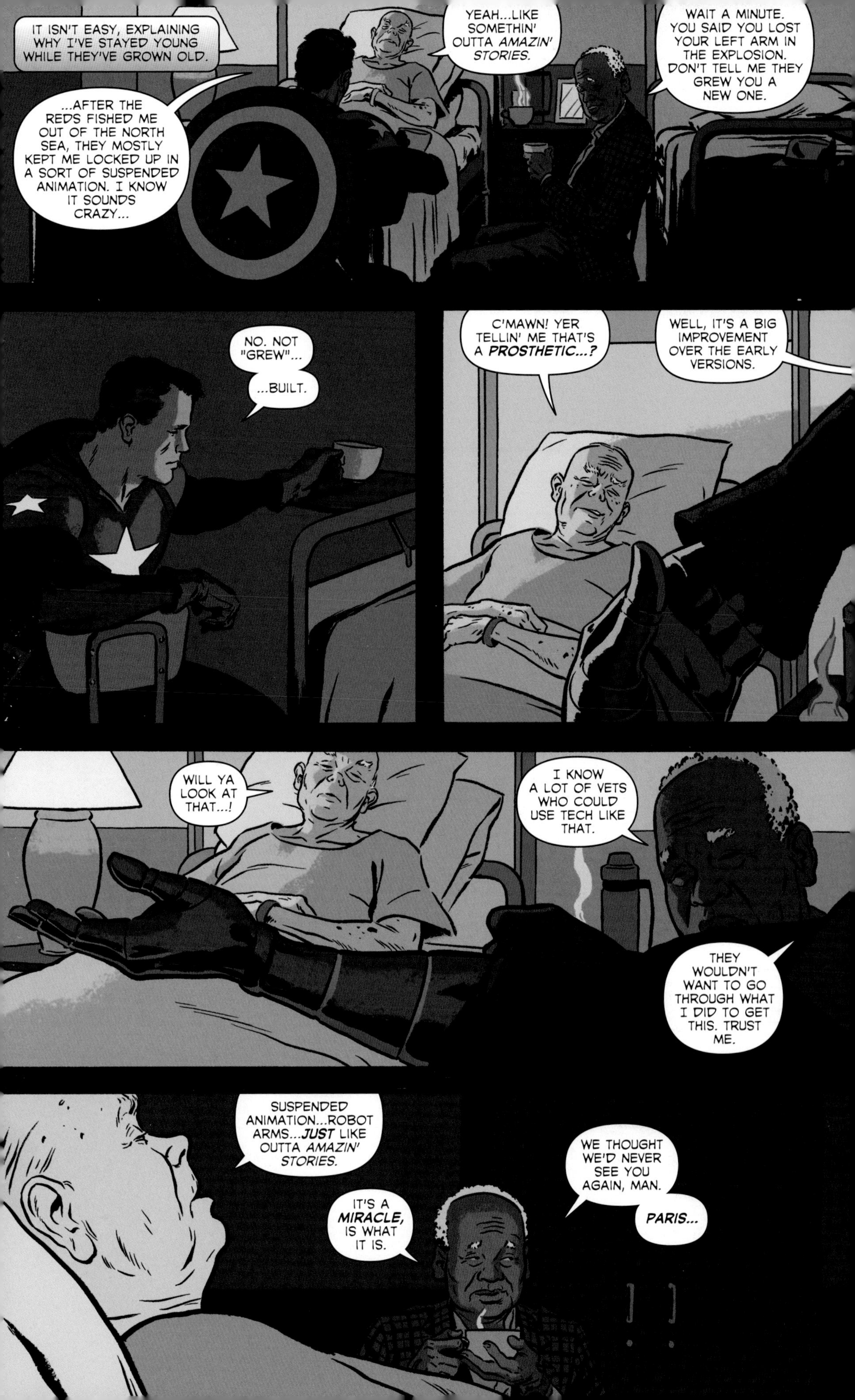
IT ISN'T EASY, EXPLAINING WHY I'VE STAYED YOUNG WHILE THEY'VE GROWN OLD.
...AFTER THE REDS FISHED ME OUT OF THE NORTH SEA, THEY MOSTLY KEPT ME LOCKED UP IN A SORT OF SUSPENDED ANIMATION. I KNOW IT SOUNDS CRAZY...
YEAH...LIKE SOMETHIN' OUTTA *AMAZIN' STORIES.*
WAIT A MINUTE. YOU SAID YOU LOST YOUR LEFT ARM IN THE EXPLOSION. DON'T TELL ME THEY GREW YOU A NEW ONE.
NO. NOT "GREW"...
...BUILT.
C'MAWN! YER TELLIN' ME THAT'S A ***PROSTHETIC...?***
WELL, IT'S A BIG IMPROVEMENT OVER THE EARLY VERSIONS.
WILL YA LOOK AT THAT...!
I KNOW A LOT OF VETS WHO COULD USE TECH LIKE THAT.
THEY WOULDN'T WANT TO GO THROUGH WHAT I DID TO GET THIS. TRUST ME.
SUSPENDED ANIMATION...ROBOT ARMS...***JUST*** LIKE OUTTA *AMAZIN' STORIES.*
IT'S A ***MIRACLE,*** IS WHAT IT IS.
WE THOUGHT WE'D NEVER SEE YOU AGAIN, MAN.
PARIS...

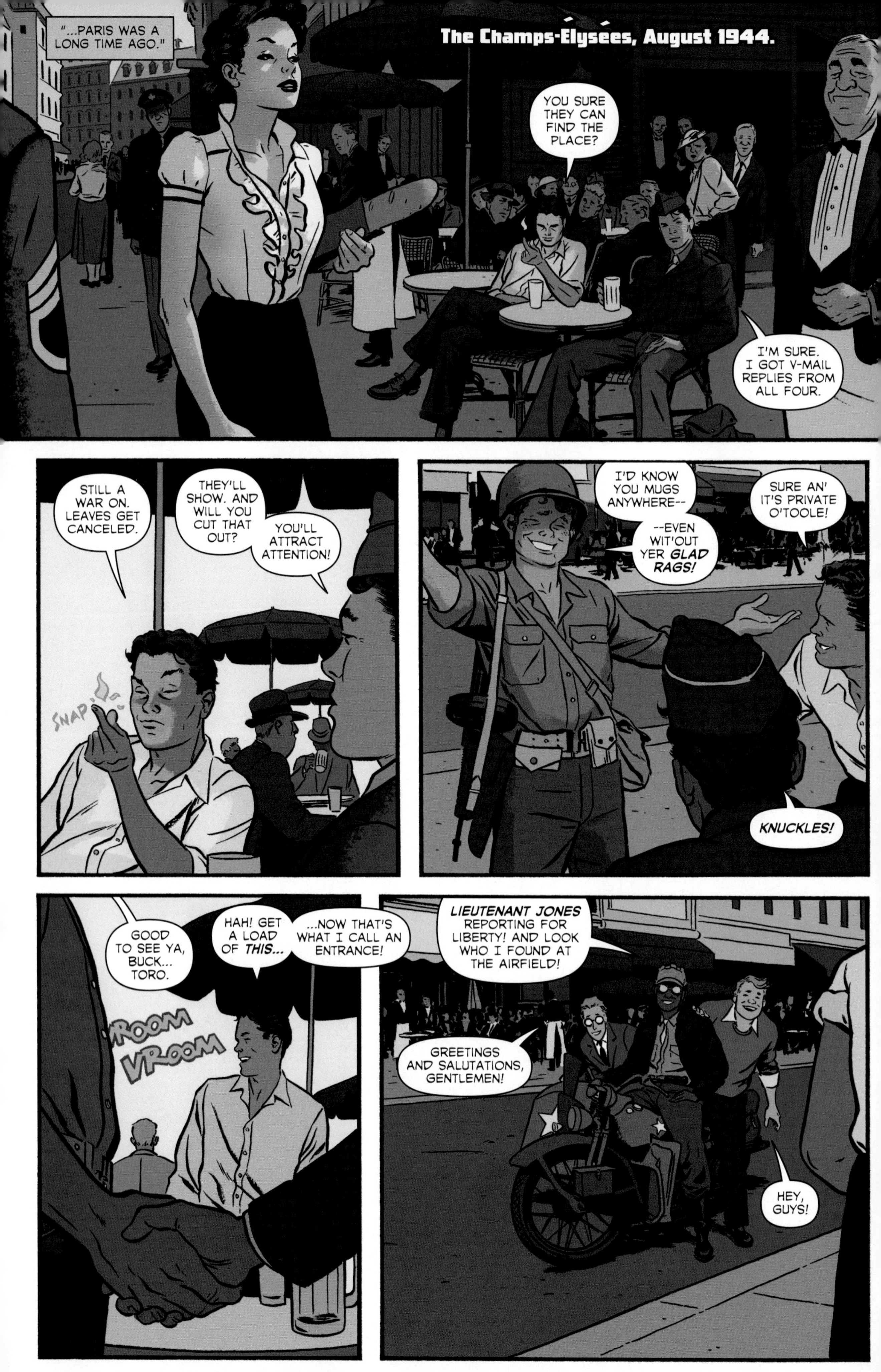
"...PARIS WAS A LONG TIME AGO."
The Champs-Elysées, August 1944.
YOU SURE THEY CAN FIND THE PLACE?
I'M SURE. I GOT V-MAIL REPLIES FROM ALL FOUR.
STILL A WAR ON. LEAVES GET CANCELED.
THEY'LL SHOW. AND WILL YOU CUT THAT OUT?
YOU'LL ATTRACT ATTENTION!
SNAP
I'D KNOW YOU MUGS ANYWHERE--
--EVEN WIT'OUT YER *GLAD RAGS!*
SURE AN' IT'S PRIVATE O'TOOLE!
KNUCKLES!
GOOD TO SEE YA, BUCK... TORO.
HAH! GET A LOAD OF *THIS...*
...NOW THAT'S WHAT I CALL AN ENTRANCE!
VROOM VROOM
LIEUTENANT JONES REPORTING FOR LIBERTY! AND LOOK WHO I FOUND AT THE AIRFIELD!
GREETINGS AND SALUTATIONS, GENTLEMEN!
HEY, GUYS!

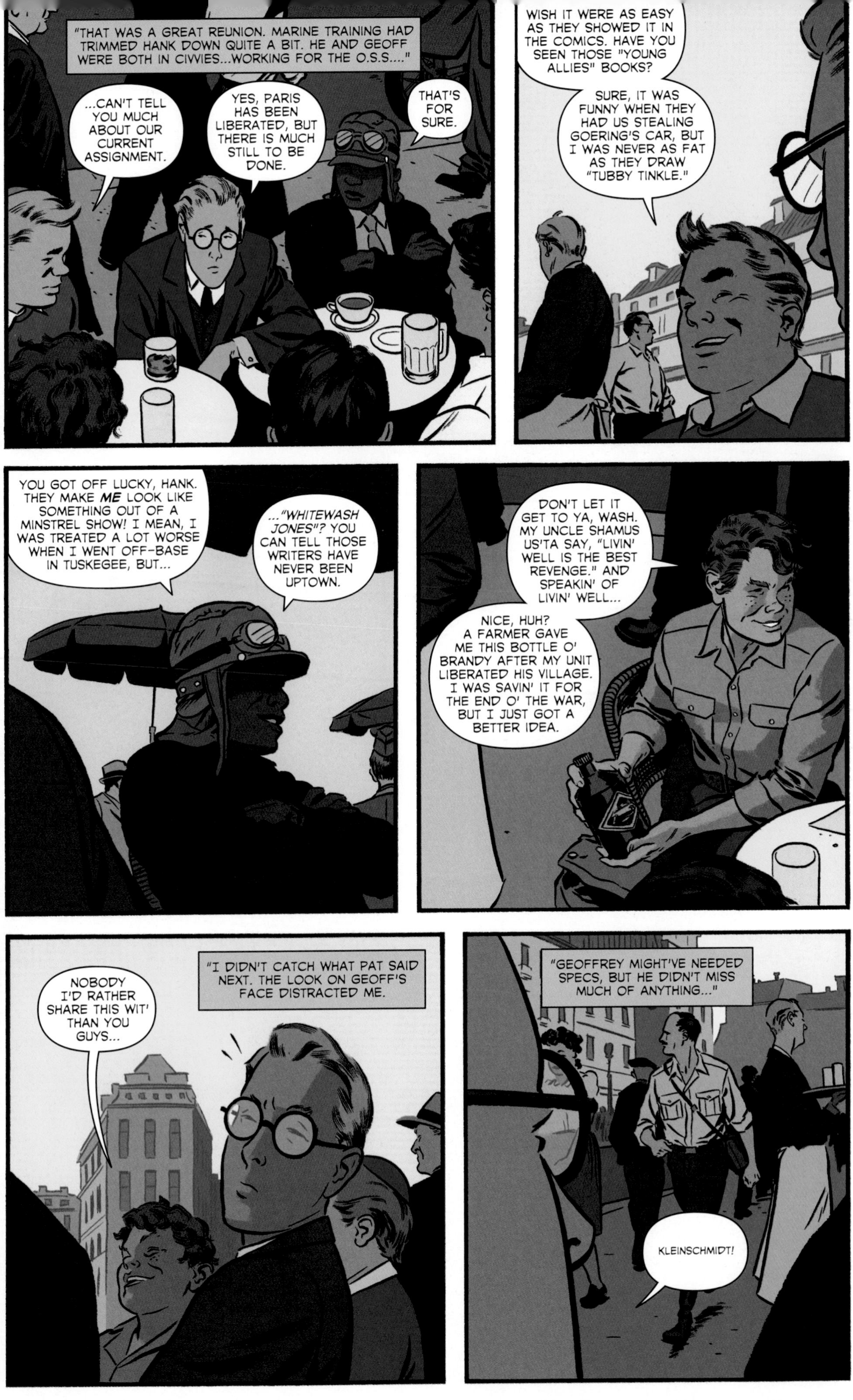
"THAT WAS A GREAT REUNION. MARINE TRAINING HAD TRIMMED HANK DOWN QUITE A BIT. HE AND GEOFF WERE BOTH IN CIVVIES...WORKING FOR THE O.S.S...."
...CAN'T TELL YOU MUCH ABOUT OUR CURRENT ASSIGNMENT.
YES, PARIS HAS BEEN LIBERATED, BUT THERE IS MUCH STILL TO BE DONE.
THAT'S FOR SURE.
WISH IT WERE AS EASY AS THEY SHOWED IT IN THE COMICS. HAVE YOU SEEN THOSE "YOUNG ALLIES" BOOKS?
SURE, IT WAS FUNNY WHEN THEY HAD US STEALING GOERING'S CAR, BUT I WAS NEVER AS FAT AS THEY DRAW "TUBBY TINKLE."
YOU GOT OFF LUCKY, HANK. THEY MAKE ***ME*** LOOK LIKE SOMETHING OUT OF A MINSTREL SHOW! I MEAN, I WAS TREATED A LOT WORSE WHEN I WENT OFF-BASE IN TUSKEGEE, BUT...
..."*WHITEWASH JONES*"? YOU CAN TELL THOSE WRITERS HAVE NEVER BEEN UPTOWN.
DON'T LET IT GET TO YA, WASH. MY UNCLE SHAMUS US'TA SAY, "LIVIN' WELL IS THE BEST REVENGE." AND SPEAKIN' OF LIVIN' WELL...
NICE, HUH? A FARMER GAVE ME THIS BOTTLE O' BRANDY AFTER MY UNIT LIBERATED HIS VILLAGE. I WAS SAVIN' IT FOR THE END O' THE WAR, BUT I JUST GOT A BETTER IDEA.
NOBODY I'D RATHER SHARE THIS WIT' THAN YOU GUYS...
"I DIDN'T CATCH WHAT PAT SAID NEXT. THE LOOK ON GEOFF'S FACE DISTRACTED ME.
"GEOFFREY MIGHT'VE NEEDED SPECS, BUT HE DIDN'T MISS MUCH OF ANYTHING..."
KLEINSCHMIDT!

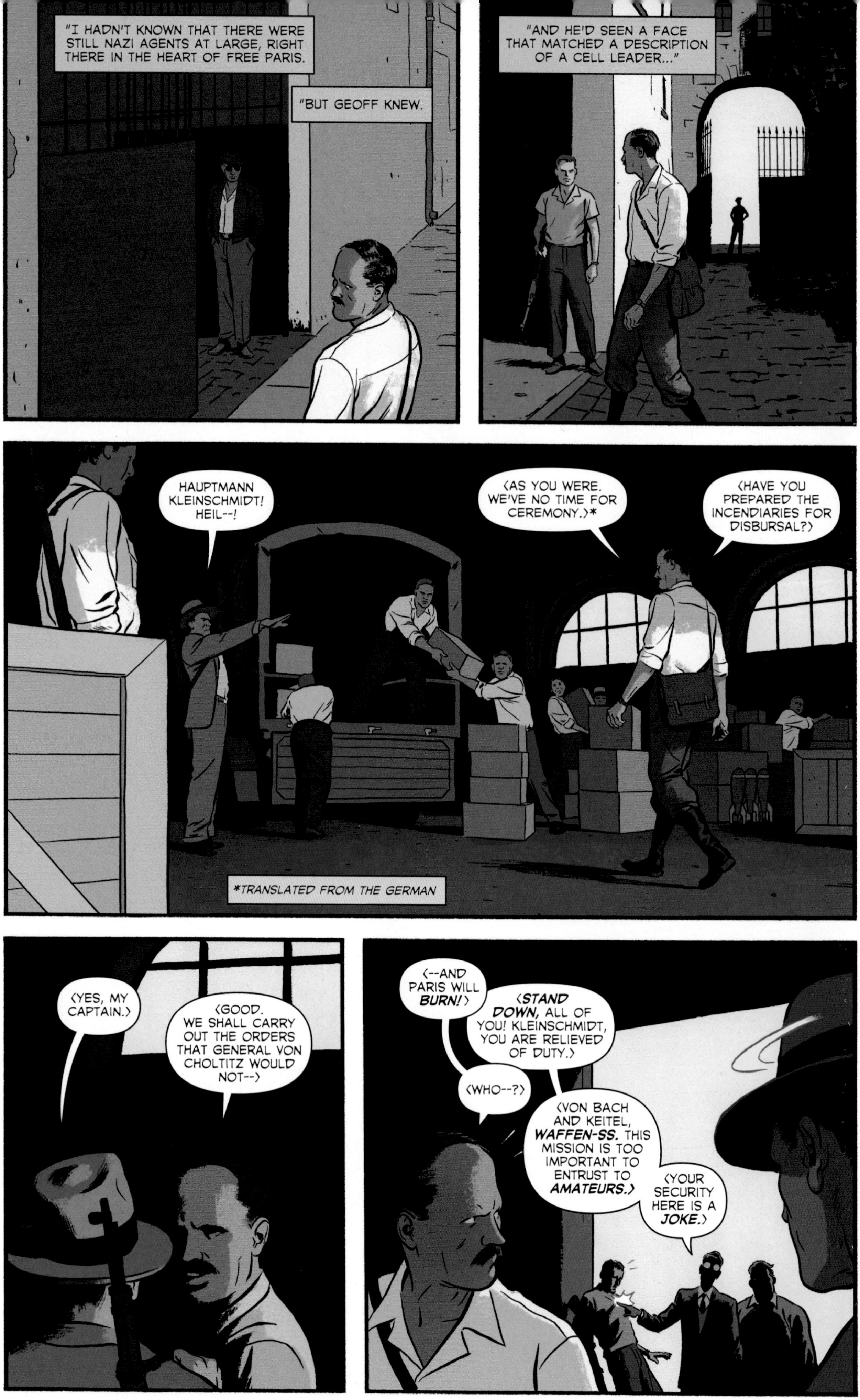
"I HADN'T KNOWN THAT THERE WERE STILL NAZI AGENTS AT LARGE, RIGHT THERE IN THE HEART OF FREE PARIS.
"BUT GEOFF KNEW.
"AND HE'D SEEN A FACE THAT MATCHED A DESCRIPTION OF A CELL LEADER..."
HAUPTMANN KLEINSCHMIDT! HEIL--!
<AS YOU WERE. WE'VE NO TIME FOR CEREMONY.>*
<HAVE YOU PREPARED THE INCENDIARIES FOR DISBURSAL?>
*TRANSLATED FROM THE GERMAN
<YES, MY CAPTAIN.>
<GOOD. WE SHALL CARRY OUT THE ORDERS THAT GENERAL VON CHOLTITZ WOULD NOT-->
<--AND PARIS WILL BURN!>
<STAND DOWN, ALL OF YOU! KLEINSCHMIDT, YOU ARE RELIEVED OF DUTY.>
<WHO--?>
<VON BACH AND KEITEL, WAFFEN-SS. THIS MISSION IS TOO IMPORTANT TO ENTRUST TO AMATEURS.>
<YOUR SECURITY HERE IS A JOKE.>

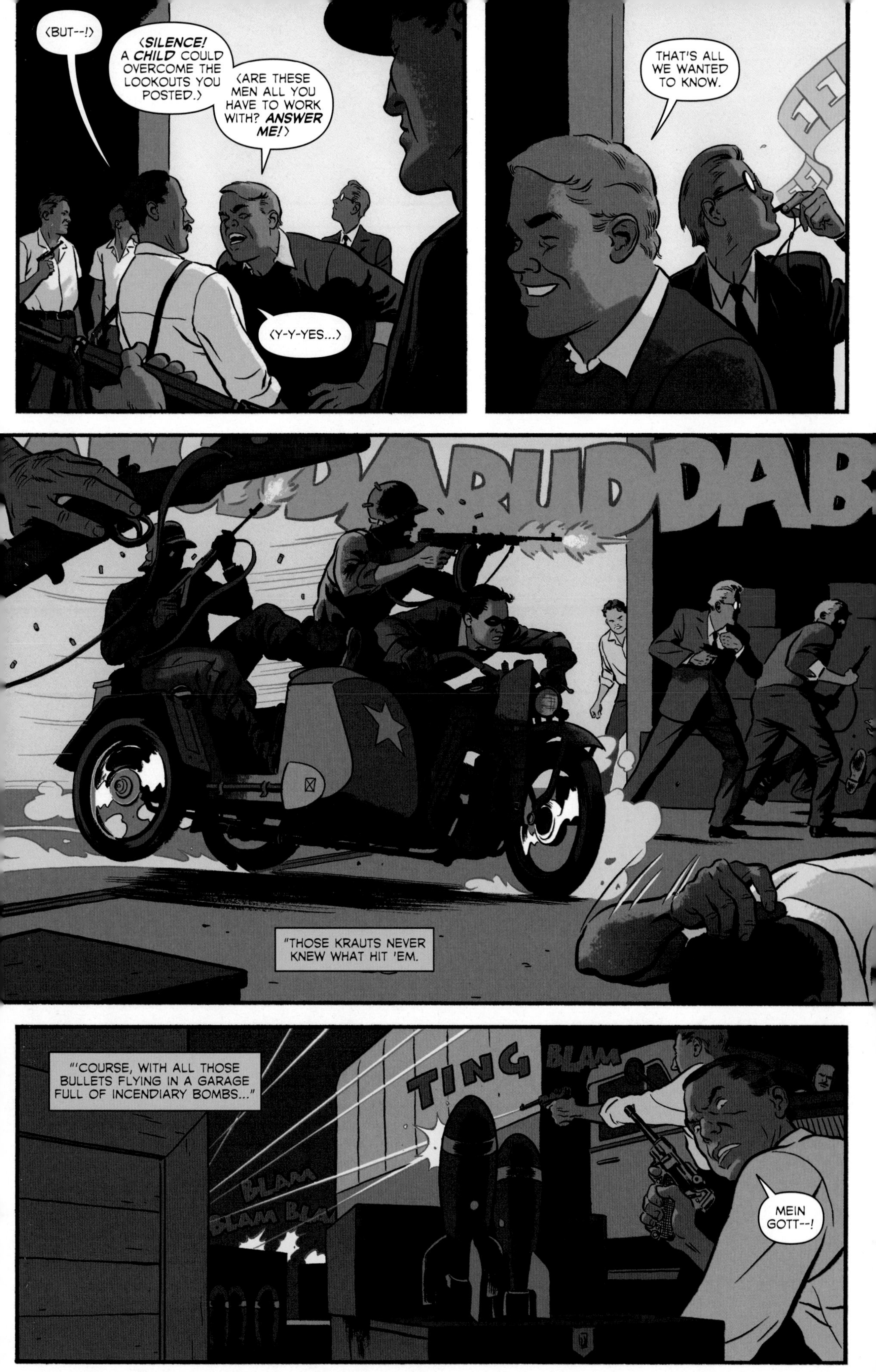

‹BUT--!›
‹SILENCE! A CHILD COULD OVERCOME THE LOOKOUTS YOU POSTED.›
‹ARE THESE MEN ALL YOU HAVE TO WORK WITH? ANSWER ME!›
‹Y-Y-YES...›
THAT'S ALL WE WANTED TO KNOW.
BUDDABUDDAB
"THOSE KRAUTS NEVER KNEW WHAT HIT 'EM.
"'COURSE, WITH ALL THOSE BULLETS FLYING IN A GARAGE FULL OF INCENDIARY BOMBS..."
TING
BLAM
BLAM
BLAM BLAM
MEIN GOTT--!

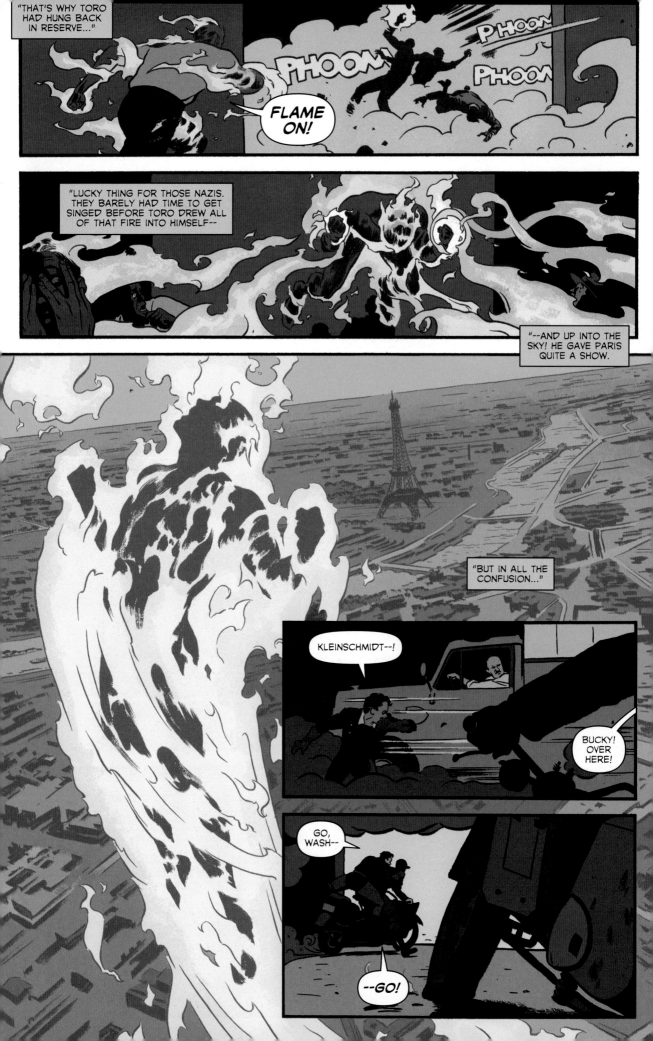

"THAT'S WHY TORO HAD HUNG BACK IN RESERVE..."

FLAME ON!

PHOOM PHOOM PHOOM

"LUCKY THING FOR THOSE NAZIS. THEY BARELY HAD TIME TO GET SINGED BEFORE TORO DREW ALL OF THAT FIRE INTO HIMSELF--

"--AND UP INTO THE SKY! HE GAVE PARIS QUITE A SHOW.

"BUT IN ALL THE CONFUSION..."

KLEINSCHMIDT--!

BUCKY! OVER HERE!

GO, WASH--

--GO!

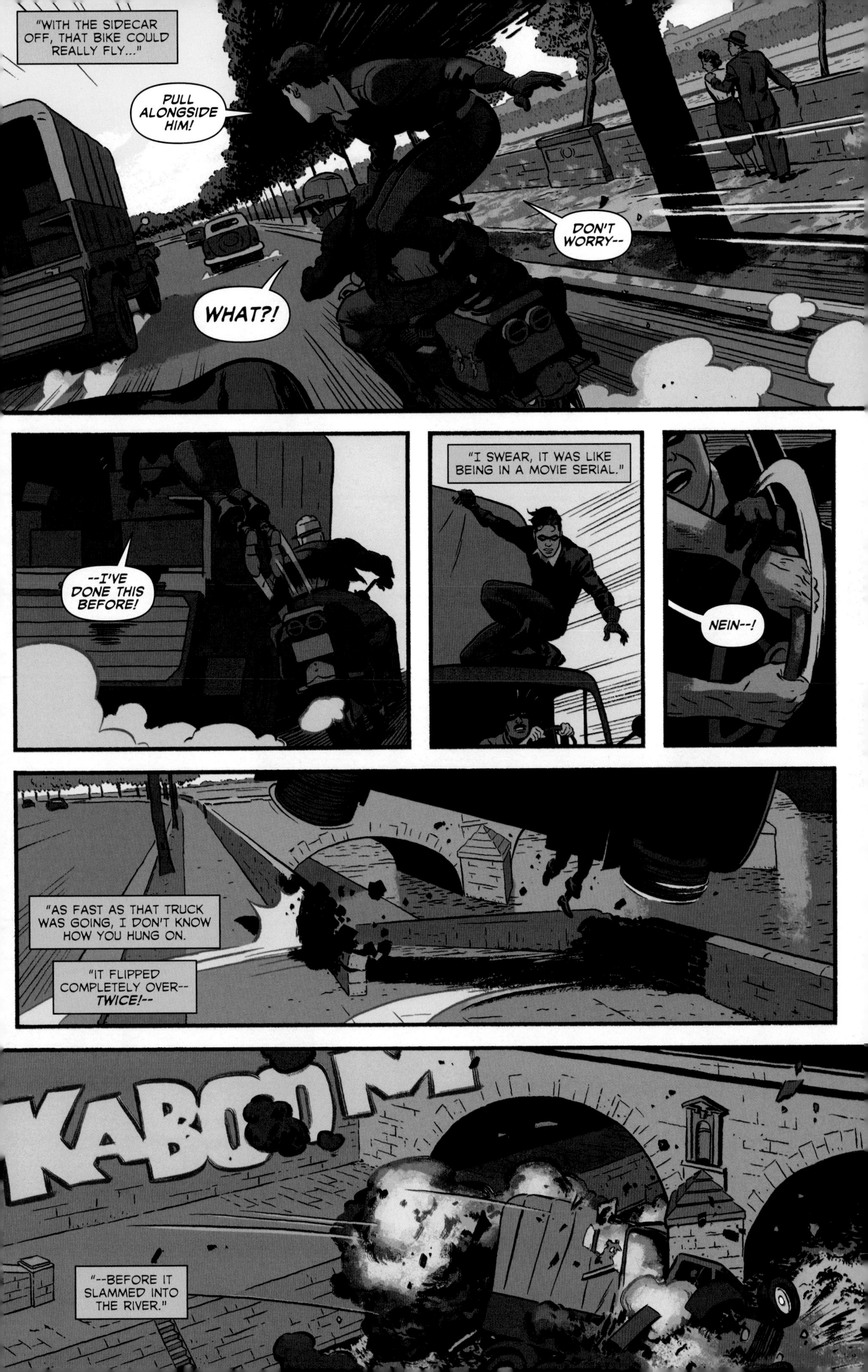
"WITH THE SIDECAR OFF, THAT BIKE COULD REALLY FLY..."
PULL ALONGSIDE HIM!
WHAT?!
DON'T WORRY--
--I'VE DONE THIS BEFORE!
"I SWEAR, IT WAS LIKE BEING IN A MOVIE SERIAL."
NEIN--!
"AS FAST AS THAT TRUCK WAS GOING, I DON'T KNOW HOW YOU HUNG ON.
"IT FLIPPED COMPLETELY OVER-- TWICE!--
KABOOM!
"--BEFORE IT SLAMMED INTO THE RIVER."

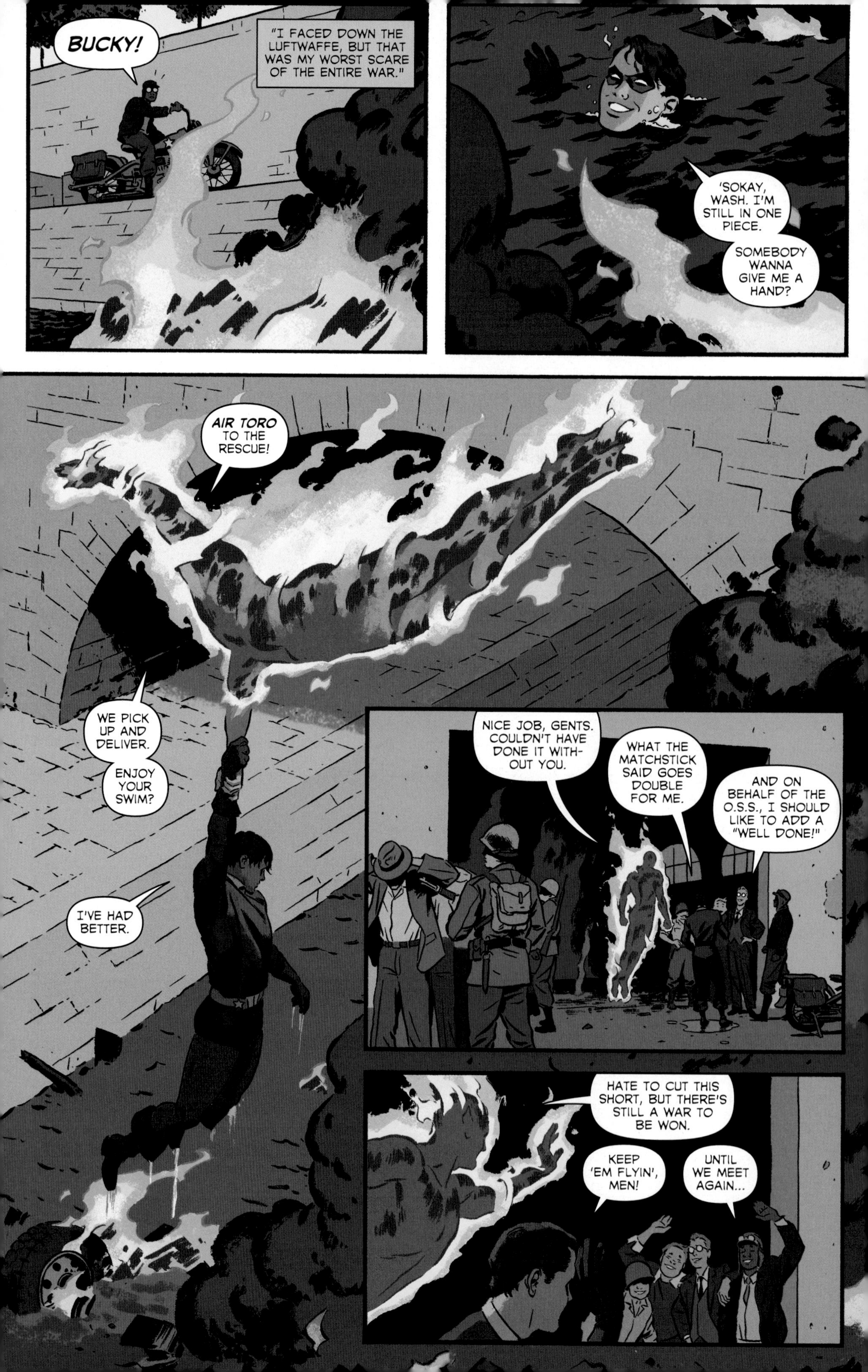
BUCKY!
"I FACED DOWN THE LUFTWAFFE, BUT THAT WAS MY WORST SCARE OF THE ENTIRE WAR."
'SOKAY, WASH. I'M STILL IN ONE PIECE.
SOMEBODY WANNA GIVE ME A HAND?
AIR TORO TO THE RESCUE!
WE PICK UP AND DELIVER.
ENJOY YOUR SWIM?
I'VE HAD BETTER.
NICE JOB, GENTS. COULDN'T HAVE DONE IT WITH-OUT YOU.
WHAT THE MATCHSTICK SAID GOES DOUBLE FOR ME.
AND ON BEHALF OF THE O.S.S., I SHOULD LIKE TO ADD A "WELL DONE!"
HATE TO CUT THIS SHORT, BUT THERE'S STILL A WAR TO BE WON.
KEEP 'EM FLYIN', MEN!
UNTIL WE MEET AGAIN...

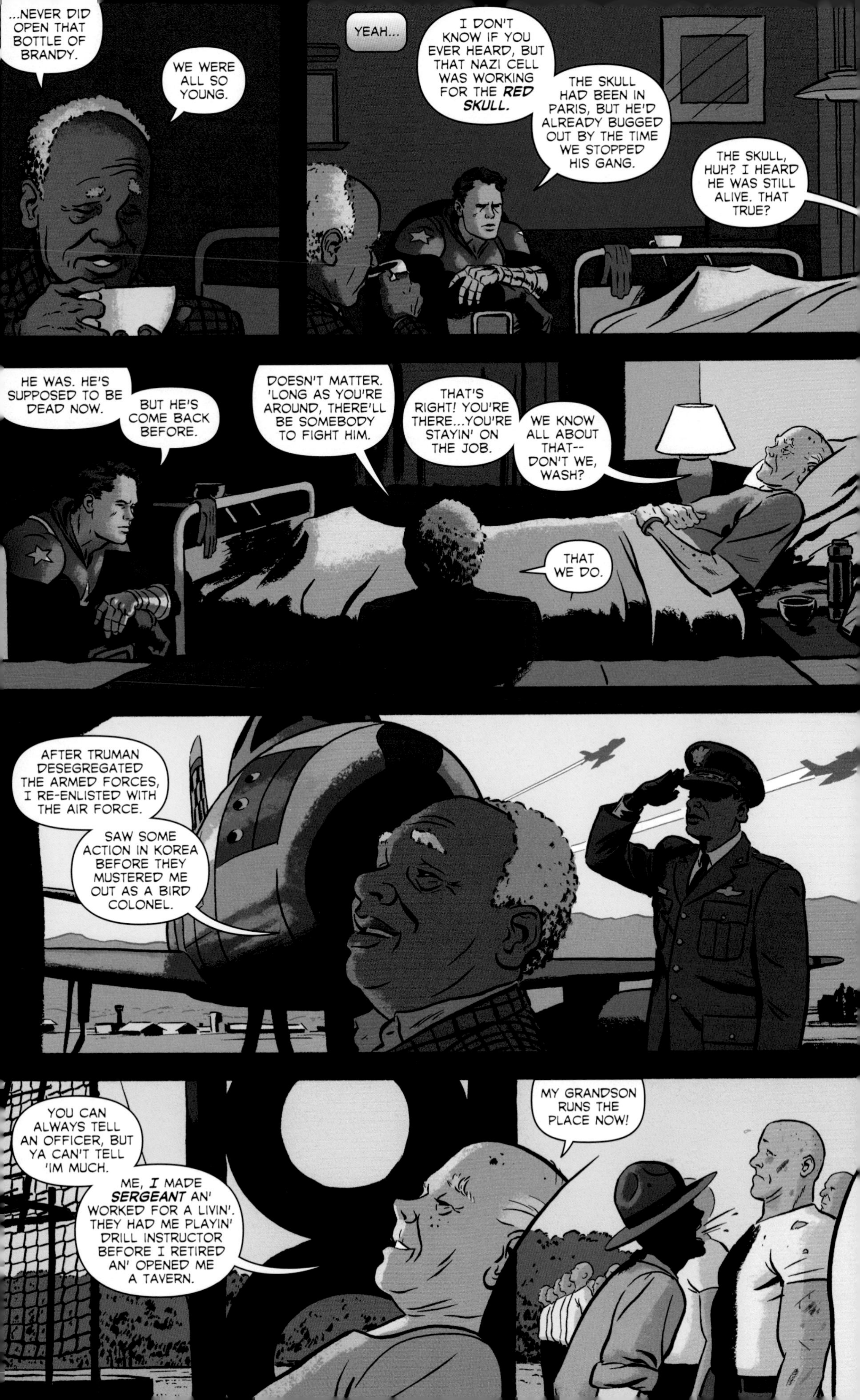
...NEVER DID OPEN THAT BOTTLE OF BRANDY.
WE WERE ALL SO YOUNG.
YEAH...
I DON'T KNOW IF YOU EVER HEARD, BUT THAT NAZI CELL WAS WORKING FOR THE ***RED SKULL.***
THE SKULL HAD BEEN IN PARIS, BUT HE'D ALREADY BUGGED OUT BY THE TIME WE STOPPED HIS GANG.
THE SKULL, HUH? I HEARD HE WAS STILL ALIVE. THAT TRUE?
HE WAS. HE'S SUPPOSED TO BE DEAD NOW.
BUT HE'S COME BACK BEFORE.
DOESN'T MATTER. 'LONG AS YOU'RE AROUND, THERE'LL BE SOMEBODY TO FIGHT HIM.
THAT'S RIGHT! YOU'RE THERE...YOU'RE STAYIN' ON THE JOB.
WE KNOW ALL ABOUT THAT-- DON'T WE, WASH?
THAT WE DO.
AFTER TRUMAN DESEGREGATED THE ARMED FORCES, I RE-ENLISTED WITH THE AIR FORCE.
SAW SOME ACTION IN KOREA BEFORE THEY MUSTERED ME OUT AS A BIRD COLONEL.
YOU CAN ALWAYS TELL AN OFFICER, BUT YA CAN'T TELL 'IM MUCH.
ME, *I* MADE ***SERGEANT*** AN' WORKED FOR A LIVIN'. THEY HAD ME PLAYIN' DRILL INSTRUCTOR BEFORE I RETIRED AN' OPENED ME A TAVERN.
MY GRANDSON RUNS THE PLACE NOW!

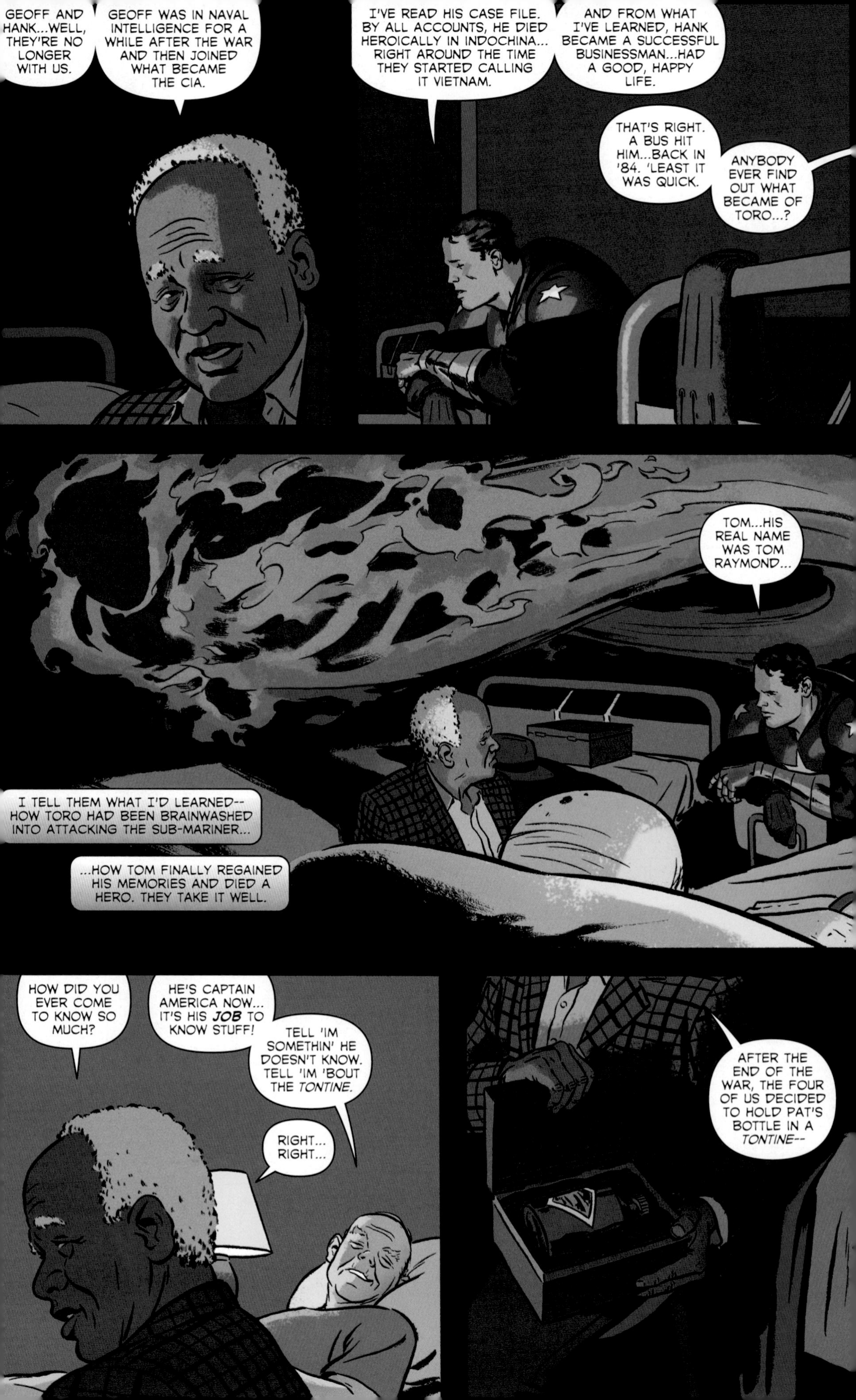

GEOFF AND HANK...WELL, THEY'RE NO LONGER WITH US.
GEOFF WAS IN NAVAL INTELLIGENCE FOR A WHILE AFTER THE WAR AND THEN JOINED WHAT BECAME THE CIA.
I'VE READ HIS CASE FILE. BY ALL ACCOUNTS, HE DIED HEROICALLY IN INDOCHINA... RIGHT AROUND THE TIME THEY STARTED CALLING IT VIETNAM.
AND FROM WHAT I'VE LEARNED, HANK BECAME A SUCCESSFUL BUSINESSMAN...HAD A GOOD, HAPPY LIFE.
THAT'S RIGHT. A BUS HIT HIM...BACK IN '84. 'LEAST IT WAS QUICK.
ANYBODY EVER FIND OUT WHAT BECAME OF TORO...?
TOM...HIS REAL NAME WAS TOM RAYMOND...
I TELL THEM WHAT I'D LEARNED-- HOW TORO HAD BEEN BRAINWASHED INTO ATTACKING THE SUB-MARINER...
...HOW TOM FINALLY REGAINED HIS MEMORIES AND DIED A HERO. THEY TAKE IT WELL.
HOW DID YOU EVER COME TO KNOW SO MUCH?
HE'S CAPTAIN AMERICA NOW... IT'S HIS JOB TO KNOW STUFF!
TELL 'IM SOMETHIN' HE DOESN'T KNOW. TELL 'IM 'BOUT THE TONTINE.
RIGHT... RIGHT...
AFTER THE END OF THE WAR, THE FOUR OF US DECIDED TO HOLD PAT'S BOTTLE IN A TONTINE--

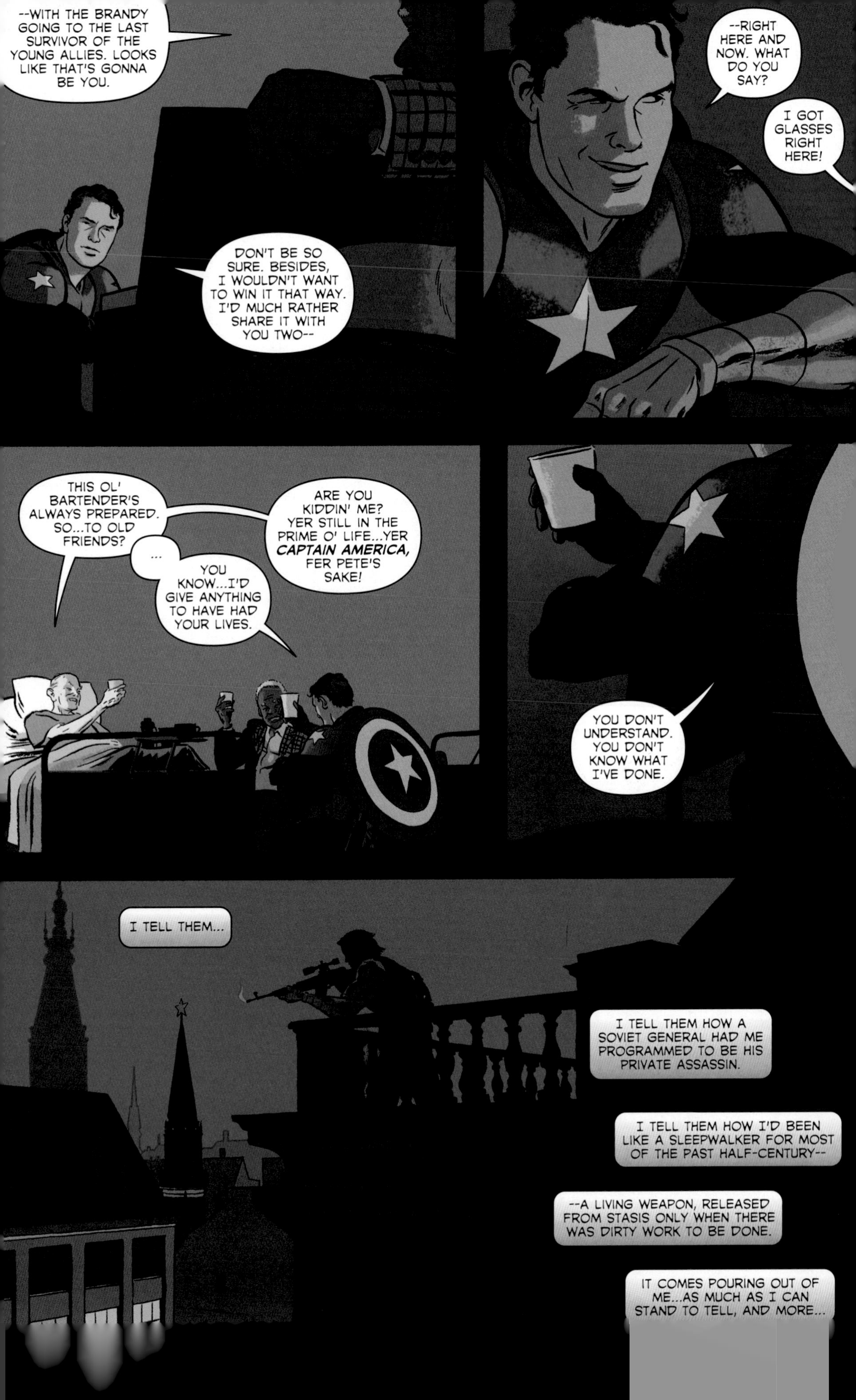
--WITH THE BRANDY GOING TO THE LAST SURVIVOR OF THE YOUNG ALLIES. LOOKS LIKE THAT'S GONNA BE YOU.
DON'T BE SO SURE. BESIDES, I WOULDN'T WANT TO WIN IT THAT WAY. I'D MUCH RATHER SHARE IT WITH YOU TWO--
--RIGHT HERE AND NOW. WHAT DO YOU SAY?
I GOT GLASSES RIGHT HERE!
THIS OL' BARTENDER'S ALWAYS PREPARED. SO...TO OLD FRIENDS?
...
YOU KNOW...I'D GIVE ANYTHING TO HAVE HAD YOUR LIVES.
ARE YOU KIDDIN' ME? YER STILL IN THE PRIME O' LIFE...YER *CAPTAIN AMERICA,* FER PETE'S SAKE!
YOU DON'T UNDERSTAND. YOU DON'T KNOW WHAT I'VE DONE.
I TELL THEM...
I TELL THEM HOW A SOVIET GENERAL HAD ME PROGRAMMED TO BE HIS PRIVATE ASSASSIN.
I TELL THEM HOW I'D BEEN LIKE A SLEEPWALKER FOR MOST OF THE PAST HALF-CENTURY--
--A LIVING WEAPON, RELEASED FROM STASIS ONLY WHEN THERE WAS DIRTY WORK TO BE DONE.
IT COMES POURING OUT OF ME...AS MUCH AS I CAN STAND TO TELL, AND MORE...

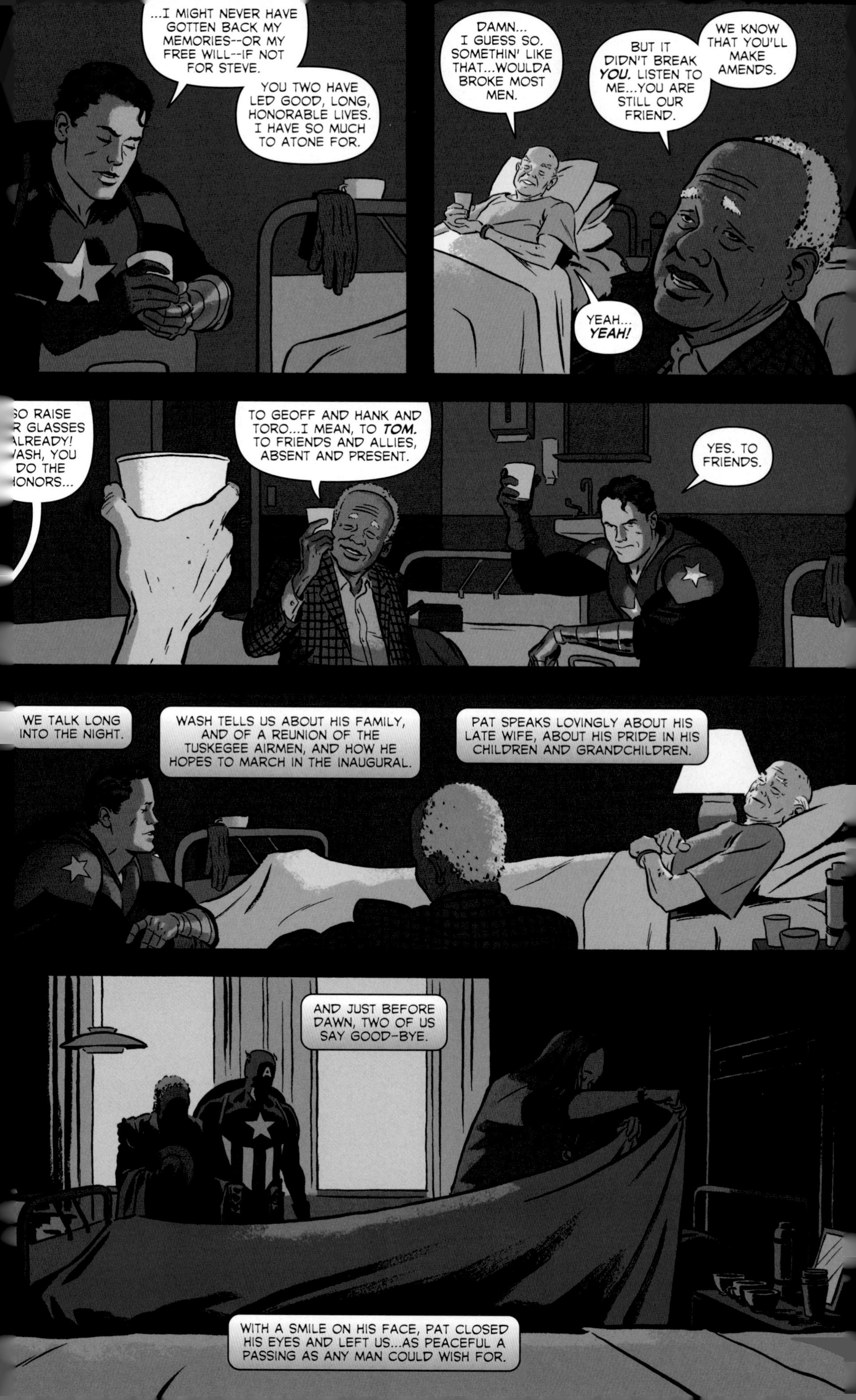
...I MIGHT NEVER HAVE GOTTEN BACK MY MEMORIES--OR MY FREE WILL--IF NOT FOR STEVE.
YOU TWO HAVE LED GOOD, LONG, HONORABLE LIVES. I HAVE SO MUCH TO ATONE FOR.
DAMN... I GUESS SO. SOMETHIN' LIKE THAT...WOULDA BROKE MOST MEN.
BUT IT DIDN'T BREAK *YOU.* LISTEN TO ME...YOU ARE STILL OUR FRIEND.
WE KNOW THAT YOU'LL MAKE AMENDS.
YEAH... *YEAH!*
SO RAISE R GLASSES ALREADY! VASH, YOU DO THE HONORS...
TO GEOFF AND HANK AND TORO...I MEAN, TO *TOM.* TO FRIENDS AND ALLIES, ABSENT AND PRESENT.
YES. TO FRIENDS.
WE TALK LONG INTO THE NIGHT.
WASH TELLS US ABOUT HIS FAMILY, AND OF A REUNION OF THE TUSKEGEE AIRMEN, AND HOW HE HOPES TO MARCH IN THE INAUGURAL.
PAT SPEAKS LOVINGLY ABOUT HIS LATE WIFE, ABOUT HIS PRIDE IN HIS CHILDREN AND GRANDCHILDREN.
AND JUST BEFORE DAWN, TWO OF US SAY GOOD-BYE.
WITH A SMILE ON HIS FACE, PAT CLOSED HIS EYES AND LEFT US...AS PEACEFUL A PASSING AS ANY MAN COULD WISH FOR.

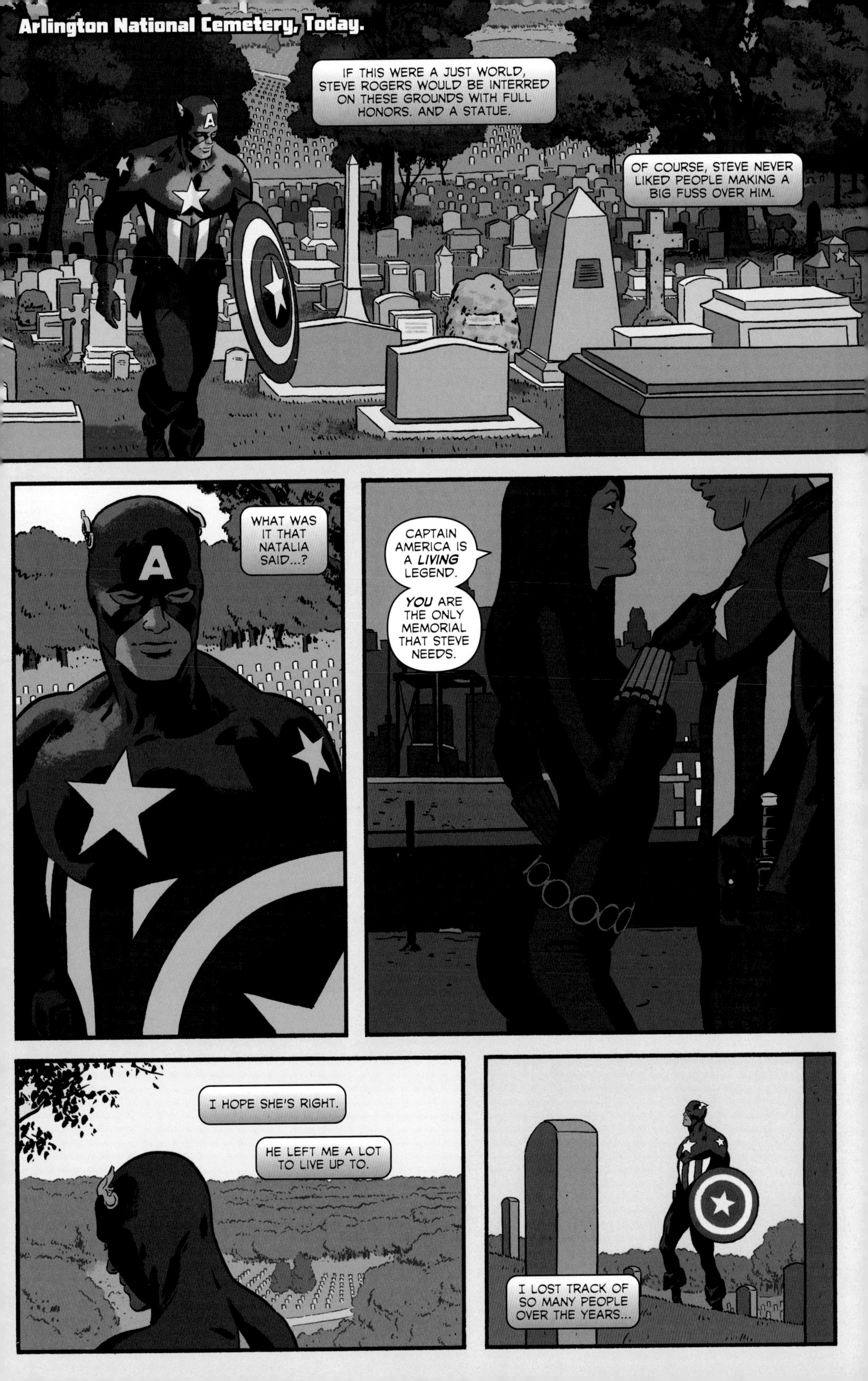
Arlington National Cemetery, Today.
IF THIS WERE A JUST WORLD, STEVE ROGERS WOULD BE INTERRED ON THESE GROUNDS WITH FULL HONORS. AND A STATUE.
OF COURSE, STEVE NEVER LIKED PEOPLE MAKING A BIG FUSS OVER HIM.
WHAT WAS IT THAT NATALIA SAID...?
CAPTAIN AMERICA IS A *LIVING* LEGEND.
YOU ARE THE ONLY MEMORIAL THAT STEVE NEEDS.
I HOPE SHE'S RIGHT.
HE LEFT ME A LOT TO LIVE UP TO.
I LOST TRACK OF SO MANY PEOPLE OVER THE YEARS...

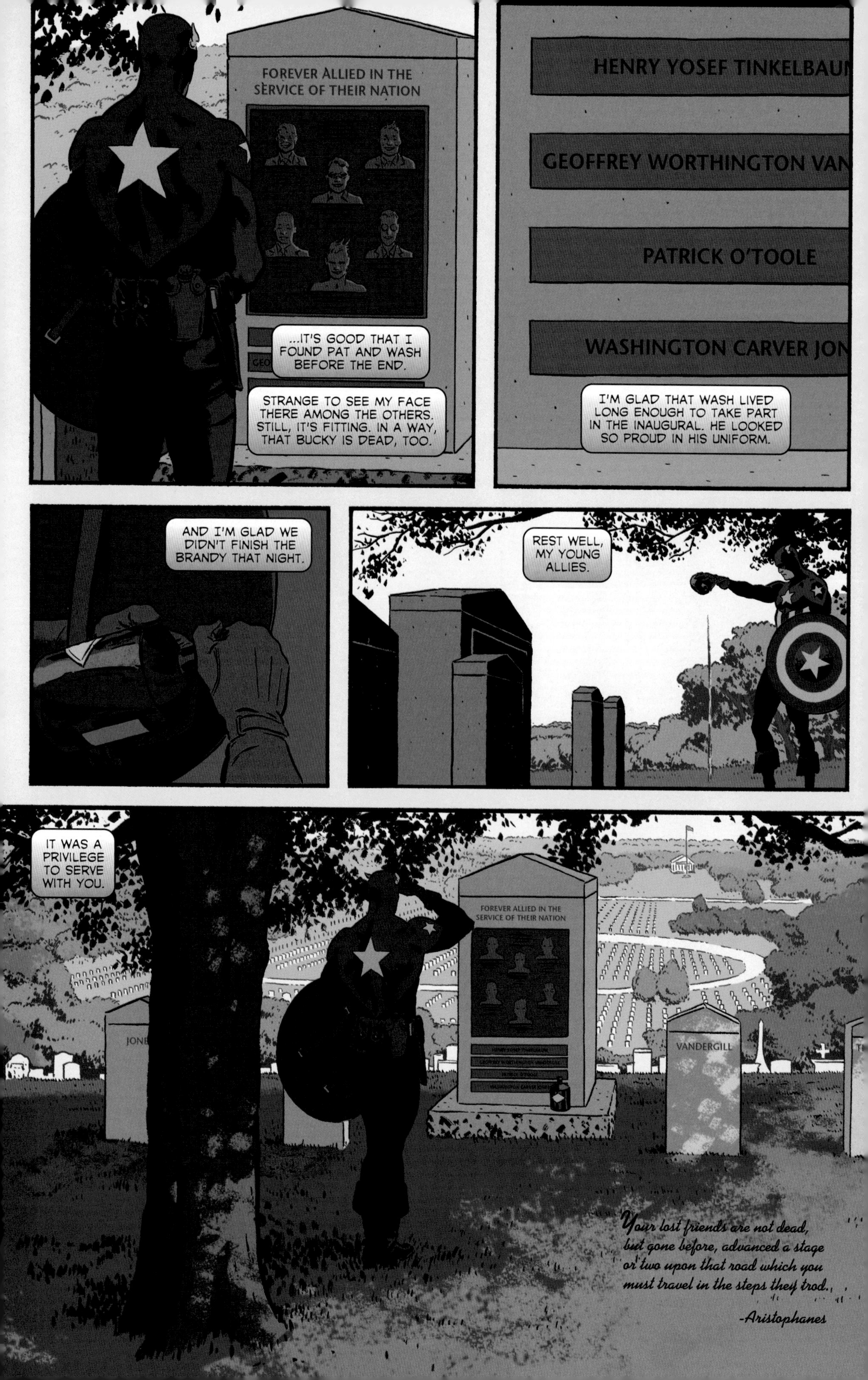
FOREVER ALLIED IN THE SERVICE OF THEIR NATION
...IT'S GOOD THAT I FOUND PAT AND WASH BEFORE THE END.
STRANGE TO SEE MY FACE THERE AMONG THE OTHERS. STILL, IT'S FITTING, IN A WAY, THAT BUCKY IS DEAD, TOO.
HENRY YOSEF TINKELBAU
GEOFFREY WORTHINGTON VAN
PATRICK O'TOOLE
WASHINGTON CARVER JON
I'M GLAD THAT WASH LIVED LONG ENOUGH TO TAKE PART IN THE INAUGURAL. HE LOOKED SO PROUD IN HIS UNIFORM.
AND I'M GLAD WE DIDN'T FINISH THE BRANDY THAT NIGHT.
REST WELL, MY YOUNG ALLIES.
IT WAS A PRIVILEGE TO SERVE WITH YOU.
FOREVER ALLIED IN THE SERVICE OF THEIR NATION
VANDERGILL
Your lost friends are not dead, but gone before, advanced a stage or two upon that road which you must travel in the steps they trod.
-Aristophanes

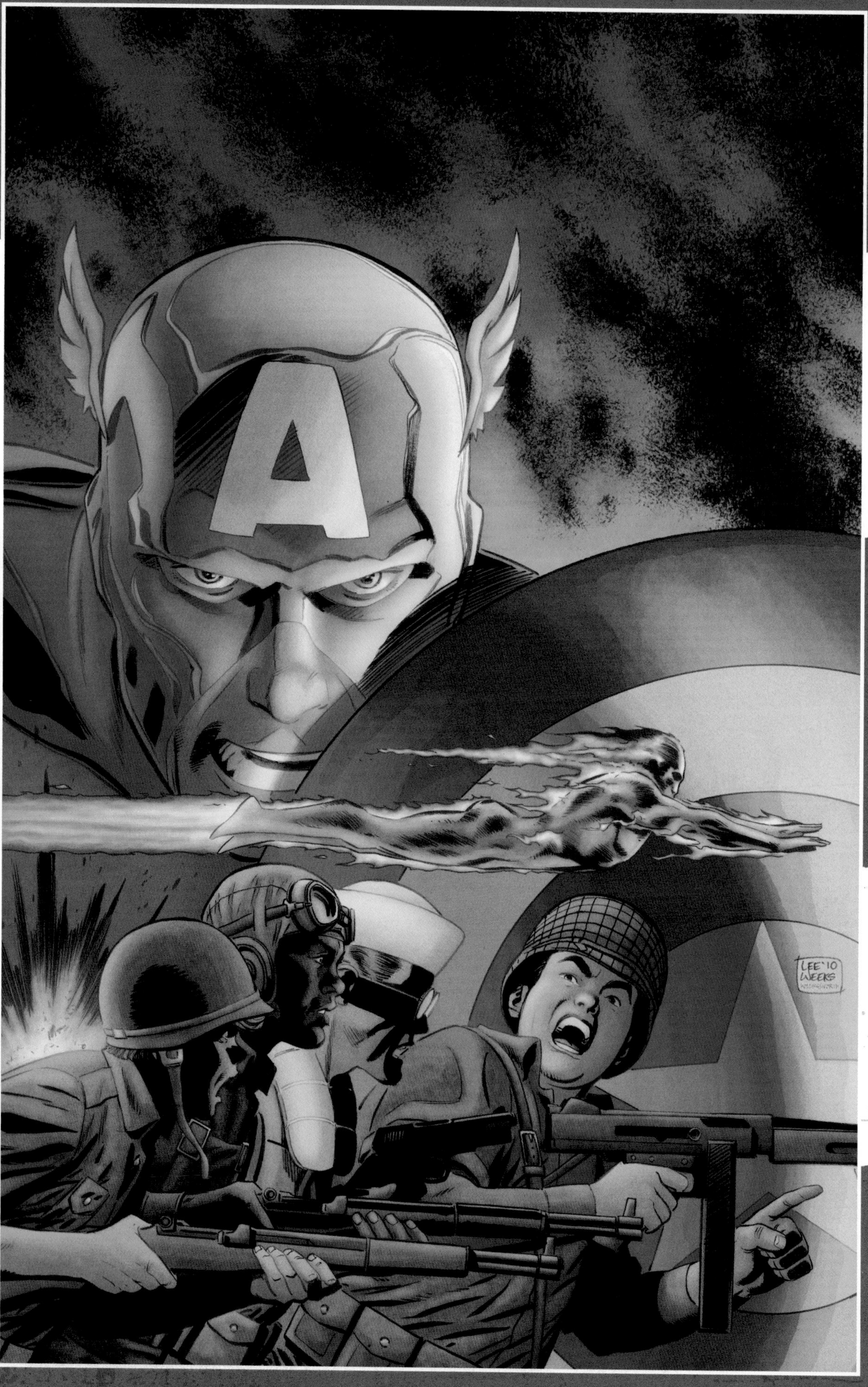
LEE '10
WEEKS

CAPTAIN AMERICA: FOREVER ALLIES #1

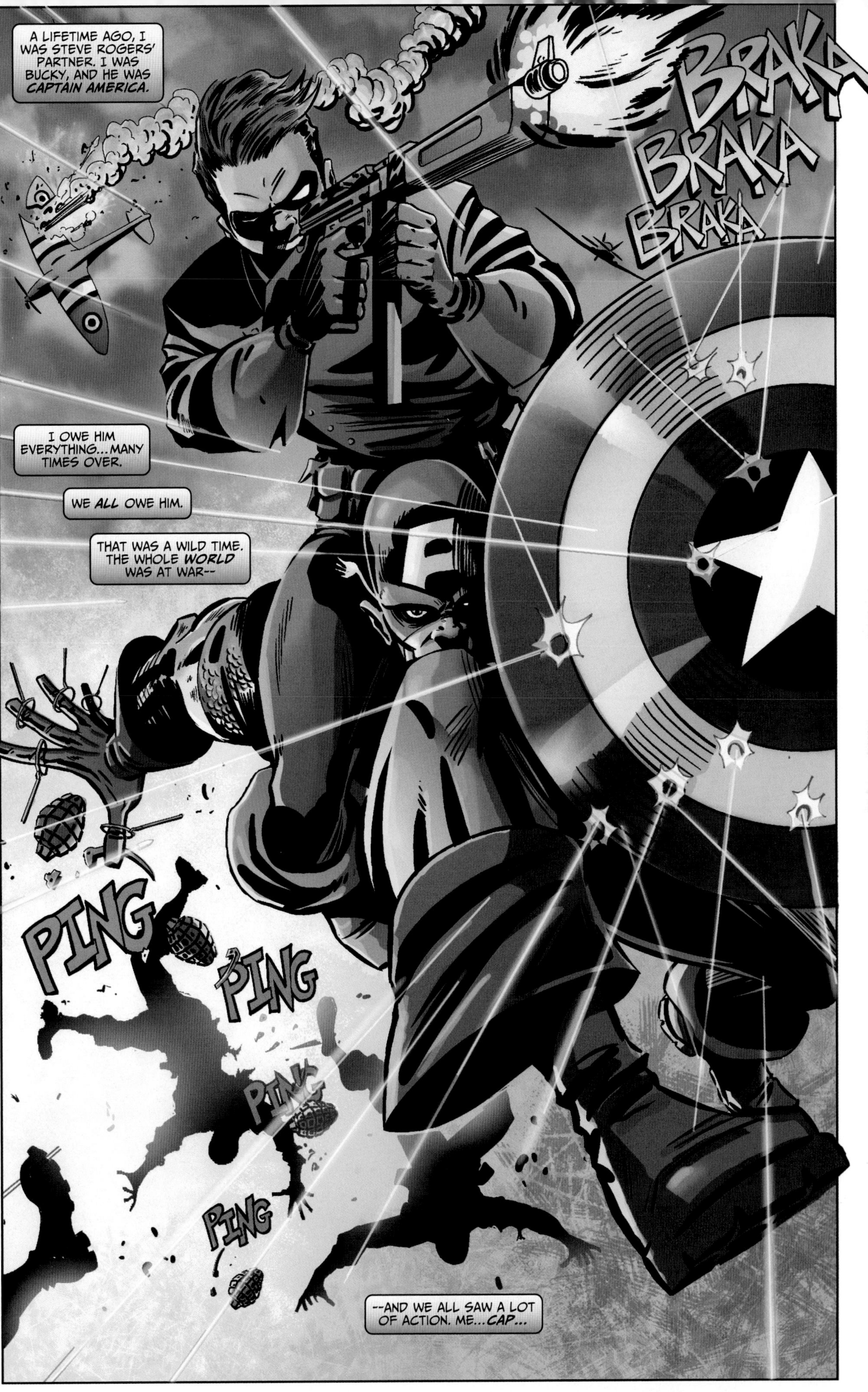

A LIFETIME AGO, I WAS STEVE ROGERS' PARTNER. I WAS BUCKY, AND HE WAS CAPTAIN AMERICA.
BRAKA
BRAKA
BRAKA
I OWE HIM EVERYTHING...MANY TIMES OVER.
WE ALL OWE HIM.
THAT WAS A WILD TIME. THE WHOLE WORLD WAS AT WAR--
PING
PING
PING
PING
--AND WE ALL SAW A LOT OF ACTION. ME...CAP...

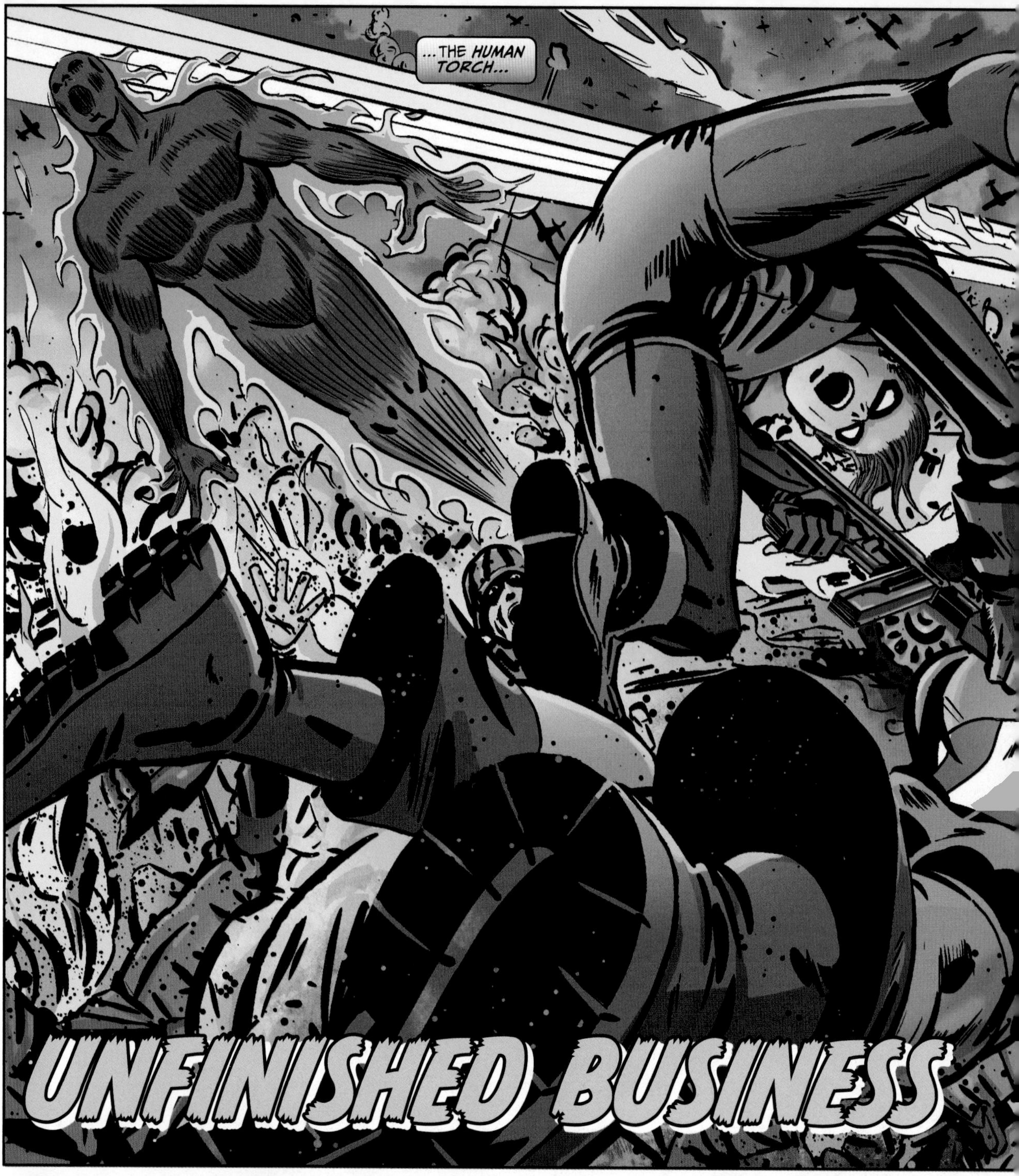
...THE *HUMAN TORCH*...
UNFINISHED BUSINESS

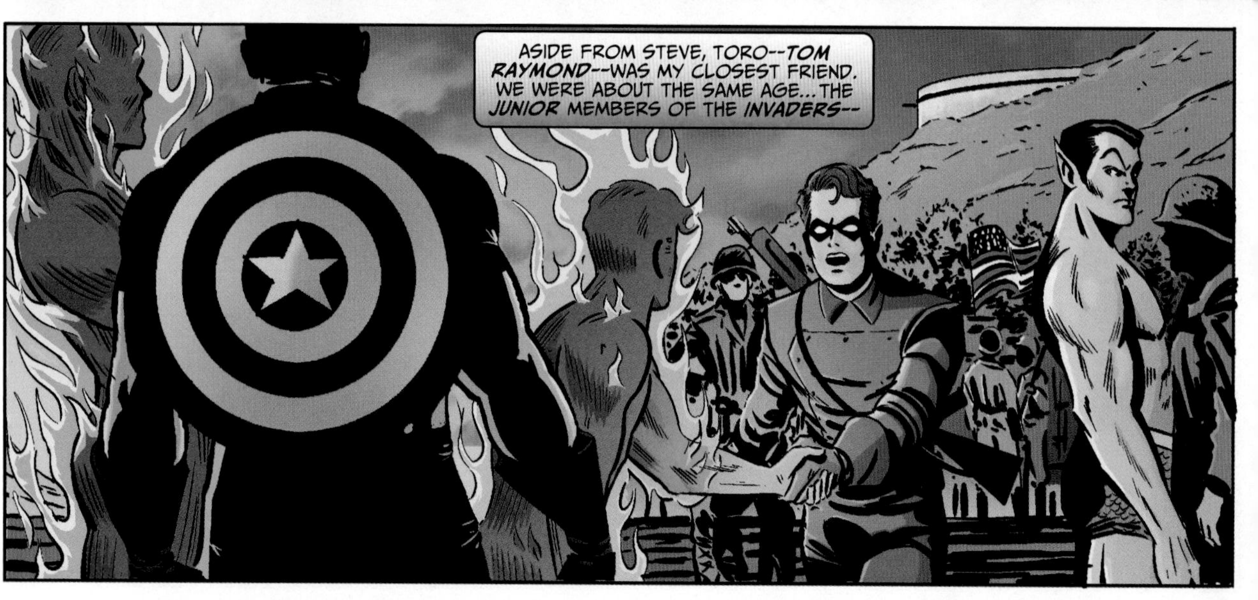
ASIDE FROM STEVE, TORO--*TOM RAYMOND*--WAS MY CLOSEST FRIEND. WE WERE ABOUT THE SAME AGE...THE *JUNIOR* MEMBERS OF THE *INVADERS*--

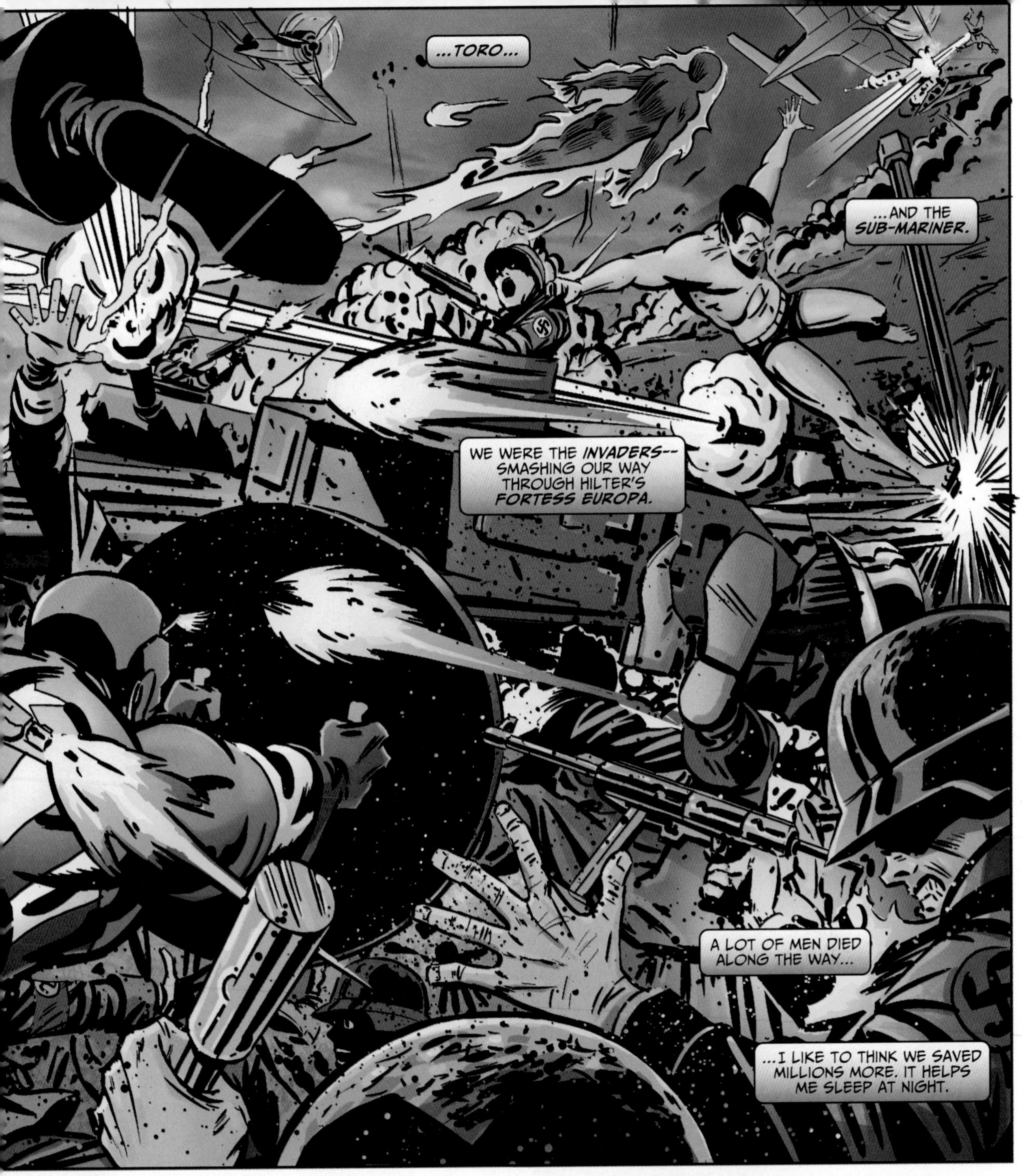
...TORO...
...AND THE SUB-MARINER.
WE WERE THE INVADERS--SMASHING OUR WAY THROUGH HILTER'S FORTESS EUROPA.
A LOT OF MEN DIED ALONG THE WAY...
...I LIKE TO THINK WE SAVED MILLIONS MORE. IT HELPS ME SLEEP AT NIGHT.

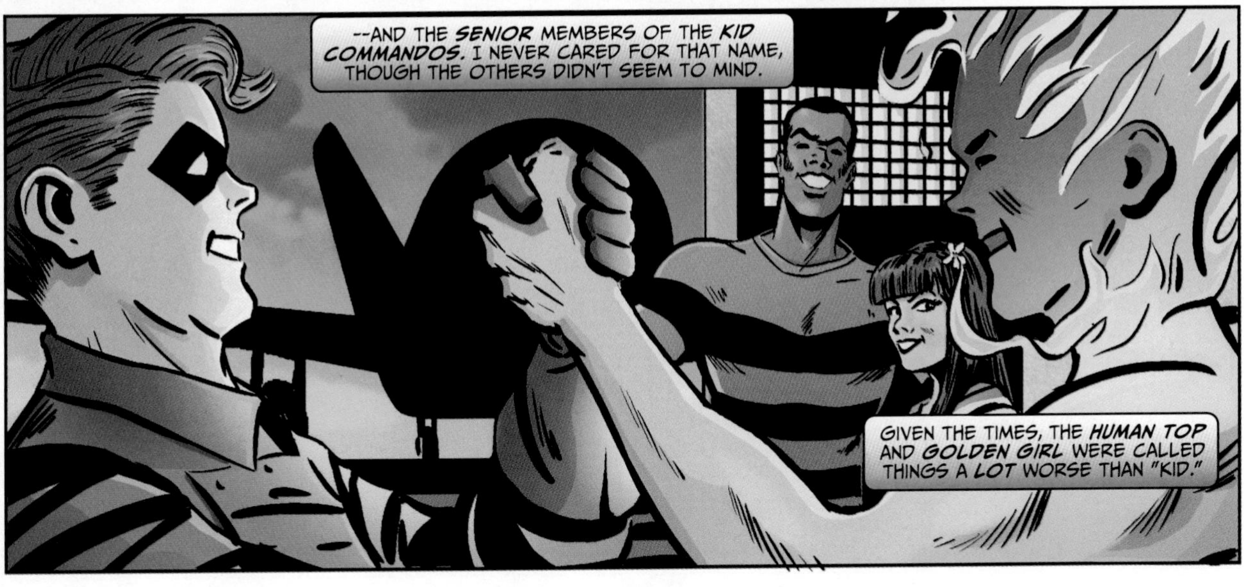
--AND THE SENIOR MEMBERS OF THE KID COMMANDOS. I NEVER CARED FOR THAT NAME, THOUGH THE OTHERS DIDN'T SEEM TO MIND.
GIVEN THE TIMES, THE HUMAN TOP AND GOLDEN GIRL WERE CALLED THINGS A LOT WORSE THAN "KID."

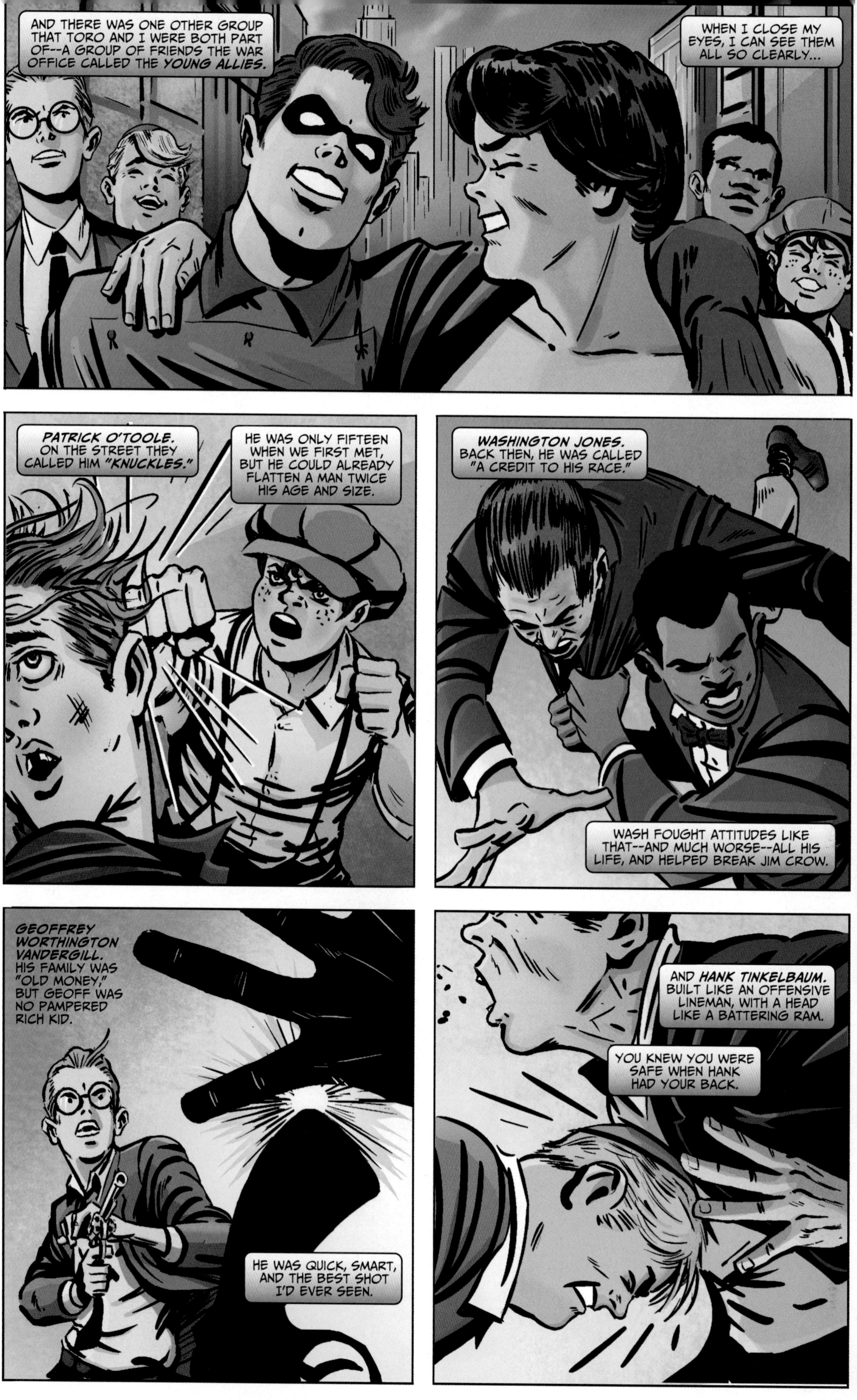
AND THERE WAS ONE OTHER GROUP THAT TORO AND I WERE BOTH PART OF--A GROUP OF FRIENDS THE WAR OFFICE CALLED THE *YOUNG ALLIES*.
WHEN I CLOSE MY EYES, I CAN SEE THEM ALL SO CLEARLY...
PATRICK O'TOOLE. ON THE STREET THEY CALLED HIM *"KNUCKLES."*
HE WAS ONLY FIFTEEN WHEN WE FIRST MET, BUT HE COULD ALREADY FLATTEN A MAN TWICE HIS AGE AND SIZE.
WASHINGTON JONES. BACK THEN, HE WAS CALLED "A CREDIT TO HIS RACE."
WASH FOUGHT ATTITUDES LIKE THAT--AND MUCH WORSE--ALL HIS LIFE, AND HELPED BREAK JIM CROW.
GEOFFREY WORTHINGTON VANDERGILL. HIS FAMILY WAS "OLD MONEY," BUT GEOFF WAS NO PAMPERED RICH KID.
HE WAS QUICK, SMART, AND THE BEST SHOT I'D EVER SEEN.
AND *HANK TINKELBAUM.* BUILT LIKE AN OFFENSIVE LINEMAN, WITH A HEAD LIKE A BATTERING RAM.
YOU KNEW YOU WERE SAFE WHEN HANK HAD YOUR BACK.

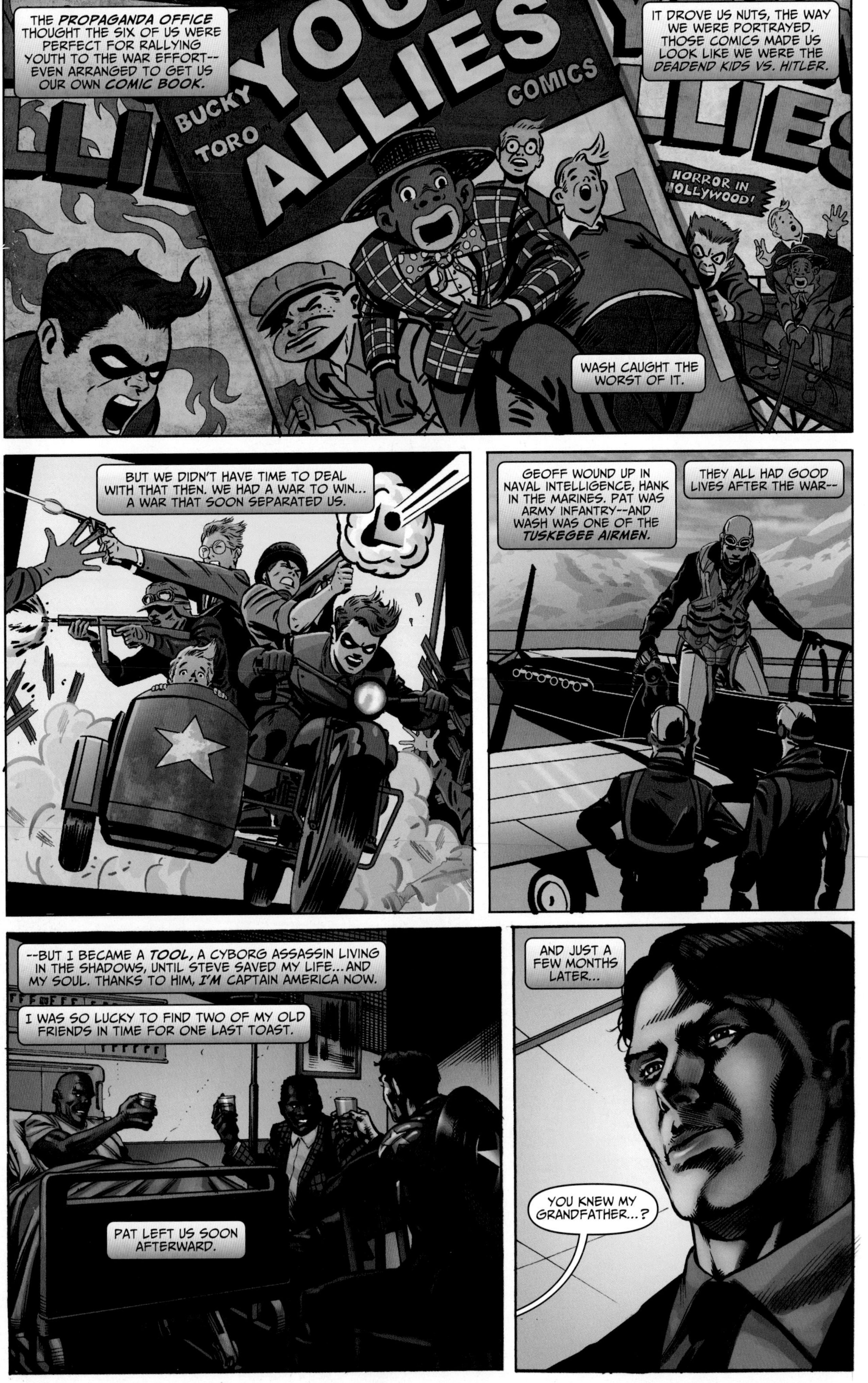
THE PROPAGANDA OFFICE THOUGHT THE SIX OF US WERE PERFECT FOR RALLYING YOUTH TO THE WAR EFFORT-- EVEN ARRANGED TO GET US OUR OWN COMIC BOOK.
BUCKY AND TORO YOUNG ALLIES COMICS
IT DROVE US NUTS, THE WAY WE WERE PORTRAYED. THOSE COMICS MADE US LOOK LIKE WE WERE THE DEADEND KIDS VS. HITLER.
HORROR IN HOLLYWOOD!
WASH CAUGHT THE WORST OF IT.
BUT WE DIDN'T HAVE TIME TO DEAL WITH THAT THEN. WE HAD A WAR TO WIN... A WAR THAT SOON SEPARATED US.
GEOFF WOUND UP IN NAVAL INTELLIGENCE, HANK IN THE MARINES. PAT WAS ARMY INFANTRY--AND WASH WAS ONE OF THE TUSKEGEE AIRMEN.
THEY ALL HAD GOOD LIVES AFTER THE WAR--
--BUT I BECAME A TOOL, A CYBORG ASSASSIN LIVING IN THE SHADOWS, UNTIL STEVE SAVED MY LIFE... AND MY SOUL. THANKS TO HIM, I'M CAPTAIN AMERICA NOW.
I WAS SO LUCKY TO FIND TWO OF MY OLD FRIENDS IN TIME FOR ONE LAST TOAST.
PAT LEFT US SOON AFTERWARD.
AND JUST A FEW MONTHS LATER...
YOU KNEW MY GRANDFATHER...?

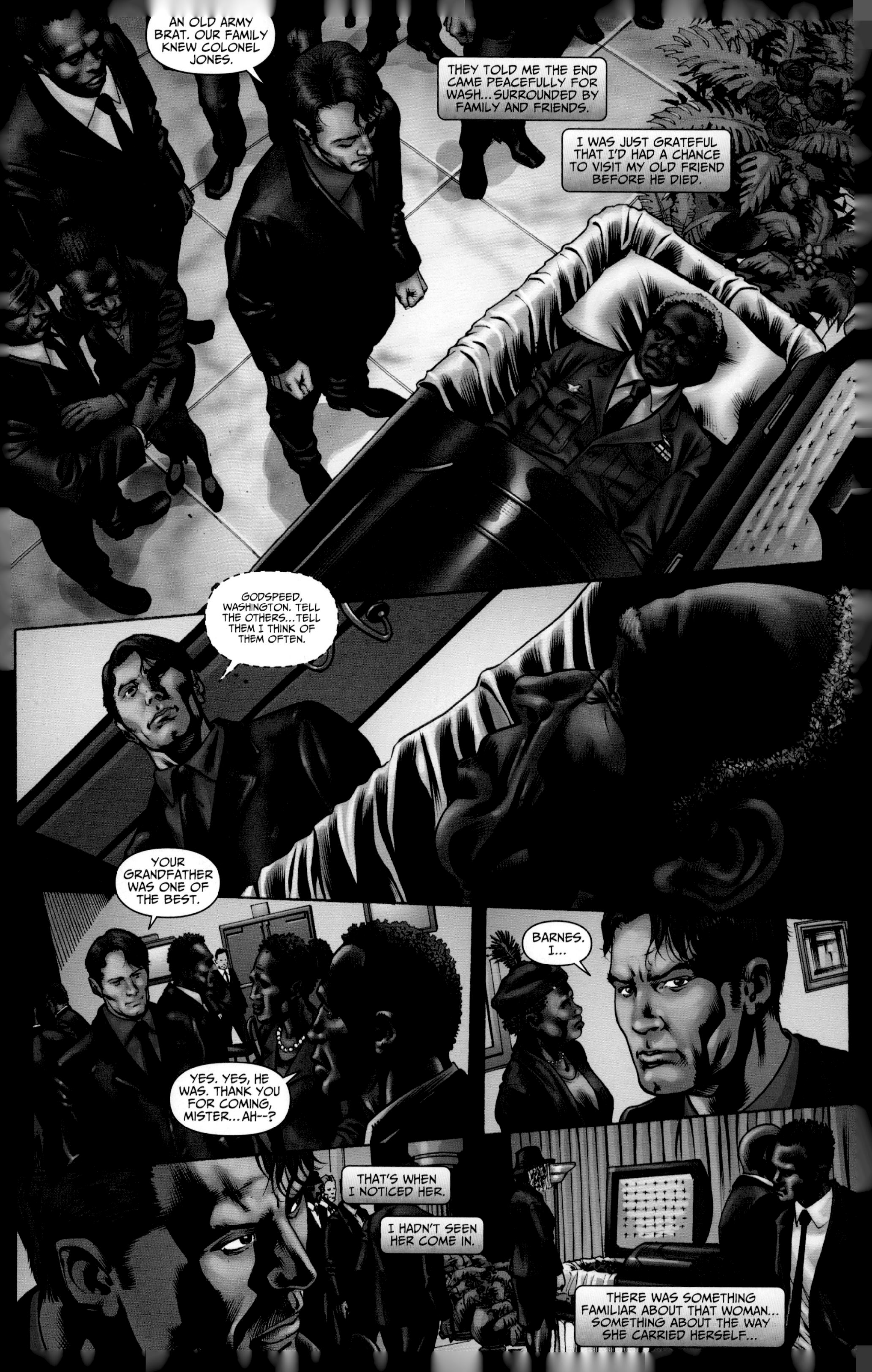
AN OLD ARMY BRAT. OUR FAMILY KNEW COLONEL JONES.
THEY TOLD ME THE END CAME PEACEFULLY FOR WASH... SURROUNDED BY FAMILY AND FRIENDS.
I WAS JUST GRATEFUL THAT I'D HAD A CHANCE TO VISIT MY OLD FRIEND BEFORE HE DIED.
GODSPEED, WASHINGTON. TELL THE OTHERS...TELL THEM I THINK OF THEM OFTEN.
YOUR GRANDFATHER WAS ONE OF THE BEST.
YES. YES, HE WAS. THANK YOU FOR COMING, MISTER...AH--?
BARNES. I...
THAT'S WHEN I NOTICED HER.
I HADN'T SEEN HER COME IN.
THERE WAS SOMETHING FAMILIAR ABOUT THAT WOMAN... SOMETHING ABOUT THE WAY SHE CARRIED HERSELF...

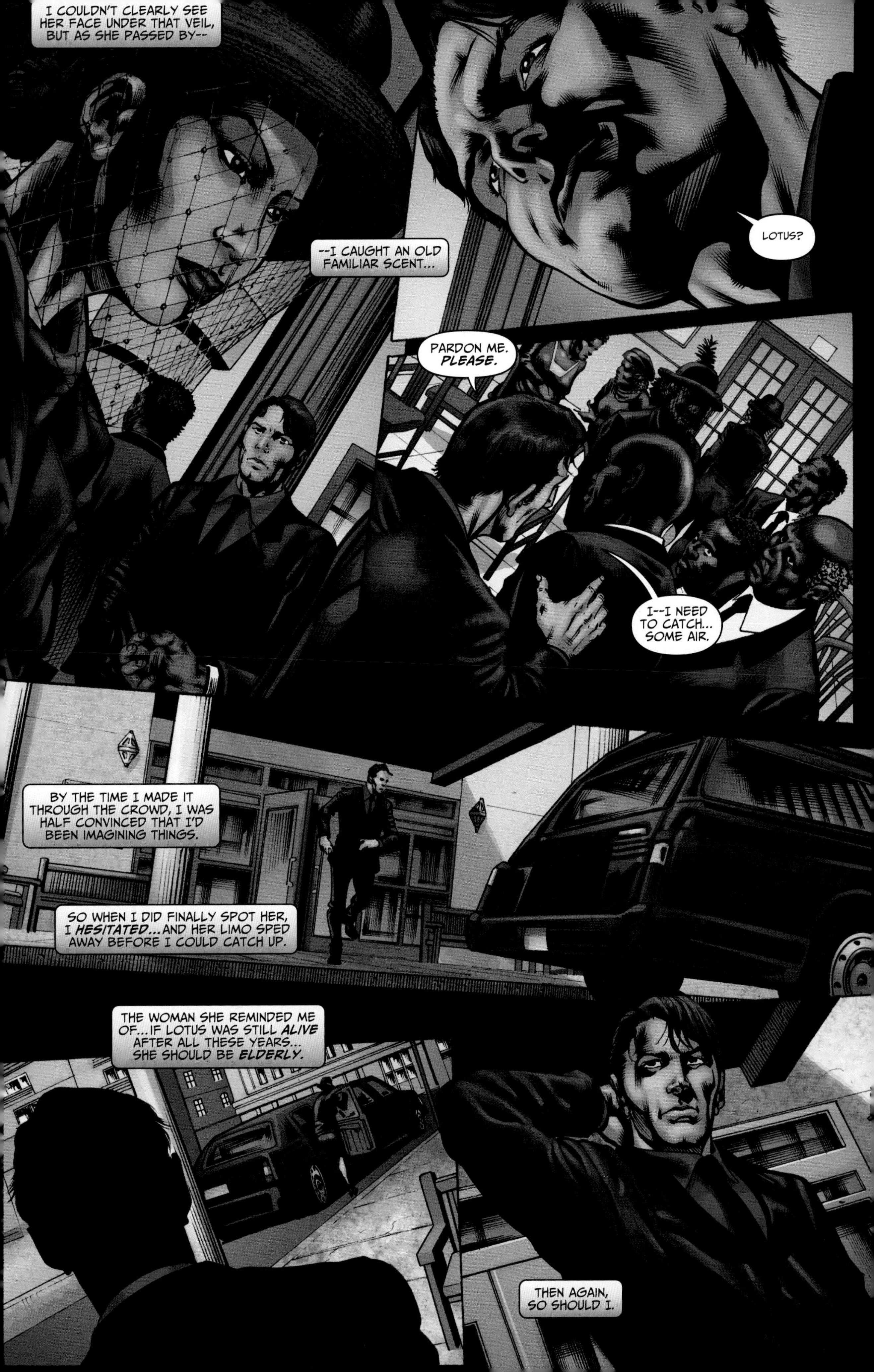
I COULDN'T CLEARLY SEE HER FACE UNDER THAT VEIL, BUT AS SHE PASSED BY--
--I CAUGHT AN OLD FAMILIAR SCENT...
LOTUS?
PARDON ME. *PLEASE.*
I--I NEED TO CATCH... SOME AIR.
BY THE TIME I MADE IT THROUGH THE CROWD, I WAS HALF CONVINCED THAT I'D BEEN IMAGINING THINGS.
SO WHEN I DID FINALLY SPOT HER, I *HESITATED...* AND HER LIMO SPED AWAY BEFORE I COULD CATCH UP.
THE WOMAN SHE REMINDED ME OF...IF LOTUS WAS STILL *ALIVE* AFTER ALL THESE YEARS... SHE SHOULD BE *ELDERLY.*
THEN AGAIN, SO SHOULD I.

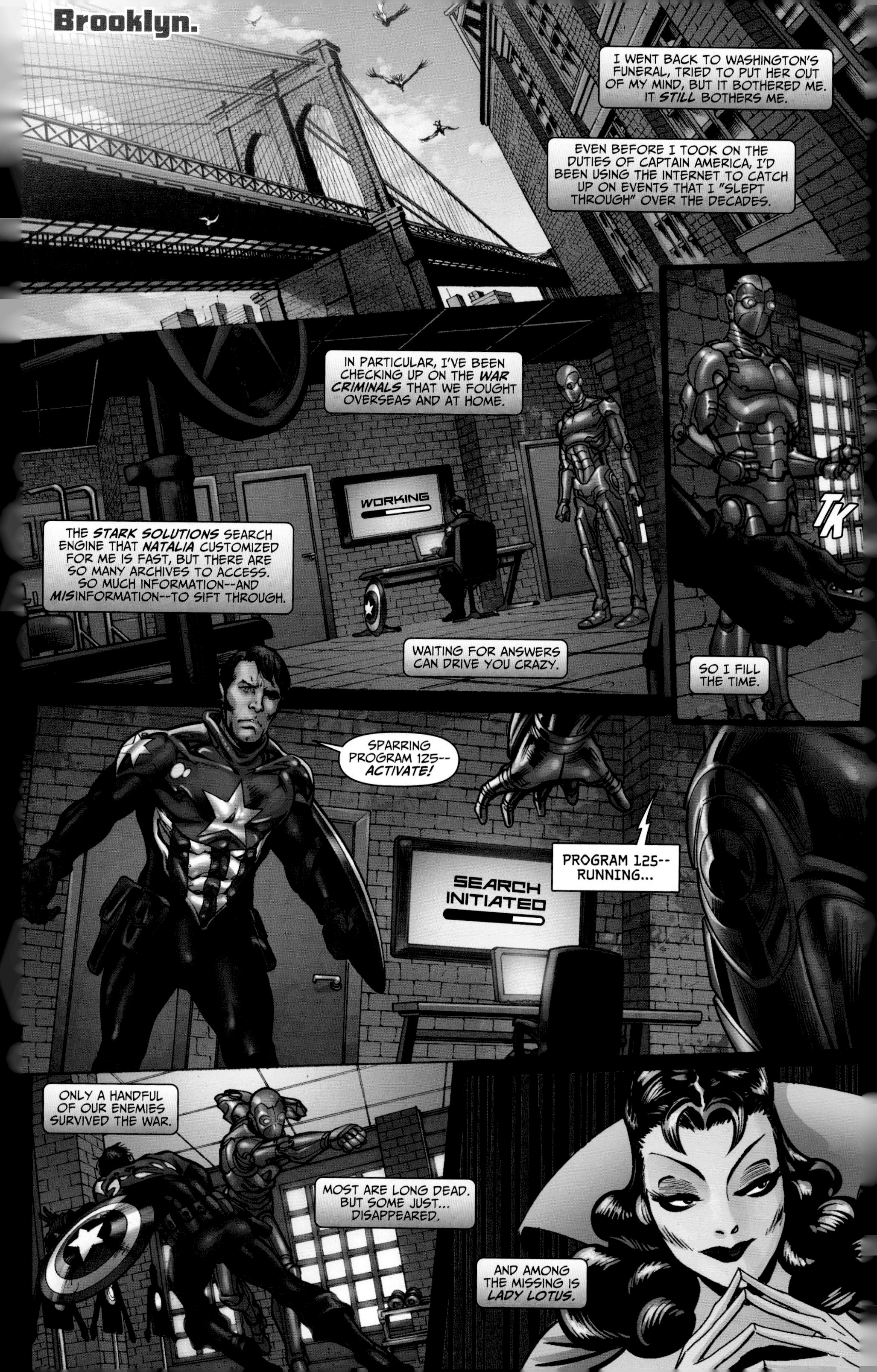

Brooklyn.
I WENT BACK TO WASHINGTON'S FUNERAL, TRIED TO PUT HER OUT OF MY MIND, BUT IT BOTHERED ME. IT *STILL* BOTHERS ME.
EVEN BEFORE I TOOK ON THE DUTIES OF CAPTAIN AMERICA, I'D BEEN USING THE INTERNET TO CATCH UP ON EVENTS THAT I "SLEPT THROUGH" OVER THE DECADES.
IN PARTICULAR, I'VE BEEN CHECKING UP ON THE *WAR CRIMINALS* THAT WE FOUGHT OVERSEAS AND AT HOME.
WORKING
THE *STARK SOLUTIONS* SEARCH ENGINE THAT *NATALIA* CUSTOMIZED FOR ME IS FAST, BUT THERE ARE SO MANY ARCHIVES TO ACCESS. SO MUCH INFORMATION--AND *MIS*INFORMATION--TO SIFT THROUGH.
WAITING FOR ANSWERS CAN DRIVE YOU CRAZY.
TK
SO I FILL THE TIME.
SPARRING PROGRAM 125-- *ACTIVATE!*
PROGRAM 125-- RUNNING...
SEARCH INITIATED
ONLY A HANDFUL OF OUR ENEMIES SURVIVED THE WAR.
MOST ARE LONG DEAD. BUT SOME JUST... DISAPPEARED.
AND AMONG THE MISSING IS *LADY LOTUS.*

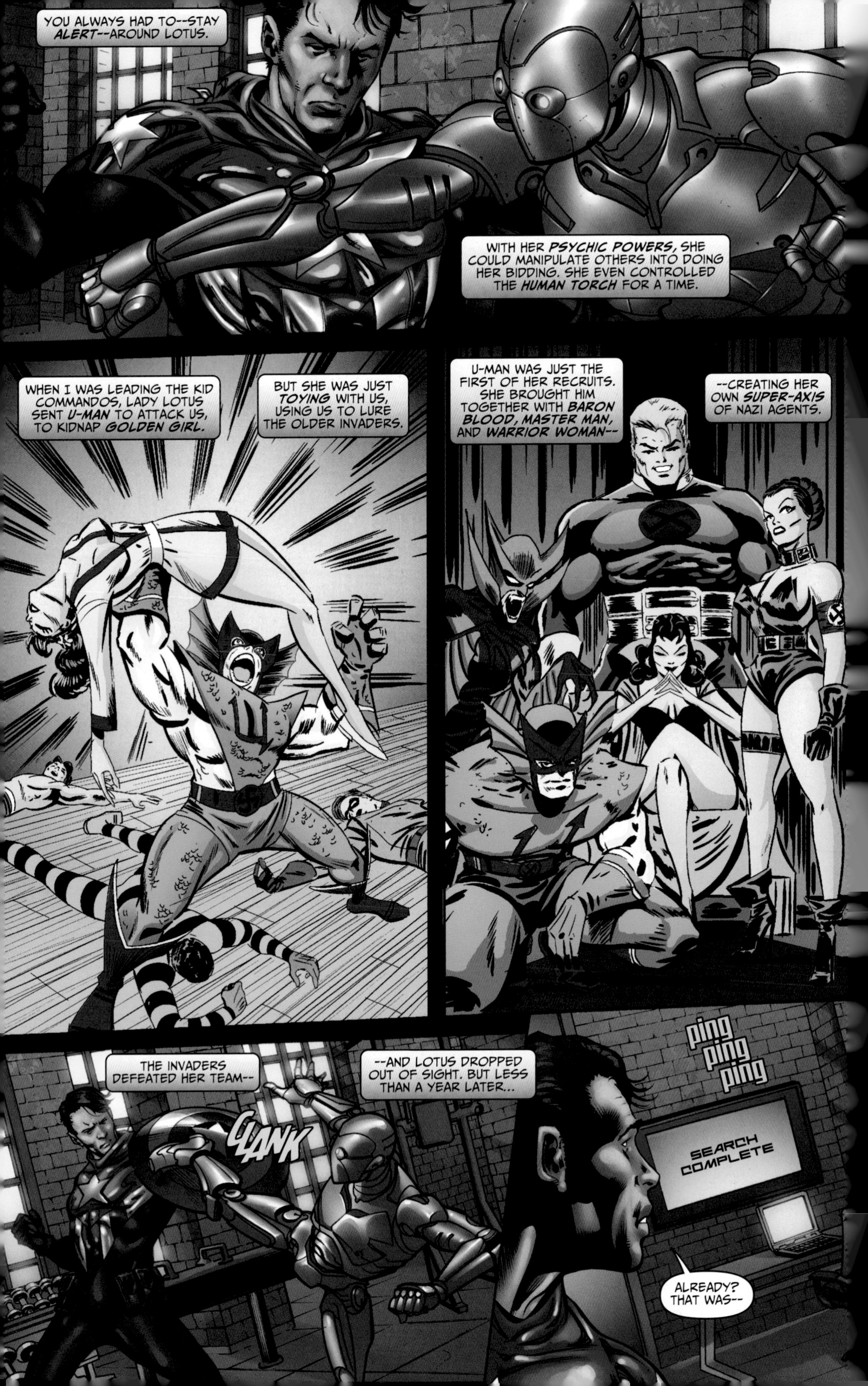
YOU ALWAYS HAD TO--STAY ALERT--AROUND LOTUS.
WITH HER PSYCHIC POWERS, SHE COULD MANIPULATE OTHERS INTO DOING HER BIDDING. SHE EVEN CONTROLLED THE HUMAN TORCH FOR A TIME.
WHEN I WAS LEADING THE KID COMMANDOS, LADY LOTUS SENT U-MAN TO ATTACK US, TO KIDNAP GOLDEN GIRL.
BUT SHE WAS JUST TOYING WITH US, USING US TO LURE THE OLDER INVADERS.
U-MAN WAS JUST THE FIRST OF HER RECRUITS. SHE BROUGHT HIM TOGETHER WITH BARON BLOOD, MASTER MAN, AND WARRIOR WOMAN--
--CREATING HER OWN SUPER-AXIS OF NAZI AGENTS.
THE INVADERS DEFEATED HER TEAM--
--AND LOTUS DROPPED OUT OF SIGHT. BUT LESS THAN A YEAR LATER...
CLANK
ping ping ping
SEARCH COMPLETE
ALREADY? THAT WAS--

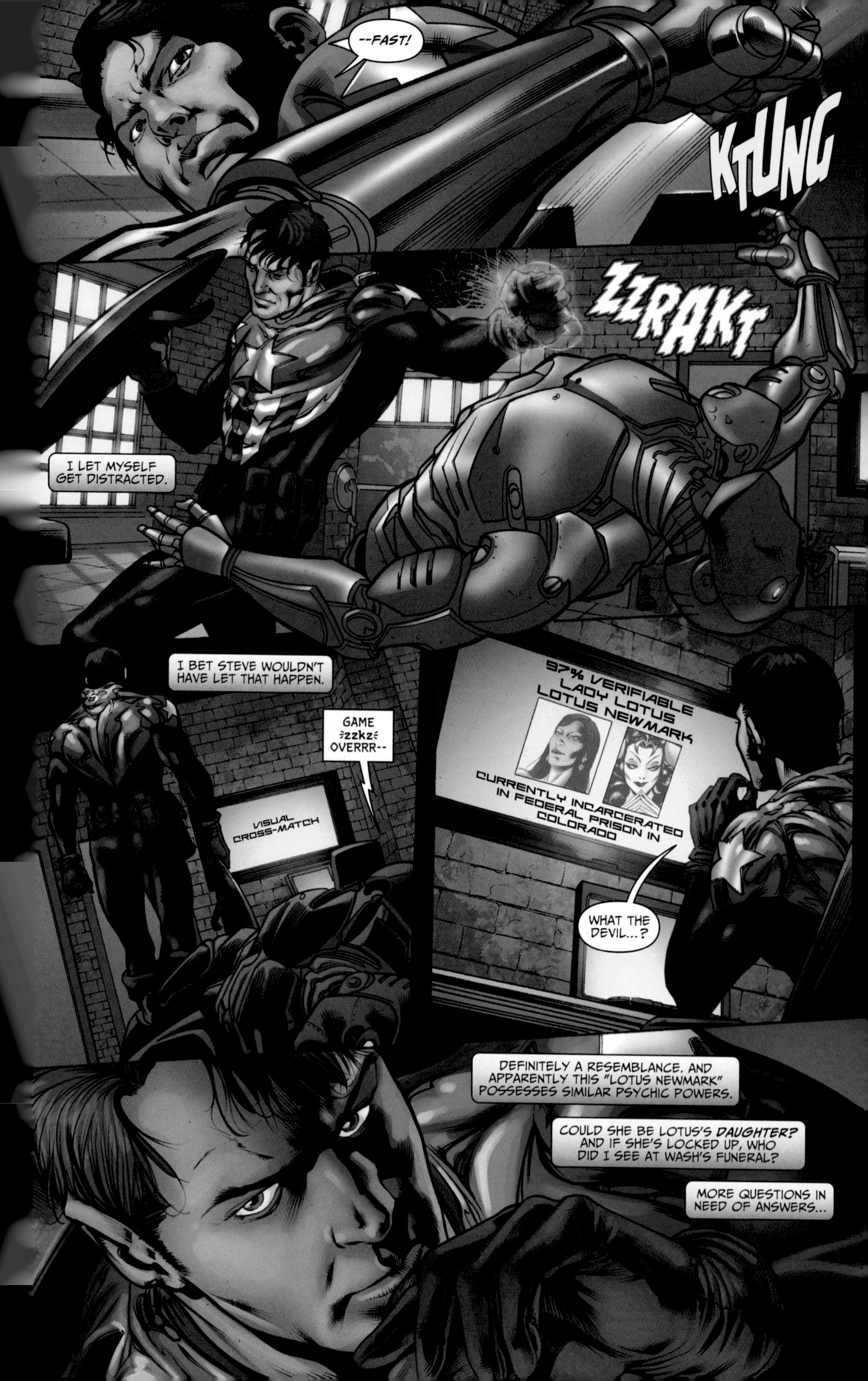
--FAST!
KTUNG
ZZRAKT
I LET MYSELF GET DISTRACTED.
I BET STEVE WOULDN'T HAVE LET THAT HAPPEN.
GAME zzkz OVERRR--
VISUAL CROSS-MATCH
97% VERIFIABLE LADY LOTUS LOTUS NEWMARK
CURRENTLY INCARCERATED IN FEDERAL PRISON IN COLORADO
WHAT THE DEVIL...?
DEFINITELY A RESEMBLANCE. AND APPARENTLY THIS "LOTUS NEWMARK" POSSESSES SIMILAR PSYCHIC POWERS.
COULD SHE BE LOTUS'S DAUGHTER? AND IF SHE'S LOCKED UP, WHO DID I SEE AT WASH'S FUNERAL?
MORE QUESTIONS IN NEED OF ANSWERS...

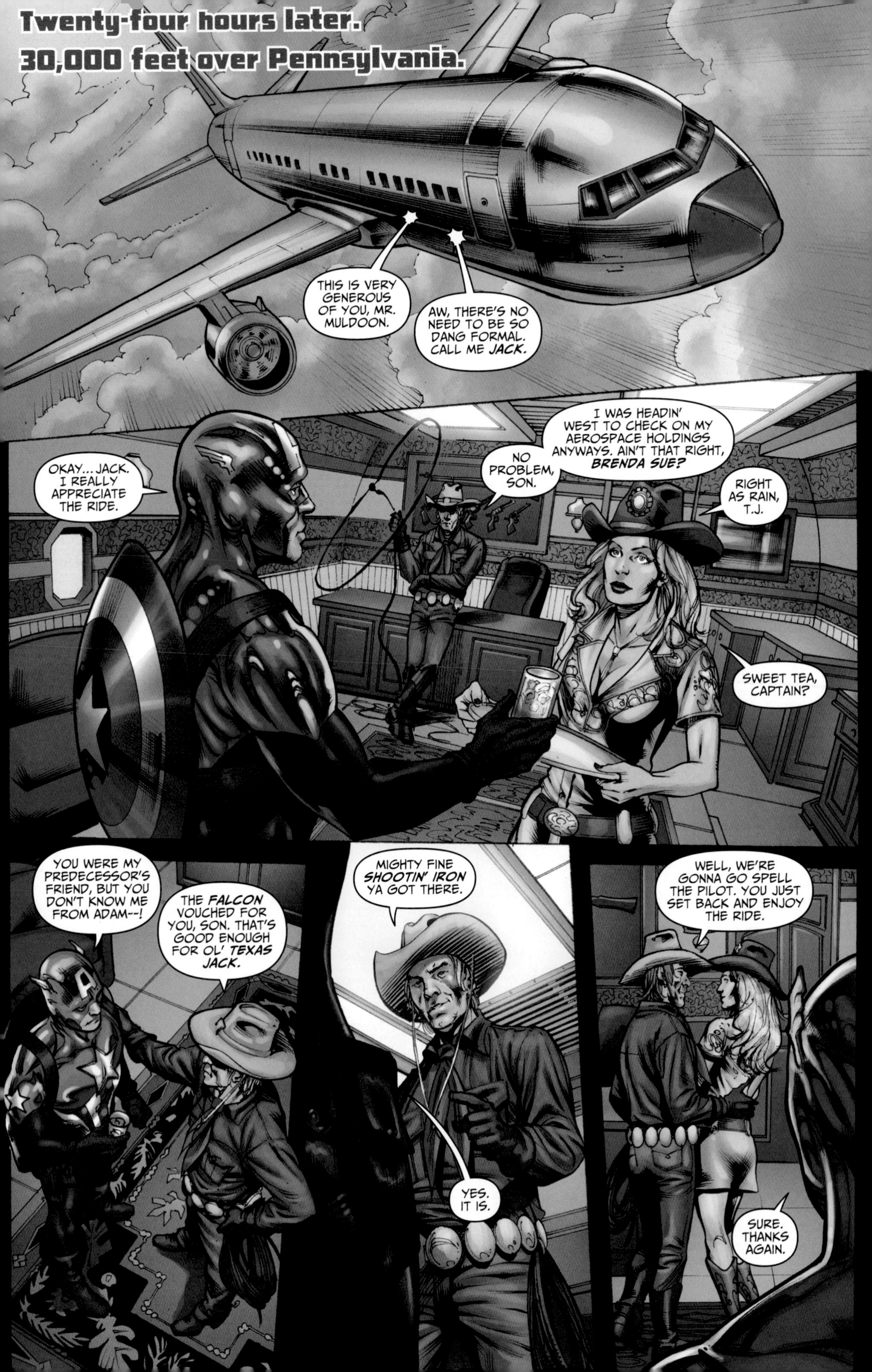
Twenty-four hours later.
30,000 feet over Pennsylvania.
THIS IS VERY GENEROUS OF YOU, MR. MULDOON.
AW, THERE'S NO NEED TO BE SO DANG FORMAL. CALL ME JACK.
OKAY... JACK. I REALLY APPRECIATE THE RIDE.
NO PROBLEM, SON.
I WAS HEADIN' WEST TO CHECK ON MY AEROSPACE HOLDINGS ANYWAYS. AIN'T THAT RIGHT, BRENDA SUE?
RIGHT AS RAIN, T.J.
SWEET TEA, CAPTAIN?
YOU WERE MY PREDECESSOR'S FRIEND, BUT YOU DON'T KNOW ME FROM ADAM--!
THE FALCON VOUCHED FOR YOU, SON. THAT'S GOOD ENOUGH FOR OL' TEXAS JACK.
MIGHTY FINE SHOOTIN' IRON YA GOT THERE.
YES. IT IS.
WELL, WE'RE GONNA GO SPELL THE PILOT. YOU JUST SET BACK AND ENJOY THE RIDE.
SURE. THANKS AGAIN.

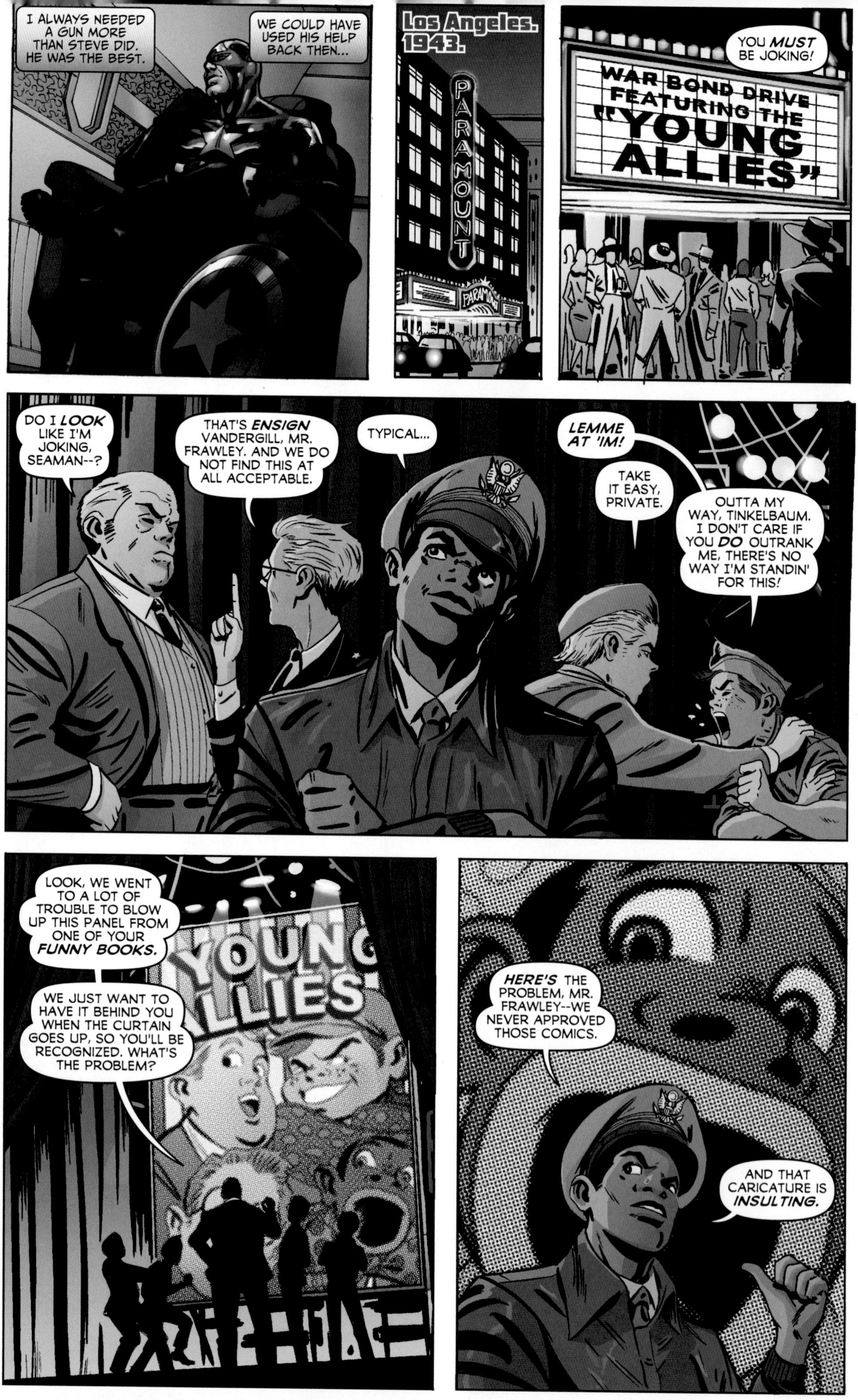

I ALWAYS NEEDED A GUN MORE THAN STEVE DID. HE WAS THE BEST.
WE COULD HAVE USED HIS HELP BACK THEN...
Los Angeles. 1943.
PARAMOUNT
YOU MUST BE JOKING!
WAR BOND DRIVE FEATURING THE "YOUNG ALLIES"
DO I LOOK LIKE I'M JOKING, SEAMAN--?
THAT'S ENSIGN VANDERGILL, MR. FRAWLEY. AND WE DO NOT FIND THIS AT ALL ACCEPTABLE.
TYPICAL...
LEMME AT 'IM!
TAKE IT EASY, PRIVATE.
OUTTA MY WAY, TINKELBAUM. I DON'T CARE IF YOU DO OUTRANK ME, THERE'S NO WAY I'M STANDIN' FOR THIS!
LOOK, WE WENT TO A LOT OF TROUBLE TO BLOW UP THIS PANEL FROM ONE OF YOUR FUNNY BOOKS.
WE JUST WANT TO HAVE IT BEHIND YOU WHEN THE CURTAIN GOES UP, SO YOU'LL BE RECOGNIZED. WHAT'S THE PROBLEM?
HERE'S THE PROBLEM, MR. FRAWLEY--WE NEVER APPROVED THOSE COMICS.
AND THAT CARICATURE IS INSULTING.

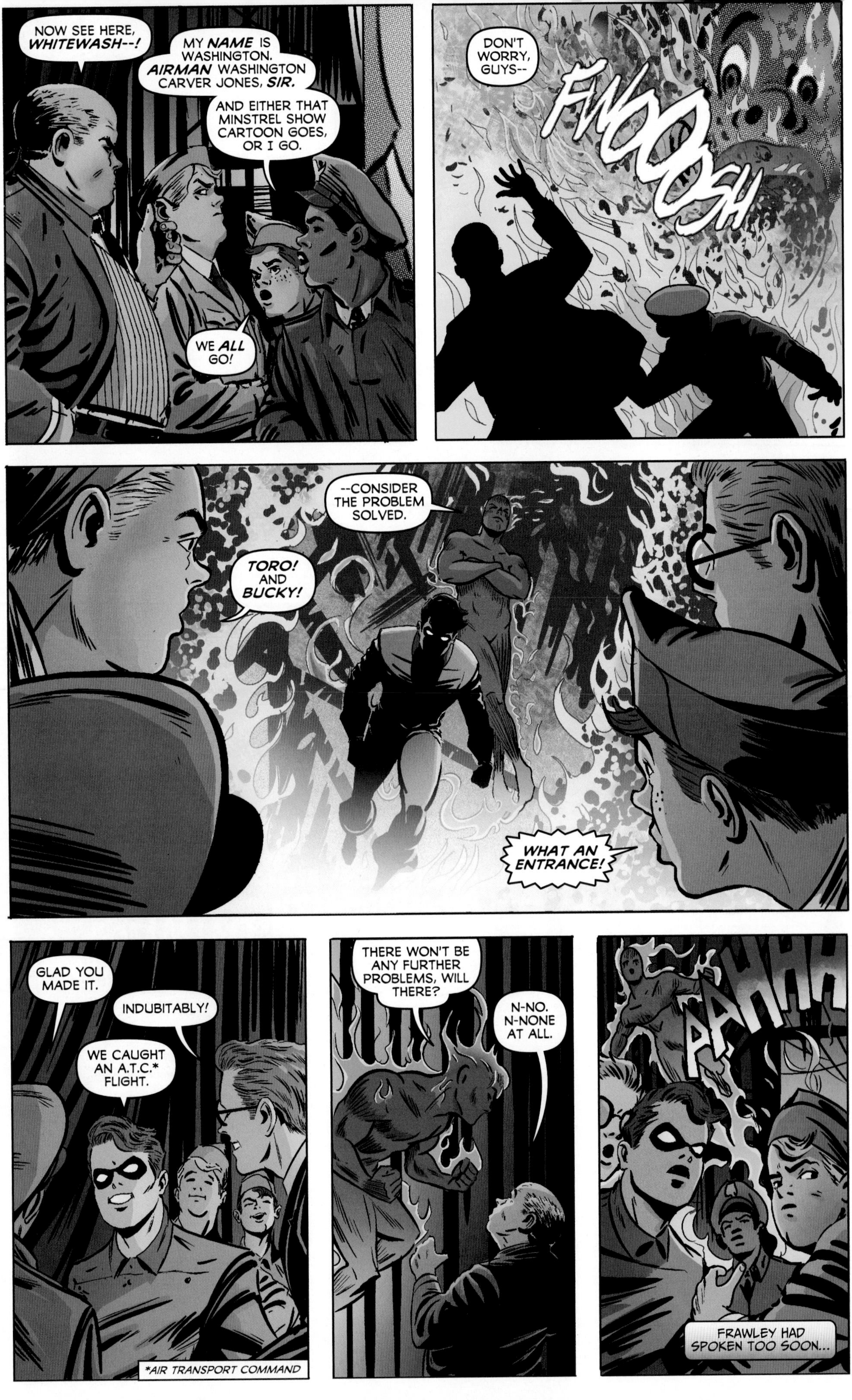
NOW SEE HERE, WHITEWASH--!
MY NAME IS WASHINGTON. AIRMAN WASHINGTON CARVER JONES, SIR.
AND EITHER THAT MINSTREL SHOW CARTOON GOES, OR I GO.
WE ALL GO!
DON'T WORRY, GUYS--
FWOOOSH
--CONSIDER THE PROBLEM SOLVED.
TORO! AND BUCKY!
WHAT AN ENTRANCE!
GLAD YOU MADE IT.
INDUBITABLY!
WE CAUGHT AN A.T.C.* FLIGHT.
*AIR TRANSPORT COMMAND
THERE WON'T BE ANY FURTHER PROBLEMS, WILL THERE?
N-NO. N-NONE AT ALL.
AAHHH
FRAWLEY HAD SPOKEN TOO SOON...

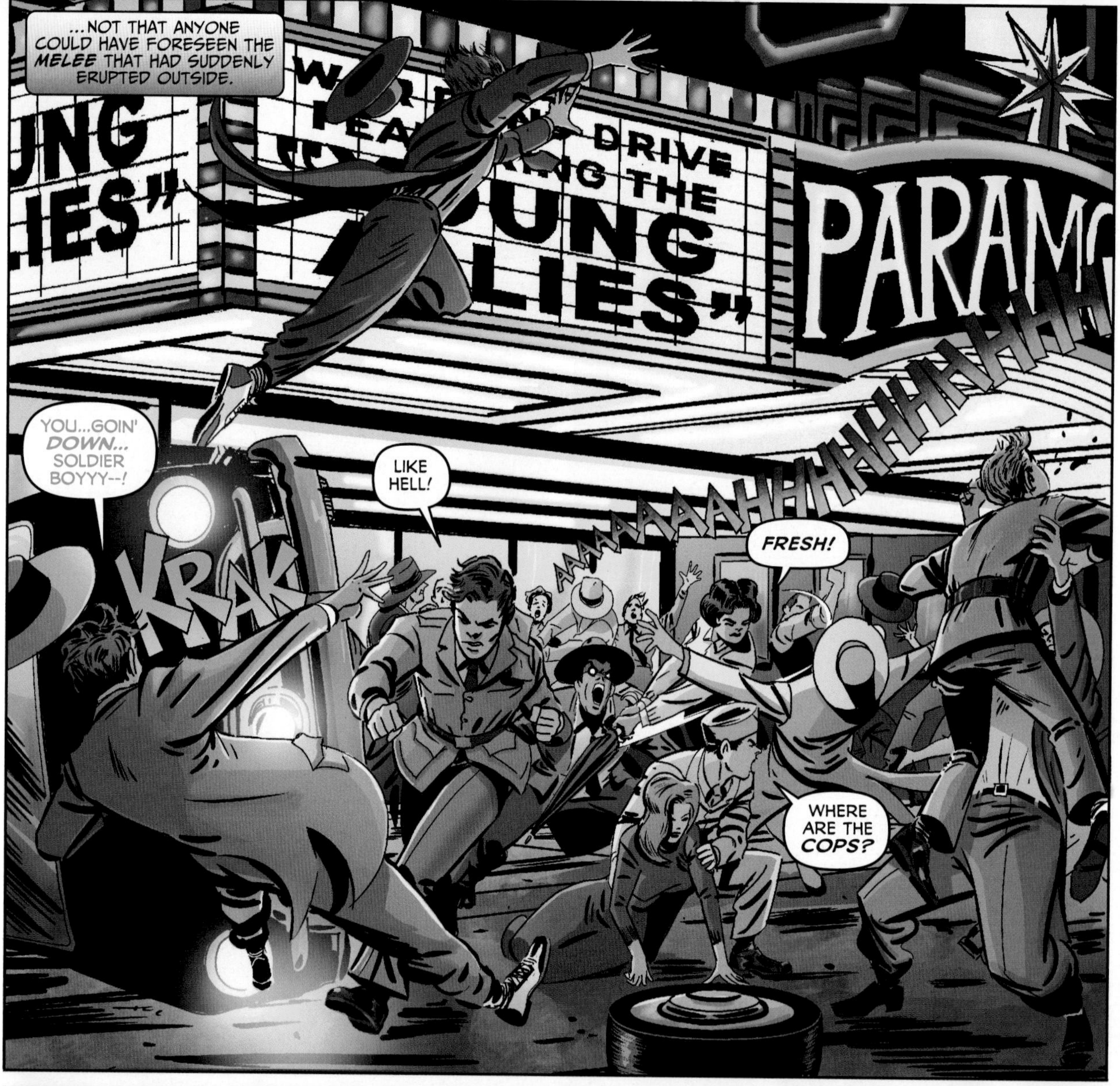
...NOT THAT ANYONE COULD HAVE FORESEEN THE *MELEE* THAT HAD SUDDENLY ERUPTED OUTSIDE.
YOU...GOIN' *DOWN*... SOLDIER BOYYY--!
KRAK
LIKE HELL!
FRESH!
WHERE ARE THE *COPS?*

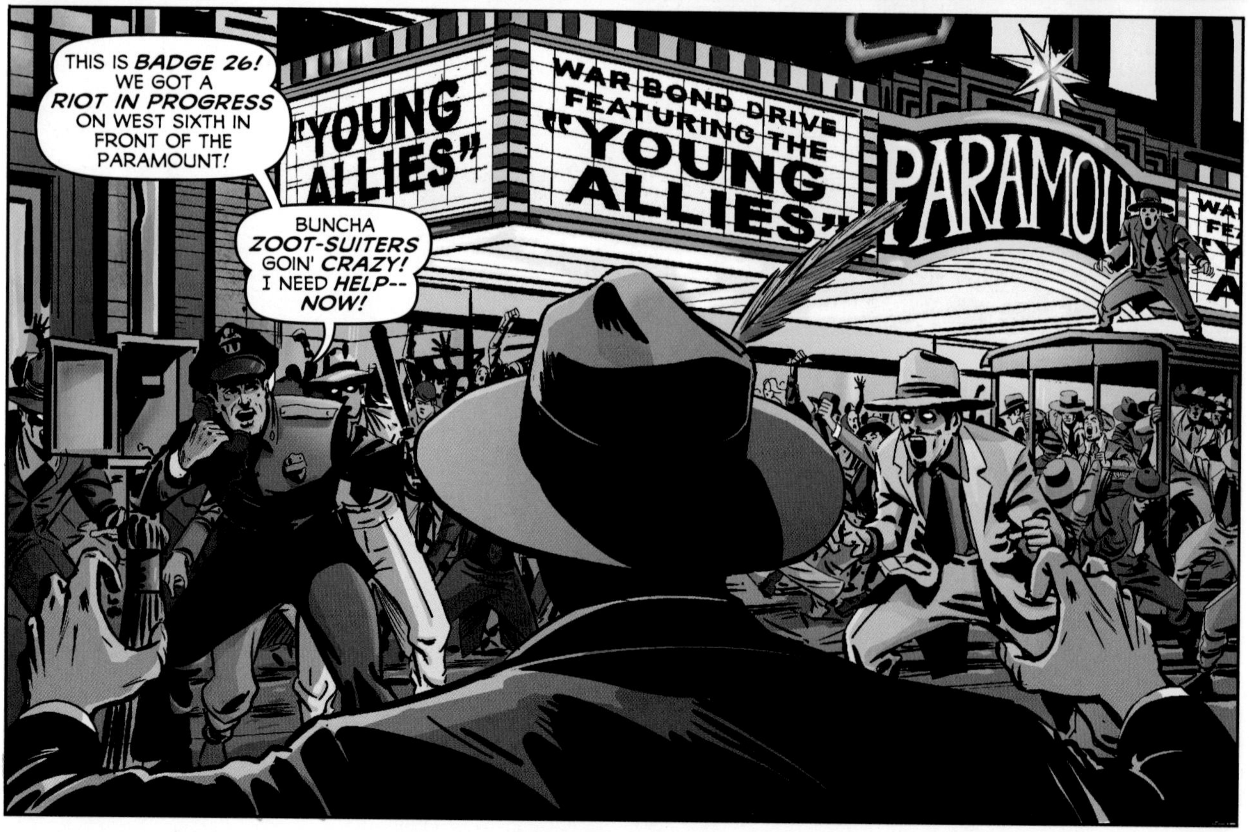
"YOUNG ALLIES"
WAR BOND DRIVE FEATURING THE "YOUNG ALLIES"
THIS IS *BADGE 26!* WE GOT A *RIOT IN PROGRESS* ON WEST SIXTH IN FRONT OF THE PARAMOUNT!
BUNCHA *ZOOT-SUITERS* GOIN' *CRAZY!* I NEED *HELP--NOW!*

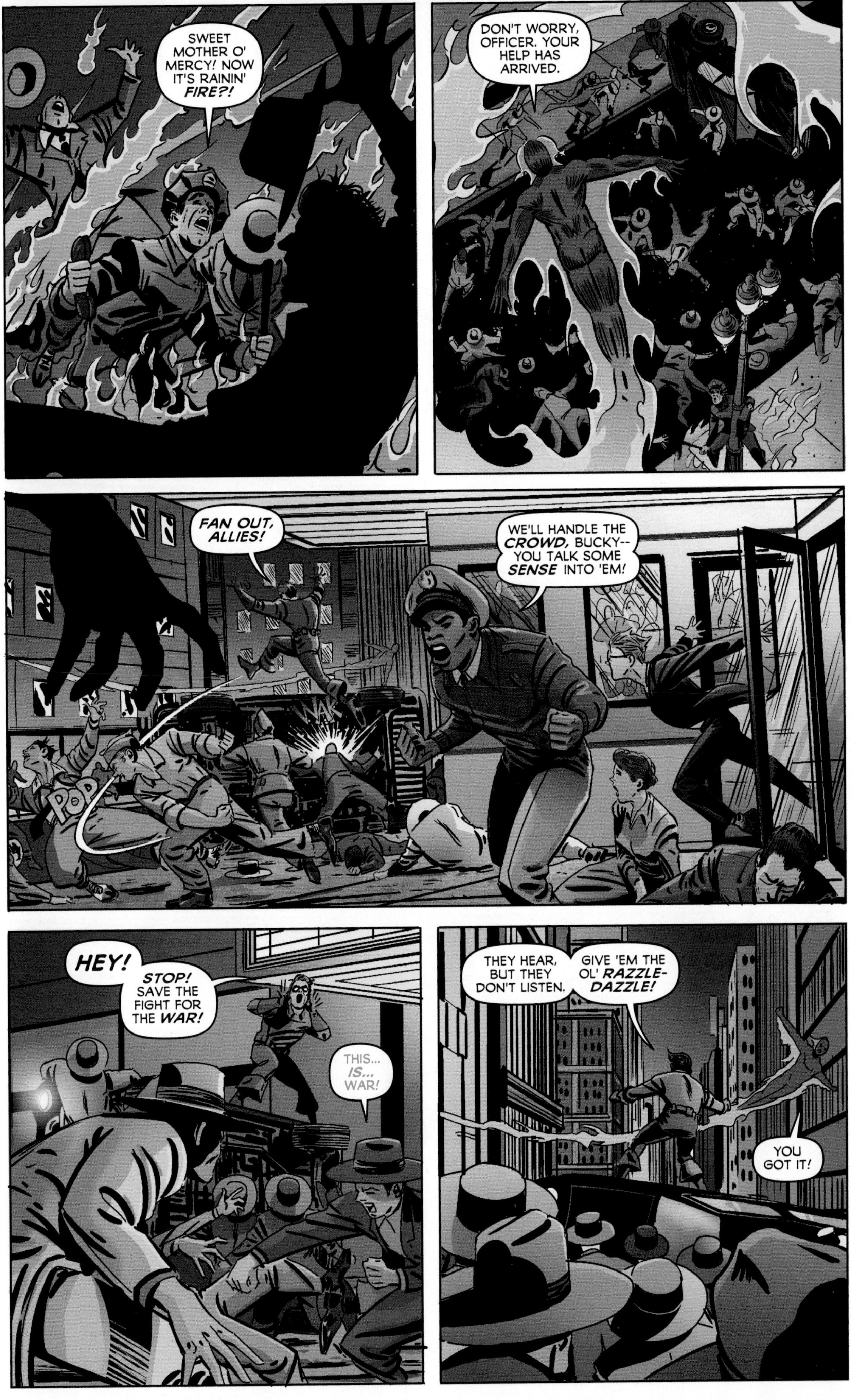
SWEET MOTHER O' MERCY! NOW IT'S RAININ' *FIRE?!*
DON'T WORRY, OFFICER. YOUR HELP HAS ARRIVED.
FAN OUT, ALLIES!
WE'LL HANDLE THE *CROWD,* BUCKY-- YOU TALK SOME *SENSE* INTO 'EM!
POP
HEY!
STOP! SAVE THE FIGHT FOR THE *WAR!*
THIS... *IS...* WAR!
THEY HEAR, BUT THEY DON'T LISTEN.
GIVE 'EM THE OL' *RAZZLE-DAZZLE!*
YOU GOT IT!

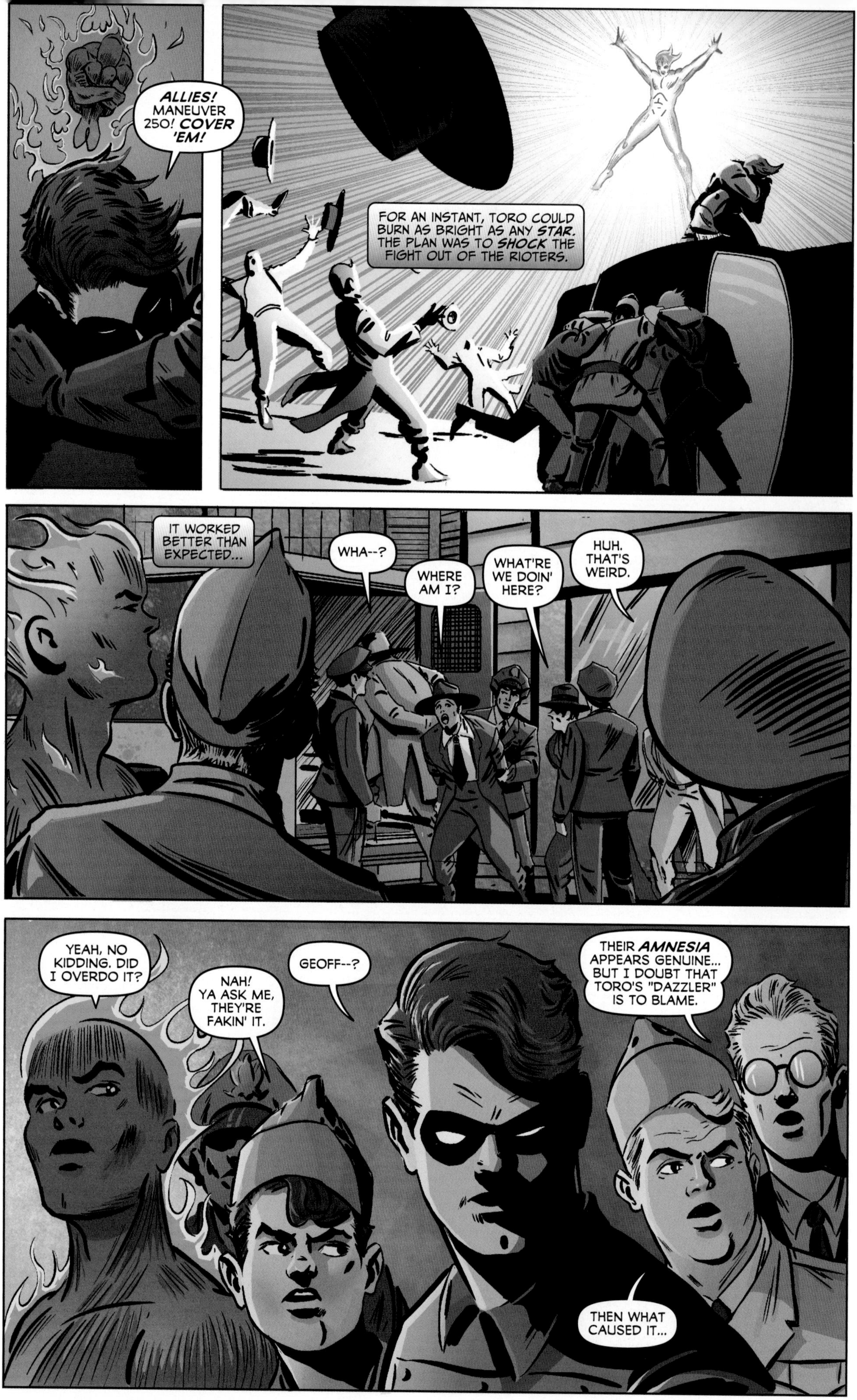
ALLIES! MANEUVER 250! COVER 'EM!
FOR AN INSTANT, TORO COULD BURN AS BRIGHT AS ANY STAR. THE PLAN WAS TO SHOCK THE FIGHT OUT OF THE RIOTERS.
IT WORKED BETTER THAN EXPECTED...
WHA--?
WHERE AM I?
WHAT'RE WE DOIN' HERE?
HUH. THAT'S WEIRD.
YEAH, NO KIDDING. DID I OVERDO IT?
NAH! YA ASK ME, THEY'RE FAKIN' IT.
GEOFF--?
THEIR AMNESIA APPEARS GENUINE... BUT I DOUBT THAT TORO'S "DAZZLER" IS TO BLAME.
THEN WHAT CAUSED IT...

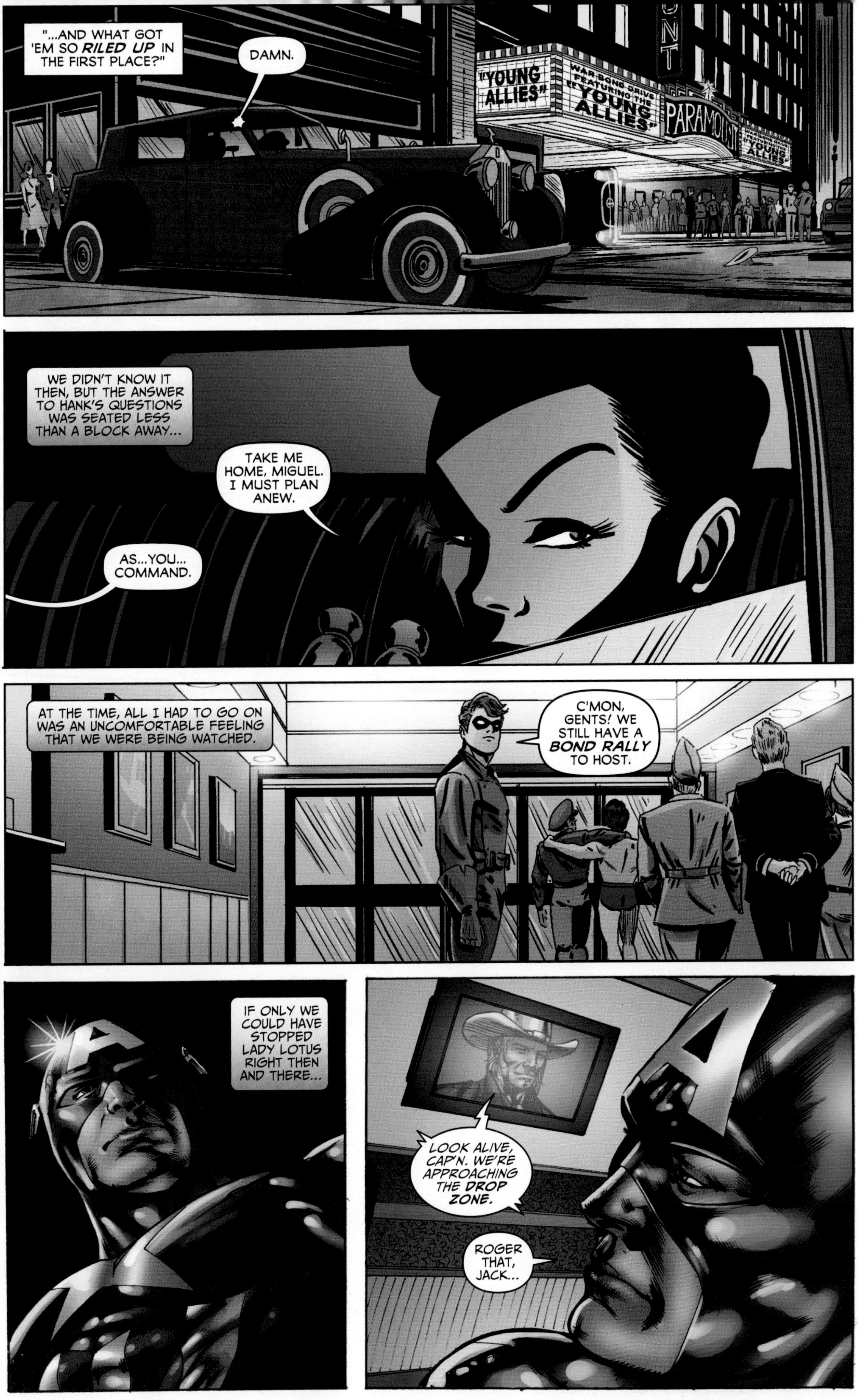
"...AND WHAT GOT 'EM SO ***RILED UP*** IN THE FIRST PLACE?"
DAMN.
"YOUNG ALLIES"
WAR BOND DRIVE FEATURING THE "YOUNG ALLIES"
PARAMOUNT
WE DIDN'T KNOW IT THEN, BUT THE ANSWER TO HANK'S QUESTIONS WAS SEATED LESS THAN A BLOCK AWAY...
TAKE ME HOME, MIGUEL. I MUST PLAN ANEW.
AS...YOU... COMMAND.
AT THE TIME, ALL I HAD TO GO ON WAS AN UNCOMFORTABLE FEELING THAT WE WERE BEING WATCHED.
C'MON, GENTS! WE STILL HAVE A ***BOND RALLY*** TO HOST.
IF ONLY WE COULD HAVE STOPPED LADY LOTUS RIGHT THEN AND THERE...
*LOOK ALIVE, CAP'N. WE'RE APPROACHING THE **DROP ZONE.***
ROGER THAT, JACK...

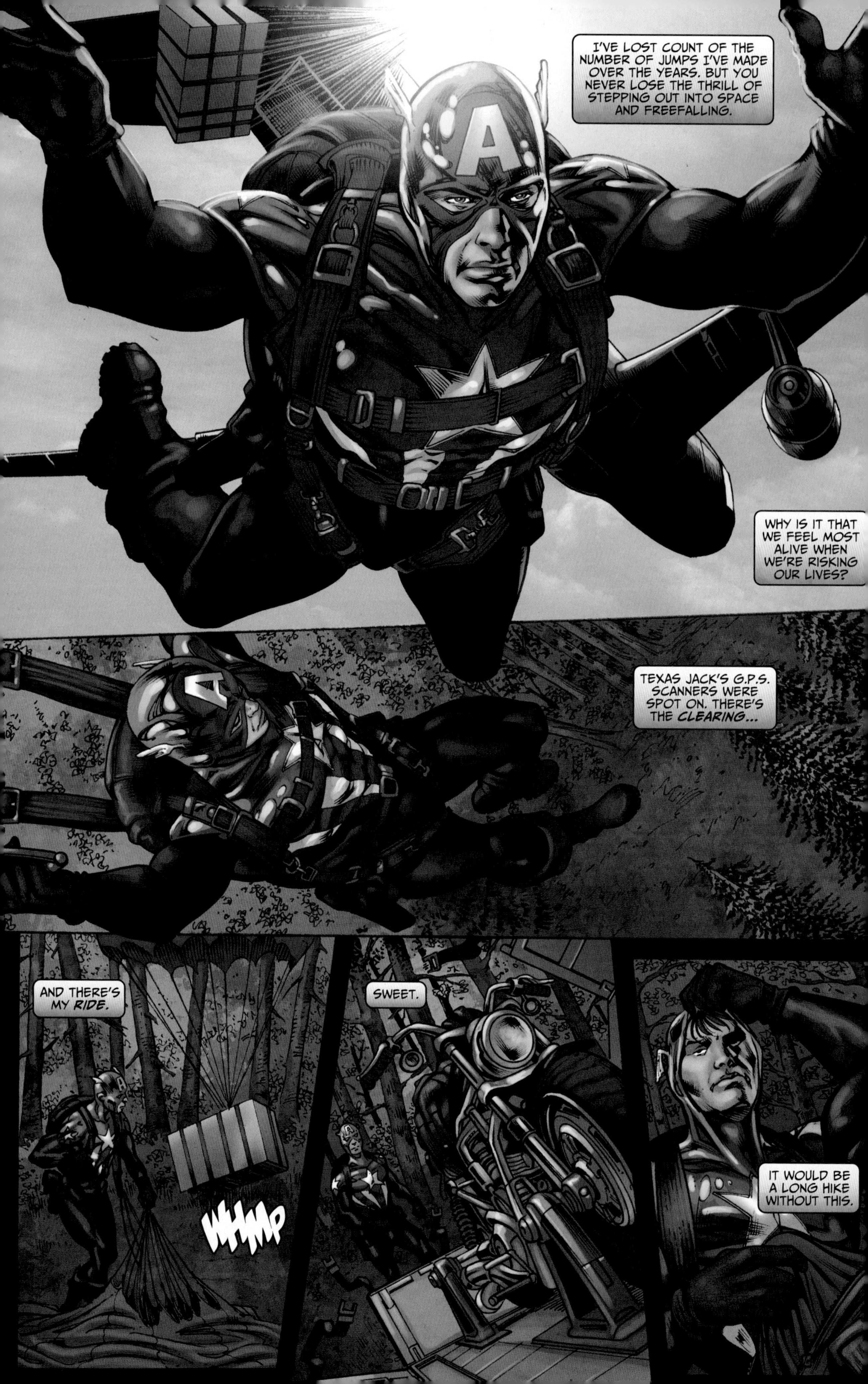
I'VE LOST COUNT OF THE NUMBER OF JUMPS I'VE MADE OVER THE YEARS. BUT YOU NEVER LOSE THE THRILL OF STEPPING OUT INTO SPACE AND FREEFALLING.
WHY IS IT THAT WE FEEL MOST ALIVE WHEN WE'RE RISKING OUR LIVES?
TEXAS JACK'S G.P.S. SCANNERS WERE SPOT ON. THERE'S THE *CLEARING*...
AND THERE'S MY *RIDE*.
WHMP
SWEET.
IT WOULD BE A LONG HIKE WITHOUT THIS.

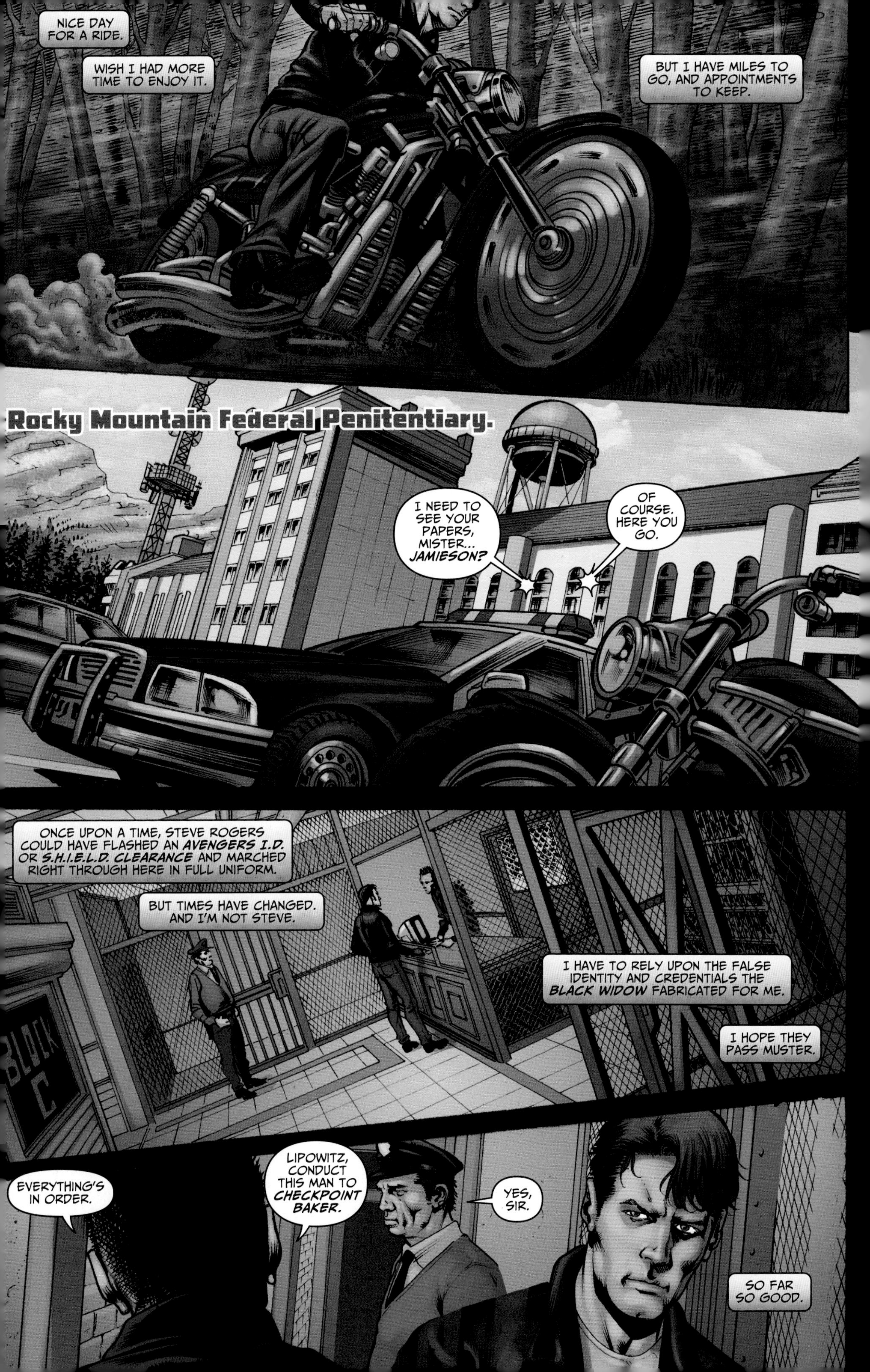
NICE DAY FOR A RIDE.
WISH I HAD MORE TIME TO ENJOY IT.
BUT I HAVE MILES TO GO, AND APPOINTMENTS TO KEEP.
Rocky Mountain Federal Penitentiary.
I NEED TO SEE YOUR PAPERS, MISTER... JAMIESON?
OF COURSE. HERE YOU GO.
ONCE UPON A TIME, STEVE ROGERS COULD HAVE FLASHED AN AVENGERS I.D. OR S.H.I.E.L.D. CLEARANCE AND MARCHED RIGHT THROUGH HERE IN FULL UNIFORM.
BUT TIMES HAVE CHANGED. AND I'M NOT STEVE.
I HAVE TO RELY UPON THE FALSE IDENTITY AND CREDENTIALS THE BLACK WIDOW FABRICATED FOR ME.
I HOPE THEY PASS MUSTER.
BLOCK C
EVERYTHING'S IN ORDER.
LIPOWITZ, CONDUCT THIS MAN TO CHECKPOINT BAKER.
YES, SIR.
SO FAR SO GOOD.

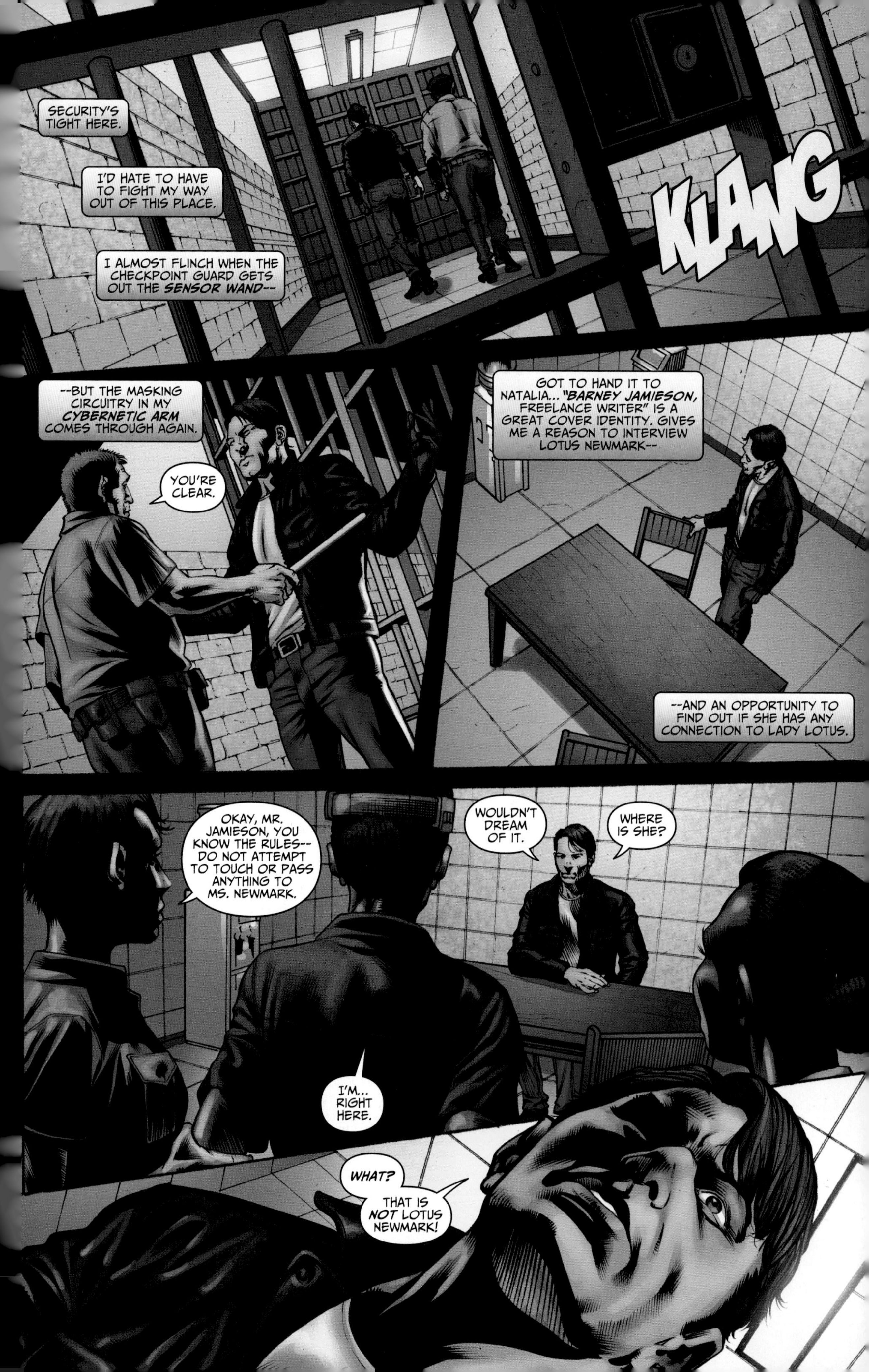
SECURITY'S TIGHT HERE.
I'D HATE TO HAVE TO FIGHT MY WAY OUT OF THIS PLACE.
I ALMOST FLINCH WHEN THE CHECKPOINT GUARD GETS OUT THE *SENSOR WAND*--
KLANG
--BUT THE MASKING CIRCUITRY IN MY *CYBERNETIC ARM* COMES THROUGH AGAIN.
YOU'RE CLEAR.
GOT TO HAND IT TO NATALIA... *"BARNEY JAMIESON,* FREELANCE WRITER" IS A GREAT COVER IDENTITY. GIVES ME A REASON TO INTERVIEW LOTUS NEWMARK--
--AND AN OPPORTUNITY TO FIND OUT IF SHE HAS ANY CONNECTION TO LADY LOTUS.
OKAY, MR. JAMIESON, YOU KNOW THE RULES-- DO NOT ATTEMPT TO TOUCH OR PASS ANYTHING TO MS. NEWMARK.
WOULDN'T DREAM OF IT.
WHERE IS SHE?
I'M... RIGHT HERE.
WHAT?
THAT IS *NOT* LOTUS NEWMARK!

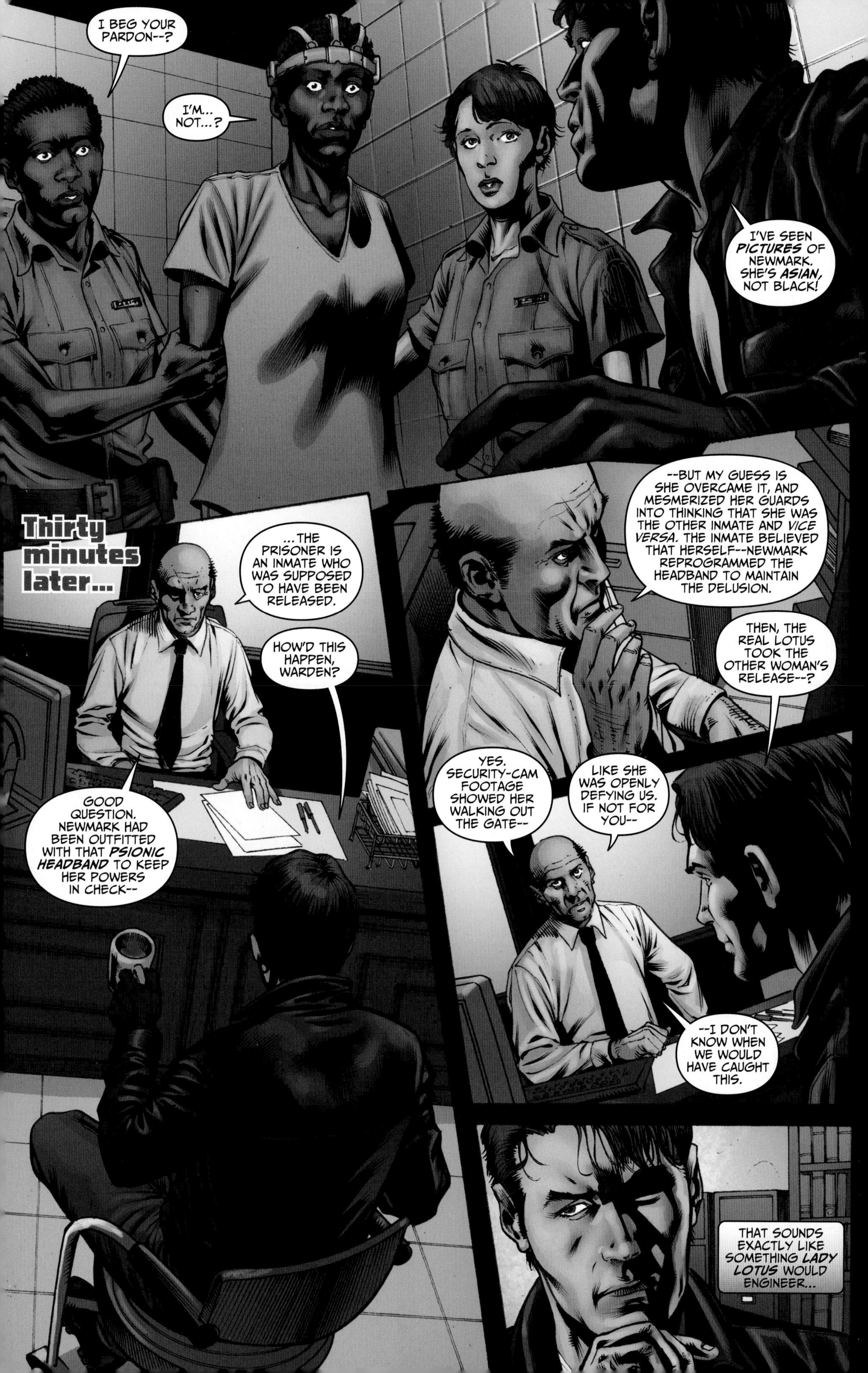
I BEG YOUR PARDON--?
I'M... NOT...?
I'VE SEEN PICTURES OF NEWMARK. SHE'S ASIAN, NOT BLACK!
Thirty minutes later...
...THE PRISONER IS AN INMATE WHO WAS SUPPOSED TO HAVE BEEN RELEASED.
HOW'D THIS HAPPEN, WARDEN?
GOOD QUESTION. NEWMARK HAD BEEN OUTFITTED WITH THAT PSIONIC HEADBAND TO KEEP HER POWERS IN CHECK--
--BUT MY GUESS IS SHE OVERCAME IT, AND MESMERIZED HER GUARDS INTO THINKING THAT SHE WAS THE OTHER INMATE AND VICE VERSA. THE INMATE BELIEVED THAT HERSELF--NEWMARK REPROGRAMMED THE HEADBAND TO MAINTAIN THE DELUSION.
THEN, THE REAL LOTUS TOOK THE OTHER WOMAN'S RELEASE--?
YES. SECURITY-CAM FOOTAGE SHOWED HER WALKING OUT THE GATE--
LIKE SHE WAS OPENLY DEFYING US. IF NOT FOR YOU--
--I DON'T KNOW WHEN WE WOULD HAVE CAUGHT THIS.
THAT SOUNDS EXACTLY LIKE SOMETHING LADY LOTUS WOULD ENGINEER...

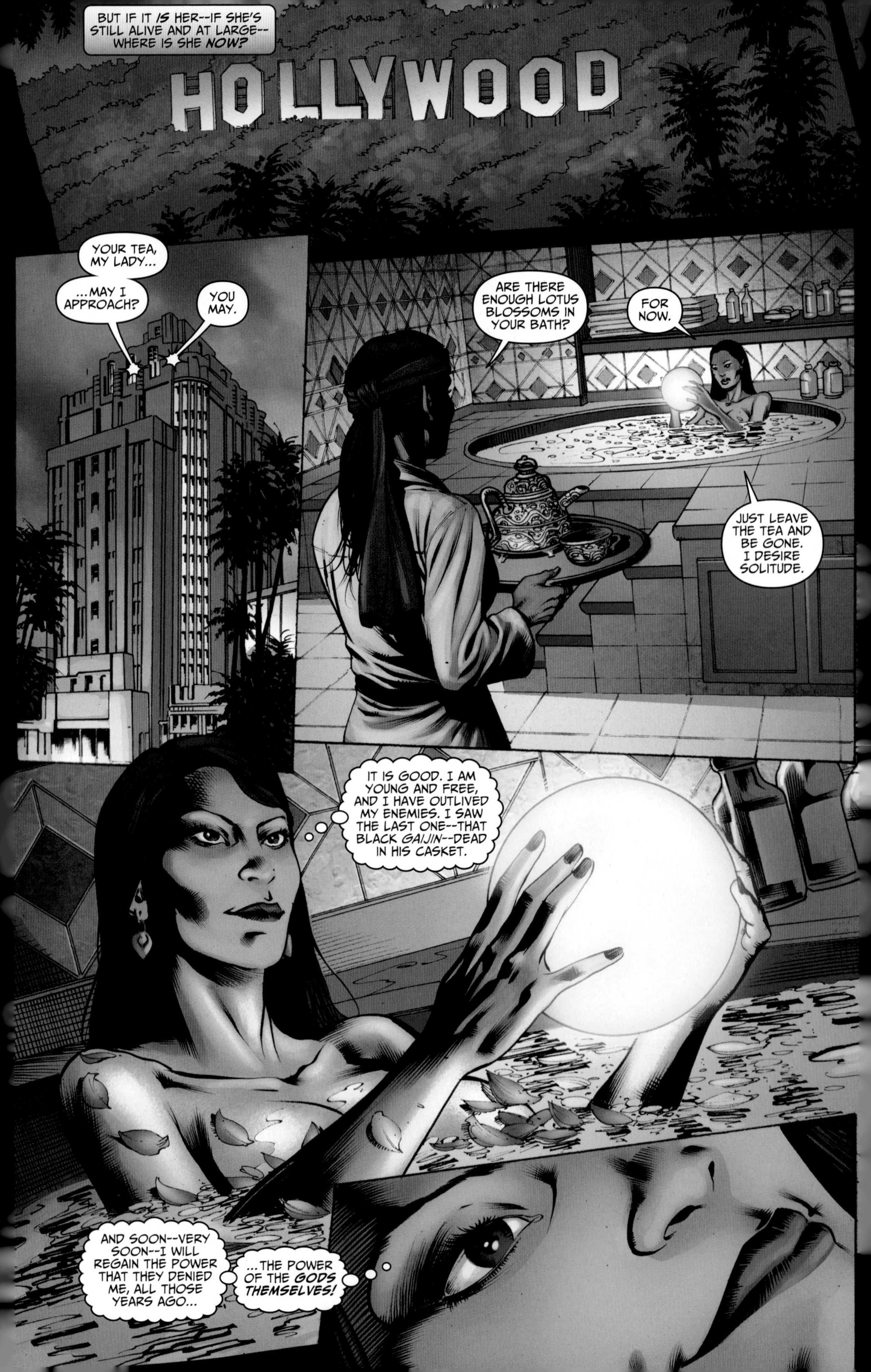
BUT IF IT *IS* HER--IF SHE'S STILL ALIVE AND AT LARGE-- WHERE IS SHE *NOW?*
HOLLYWOOD
YOUR TEA, MY LADY...
...MAY I APPROACH?
YOU MAY.
ARE THERE ENOUGH LOTUS BLOSSOMS IN YOUR BATH?
FOR NOW.
JUST LEAVE THE TEA AND BE GONE. I DESIRE SOLITUDE.
IT IS GOOD. I AM YOUNG AND FREE, AND I HAVE OUTLIVED MY ENEMIES. I SAW THE LAST ONE--THAT BLACK *GAIJIN*--DEAD IN HIS CASKET.
AND SOON--VERY SOON--I WILL REGAIN THE POWER THAT THEY DENIED ME, ALL THOSE YEARS AGO...
...THE POWER OF THE ***GODS THEMSELVES!***

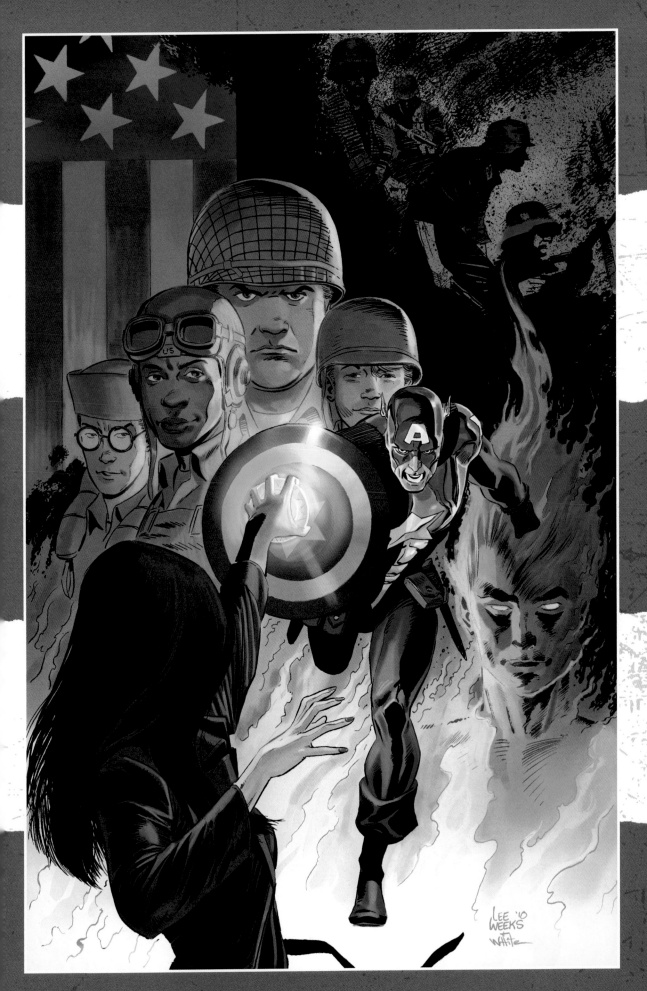

CAPTAIN AMERICA: FOREVER ALLIES #2

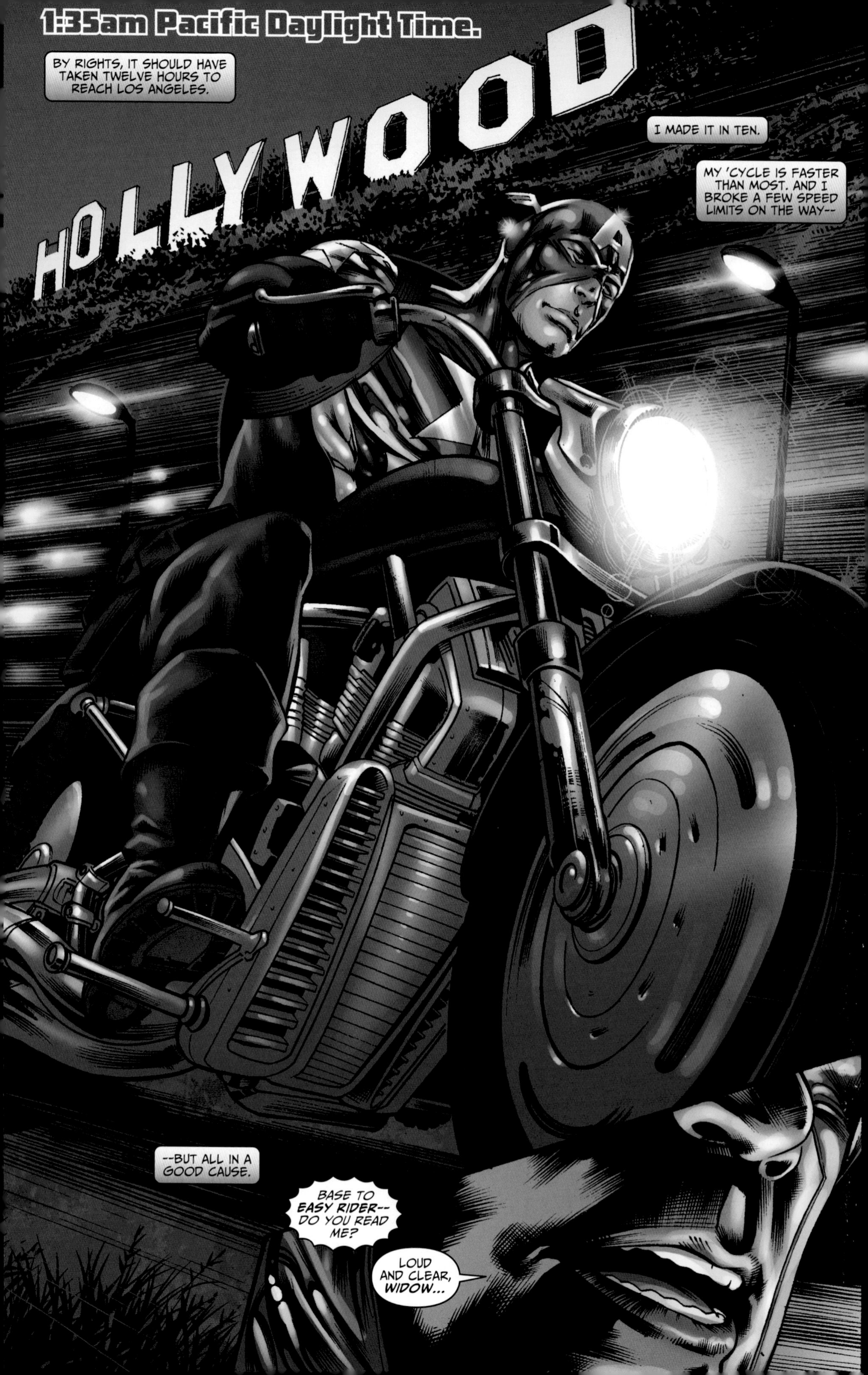
1:35am Pacific Daylight Time.
BY RIGHTS, IT SHOULD HAVE TAKEN TWELVE HOURS TO REACH LOS ANGELES.
HOLLYWOOD
I MADE IT IN TEN.
MY 'CYCLE IS FASTER THAN MOST. AND I BROKE A FEW SPEED LIMITS ON THE WAY--
--BUT ALL IN A GOOD CAUSE.
BASE TO EASY RIDER-- DO YOU READ ME?
LOUD AND CLEAR, WIDOW...

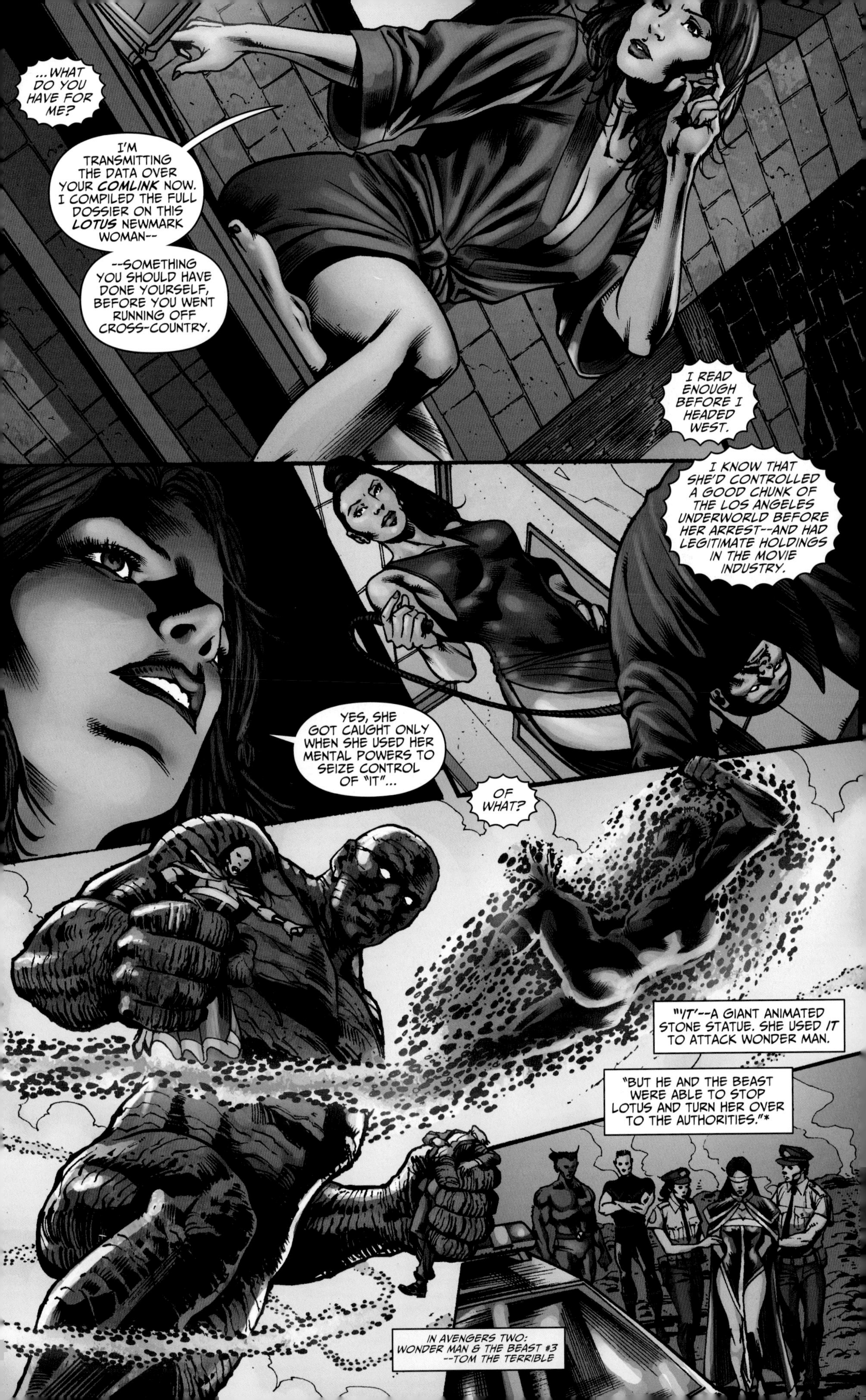
...WHAT DO YOU HAVE FOR ME?
I'M TRANSMITTING THE DATA OVER YOUR COMLINK NOW. I COMPILED THE FULL DOSSIER ON THIS LOTUS NEWMARK WOMAN--
--SOMETHING YOU SHOULD HAVE DONE YOURSELF, BEFORE YOU WENT RUNNING OFF CROSS-COUNTRY.
I READ ENOUGH BEFORE I HEADED WEST.
I KNOW THAT SHE'D CONTROLLED A GOOD CHUNK OF THE LOS ANGELES UNDERWORLD BEFORE HER ARREST--AND HAD LEGITIMATE HOLDINGS IN THE MOVIE INDUSTRY.
YES, SHE GOT CAUGHT ONLY WHEN SHE USED HER MENTAL POWERS TO SEIZE CONTROL OF "IT"...
OF WHAT?
"'IT'--A GIANT ANIMATED STONE STATUE. SHE USED IT TO ATTACK WONDER MAN.
"BUT HE AND THE BEAST WERE ABLE TO STOP LOTUS AND TURN HER OVER TO THE AUTHORITIES."*
IN AVENGERS TWO: WONDER MAN & THE BEAST #3 --TOM THE TERRIBLE

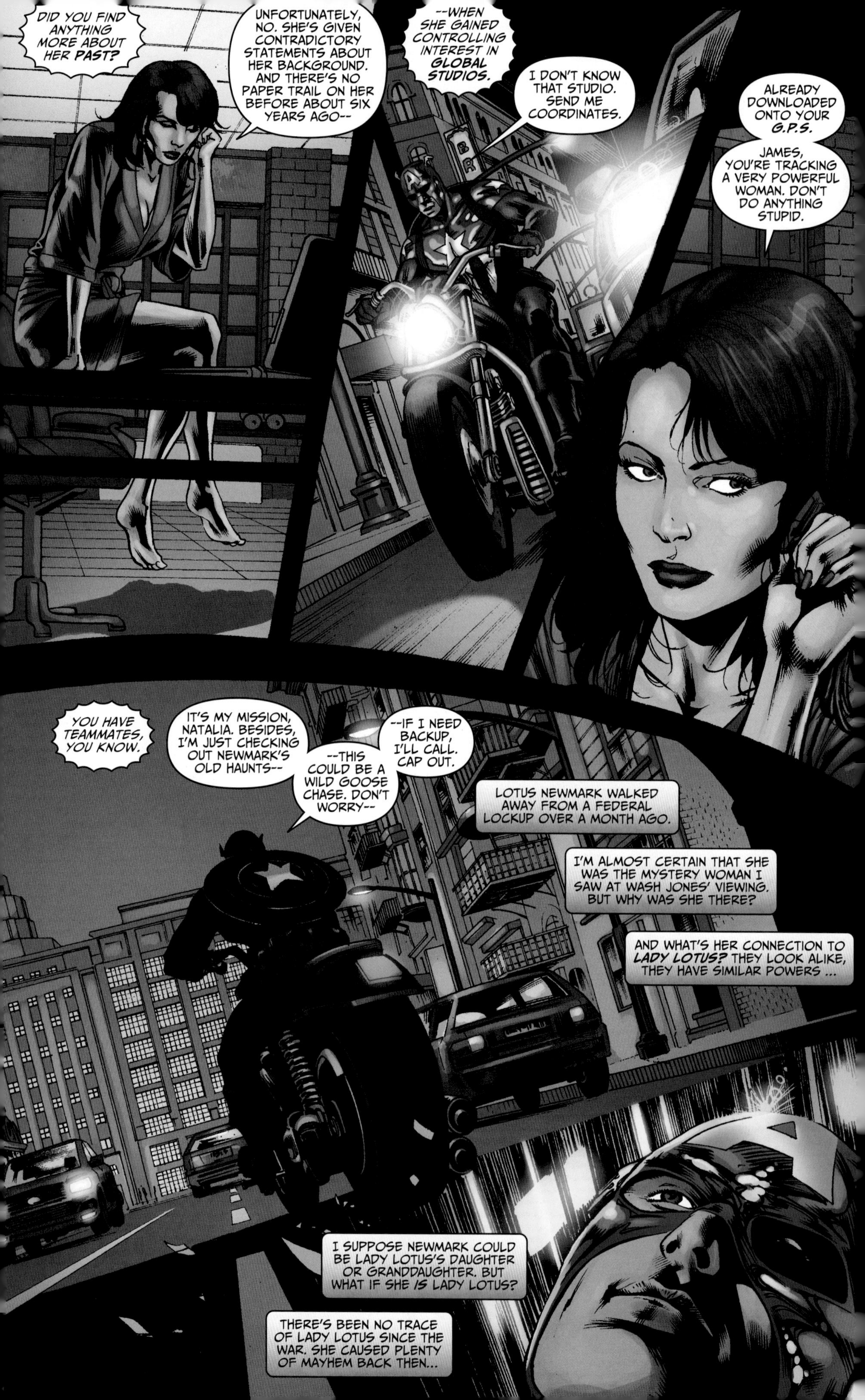
DID YOU FIND ANYTHING MORE ABOUT HER **PAST?**
UNFORTUNATELY, NO. SHE'S GIVEN CONTRADICTORY STATEMENTS ABOUT HER BACKGROUND. AND THERE'S NO PAPER TRAIL ON HER BEFORE ABOUT SIX YEARS AGO--
--WHEN SHE GAINED CONTROLLING INTEREST IN **GLOBAL STUDIOS.**
I DON'T KNOW THAT STUDIO. SEND ME COORDINATES.
ALREADY DOWNLOADED ONTO YOUR *G.P.S.*
JAMES, YOU'RE TRACKING A VERY POWERFUL WOMAN. DON'T DO ANYTHING STUPID.
YOU HAVE TEAMMATES, YOU KNOW.
IT'S MY MISSION, NATALIA. BESIDES, I'M JUST CHECKING OUT NEWMARK'S OLD HAUNTS--
--THIS COULD BE A WILD GOOSE CHASE. DON'T WORRY--
--IF I NEED BACKUP, I'LL CALL. CAP OUT.
LOTUS NEWMARK WALKED AWAY FROM A FEDERAL LOCKUP OVER A MONTH AGO.
I'M ALMOST CERTAIN THAT SHE WAS THE MYSTERY WOMAN I SAW AT WASH JONES' VIEWING. BUT WHY WAS SHE THERE?
AND WHAT'S HER CONNECTION TO *LADY LOTUS?* THEY LOOK ALIKE, THEY HAVE SIMILAR POWERS ...
I SUPPOSE NEWMARK COULD BE LADY LOTUS'S DAUGHTER OR GRANDDAUGHTER. BUT WHAT IF SHE *IS* LADY LOTUS?
THERE'S BEEN NO TRACE OF LADY LOTUS SINCE THE WAR. SHE CAUSED PLENTY OF MAYHEM BACK THEN...

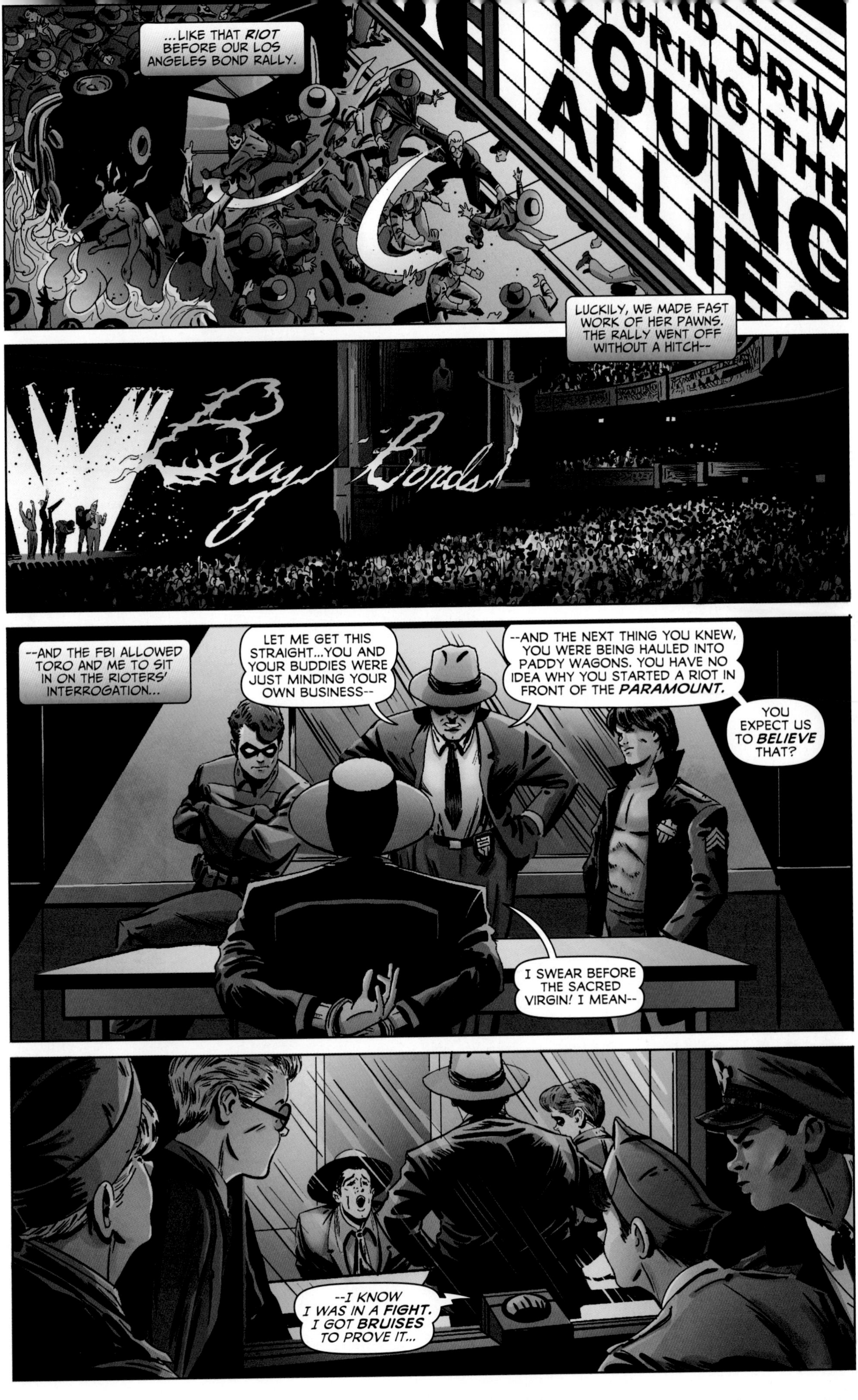
...LIKE THAT *RIOT* BEFORE OUR LOS ANGELES BOND RALLY.
LUCKILY, WE MADE FAST WORK OF HER PAWNS. THE RALLY WENT OFF WITHOUT A HITCH--
Buy Bonds!
--AND THE FBI ALLOWED TORO AND ME TO SIT IN ON THE RIOTERS' INTERROGATION...
LET ME GET THIS STRAIGHT...YOU AND YOUR BUDDIES WERE JUST MINDING YOUR OWN BUSINESS--
--AND THE NEXT THING YOU KNEW, YOU WERE BEING HAULED INTO PADDY WAGONS. YOU HAVE NO IDEA WHY YOU STARTED A RIOT IN FRONT OF THE *PARAMOUNT.*
YOU EXPECT US TO *BELIEVE* THAT?
I SWEAR BEFORE THE SACRED VIRGIN! I MEAN--
--I KNOW I WAS IN A *FIGHT.* I GOT *BRUISES* TO PROVE IT...

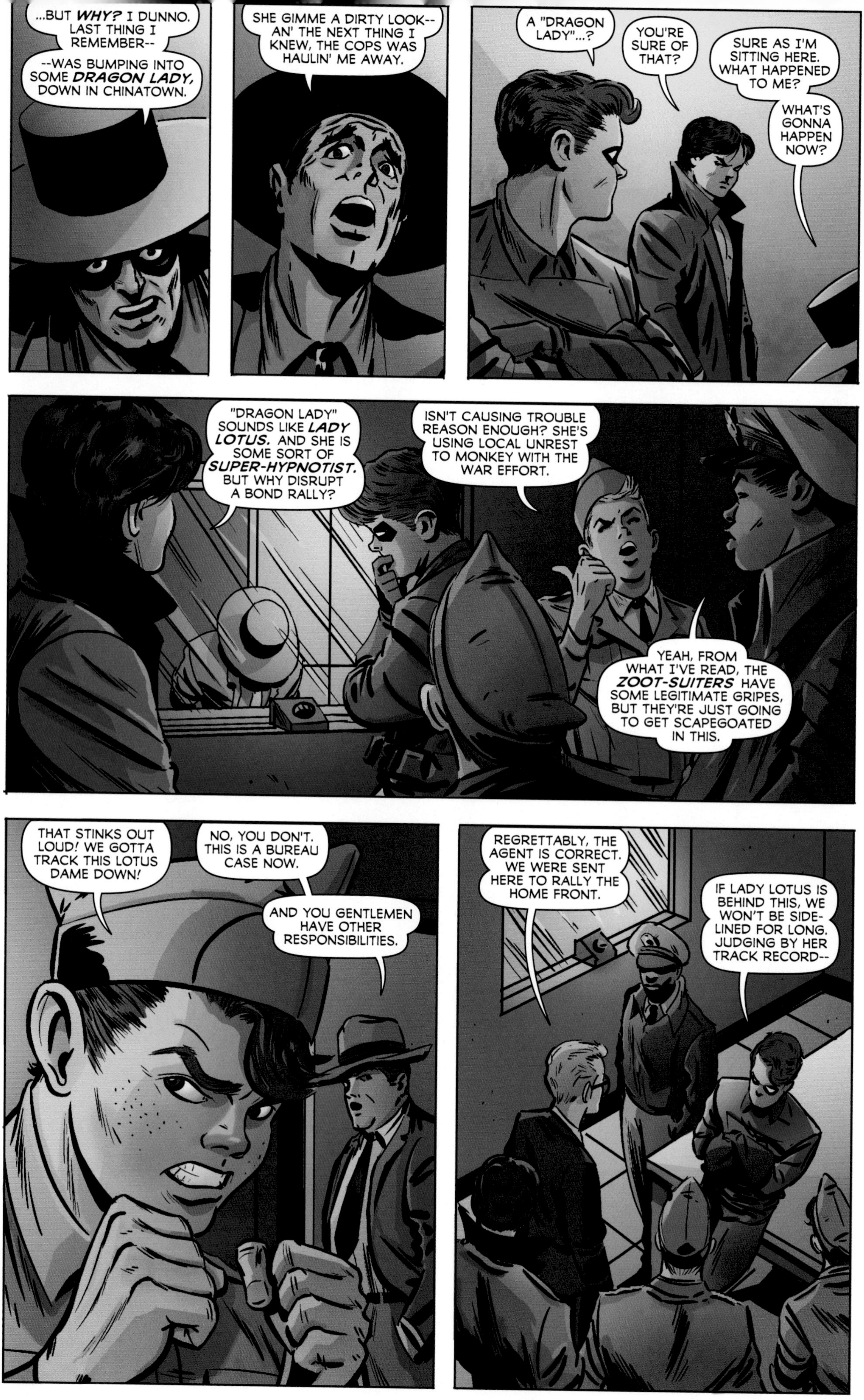
...BUT WHY? I DUNNO. LAST THING I REMEMBER--
--WAS BUMPING INTO SOME DRAGON LADY, DOWN IN CHINATOWN.
SHE GIMME A DIRTY LOOK-- AN' THE NEXT THING I KNEW, THE COPS WAS HAULIN' ME AWAY.
A "DRAGON LADY"...?
YOU'RE SURE OF THAT?
SURE AS I'M SITTING HERE. WHAT HAPPENED TO ME?
WHAT'S GONNA HAPPEN NOW?
"DRAGON LADY" SOUNDS LIKE LADY LOTUS. AND SHE IS SOME SORT OF SUPER-HYPNOTIST. BUT WHY DISRUPT A BOND RALLY?
ISN'T CAUSING TROUBLE REASON ENOUGH? SHE'S USING LOCAL UNREST TO MONKEY WITH THE WAR EFFORT.
YEAH, FROM WHAT I'VE READ, THE ZOOT-SUITERS HAVE SOME LEGITIMATE GRIPES, BUT THEY'RE JUST GOING TO GET SCAPEGOATED IN THIS.
THAT STINKS OUT LOUD! WE GOTTA TRACK THIS LOTUS DAME DOWN!
NO, YOU DON'T. THIS IS A BUREAU CASE NOW.
AND YOU GENTLEMEN HAVE OTHER RESPONSIBILITIES.
REGRETTABLY, THE AGENT IS CORRECT. WE WERE SENT HERE TO RALLY THE HOME FRONT.
IF LADY LOTUS IS BEHIND THIS, WE WON'T BE SIDE-LINED FOR LONG. JUDGING BY HER TRACK RECORD--

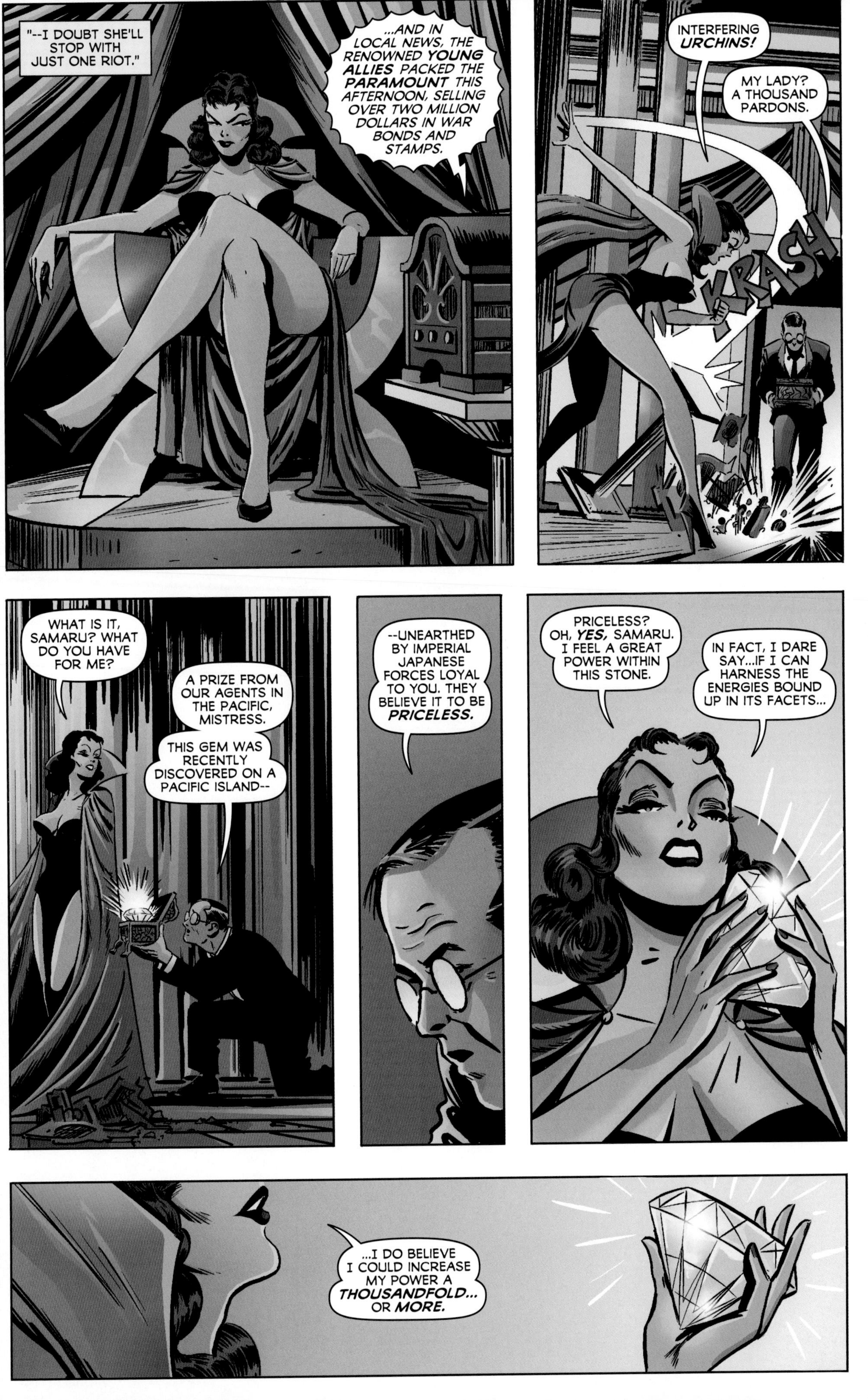
"--I DOUBT SHE'LL STOP WITH JUST ONE RIOT."
...AND IN LOCAL NEWS, THE RENOWNED YOUNG ALLIES PACKED THE PARAMOUNT THIS AFTERNOON, SELLING OVER TWO MILLION DOLLARS IN WAR BONDS AND STAMPS.
INTERFERING URCHINS!
MY LADY? A THOUSAND PARDONS.
KRASH
WHAT IS IT, SAMARU? WHAT DO YOU HAVE FOR ME?
A PRIZE FROM OUR AGENTS IN THE PACIFIC, MISTRESS.
THIS GEM WAS RECENTLY DISCOVERED ON A PACIFIC ISLAND--
--UNEARTHED BY IMPERIAL JAPANESE FORCES LOYAL TO YOU. THEY BELIEVE IT TO BE PRICELESS.
PRICELESS? OH, YES, SAMARU. I FEEL A GREAT POWER WITHIN THIS STONE.
IN FACT, I DARE SAY...IF I CAN HARNESS THE ENERGIES BOUND UP IN ITS FACETS...
...I DO BELIEVE I COULD INCREASE MY POWER A THOUSANDFOLD... OR MORE.

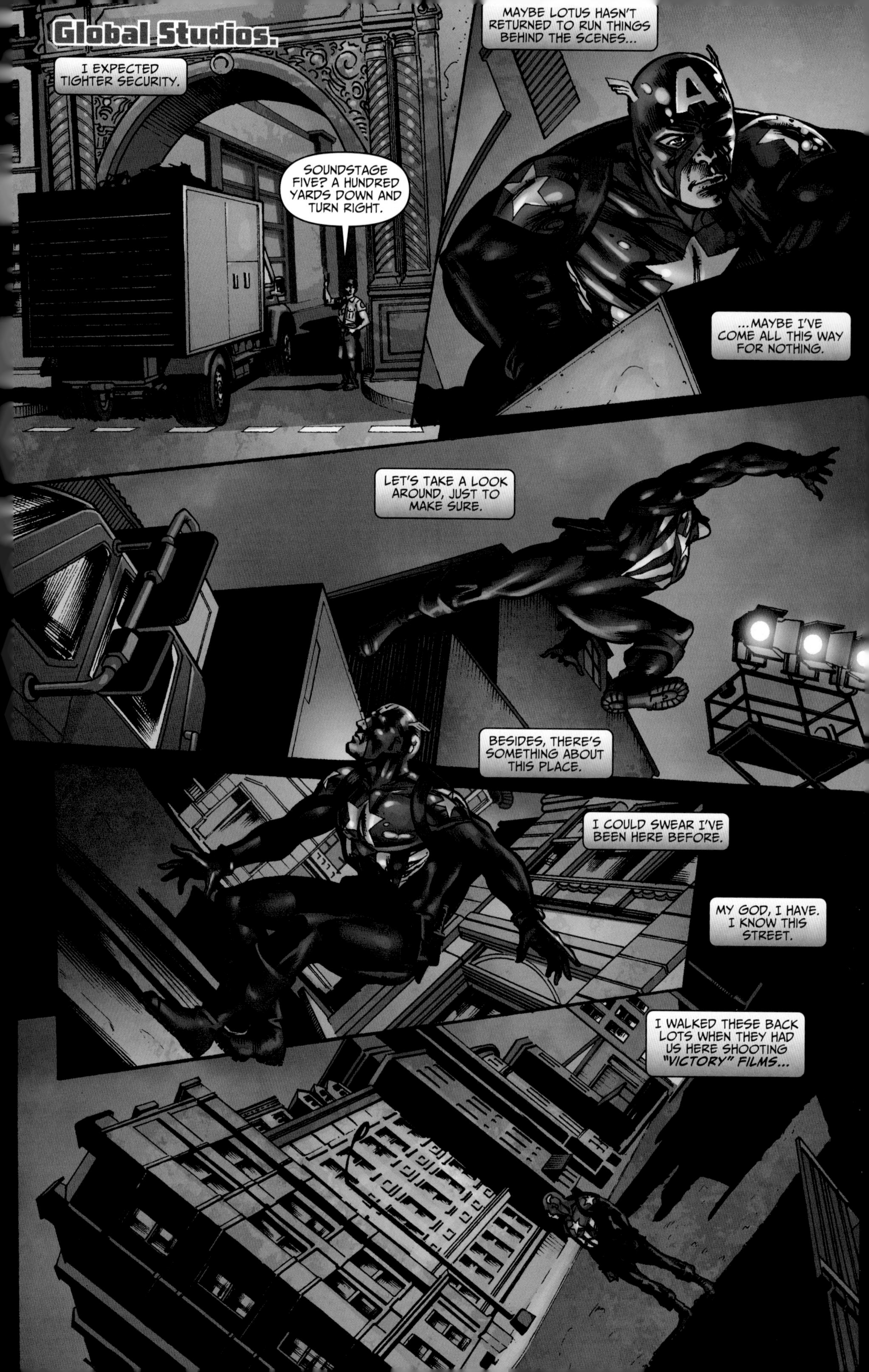
Global Studios.
I EXPECTED TIGHTER SECURITY.
SOUNDSTAGE FIVE? A HUNDRED YARDS DOWN AND TURN RIGHT.
MAYBE LOTUS HASN'T RETURNED TO RUN THINGS BEHIND THE SCENES...
...MAYBE I'VE COME ALL THIS WAY FOR NOTHING.
LET'S TAKE A LOOK AROUND, JUST TO MAKE SURE.
BESIDES, THERE'S SOMETHING ABOUT THIS PLACE.
I COULD SWEAR I'VE BEEN HERE BEFORE.
MY GOD, I HAVE. I KNOW THIS STREET.
I WALKED THESE BACK LOTS WHEN THEY HAD US HERE SHOOTING "VICTORY" FILMS...

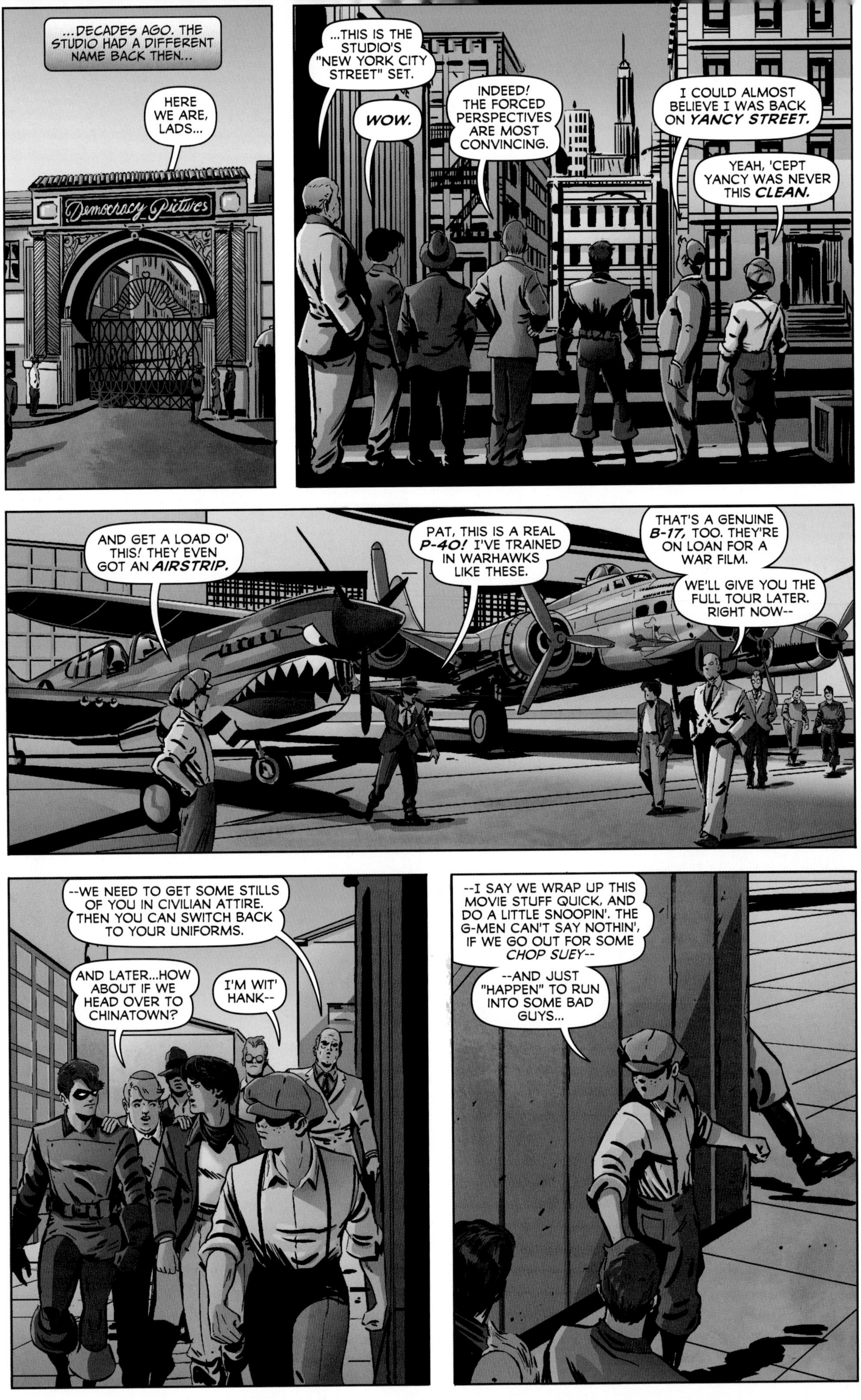
...DECADES AGO. THE STUDIO HAD A DIFFERENT NAME BACK THEN...
HERE WE ARE, LADS...
Democracy Pictures
...THIS IS THE STUDIO'S "NEW YORK CITY STREET" SET.
WOW.
INDEED! THE FORCED PERSPECTIVES ARE MOST CONVINCING.
I COULD ALMOST BELIEVE I WAS BACK ON YANCY STREET.
YEAH, 'CEPT YANCY WAS NEVER THIS CLEAN.
AND GET A LOAD O' THIS! THEY EVEN GOT AN AIRSTRIP.
PAT, THIS IS A REAL P-40! I'VE TRAINED IN WARHAWKS LIKE THESE.
THAT'S A GENUINE B-17, TOO. THEY'RE ON LOAN FOR A WAR FILM.
WE'LL GIVE YOU THE FULL TOUR LATER. RIGHT NOW--
--WE NEED TO GET SOME STILLS OF YOU IN CIVILIAN ATTIRE. THEN YOU CAN SWITCH BACK TO YOUR UNIFORMS.
AND LATER...HOW ABOUT IF WE HEAD OVER TO CHINATOWN?
I'M WIT' HANK--
--I SAY WE WRAP UP THIS MOVIE STUFF QUICK, AND DO A LITTLE SNOOPIN'. THE G-MEN CAN'T SAY NOTHIN', IF WE GO OUT FOR SOME CHOP SUEY--
--AND JUST "HAPPEN" TO RUN INTO SOME BAD GUYS...

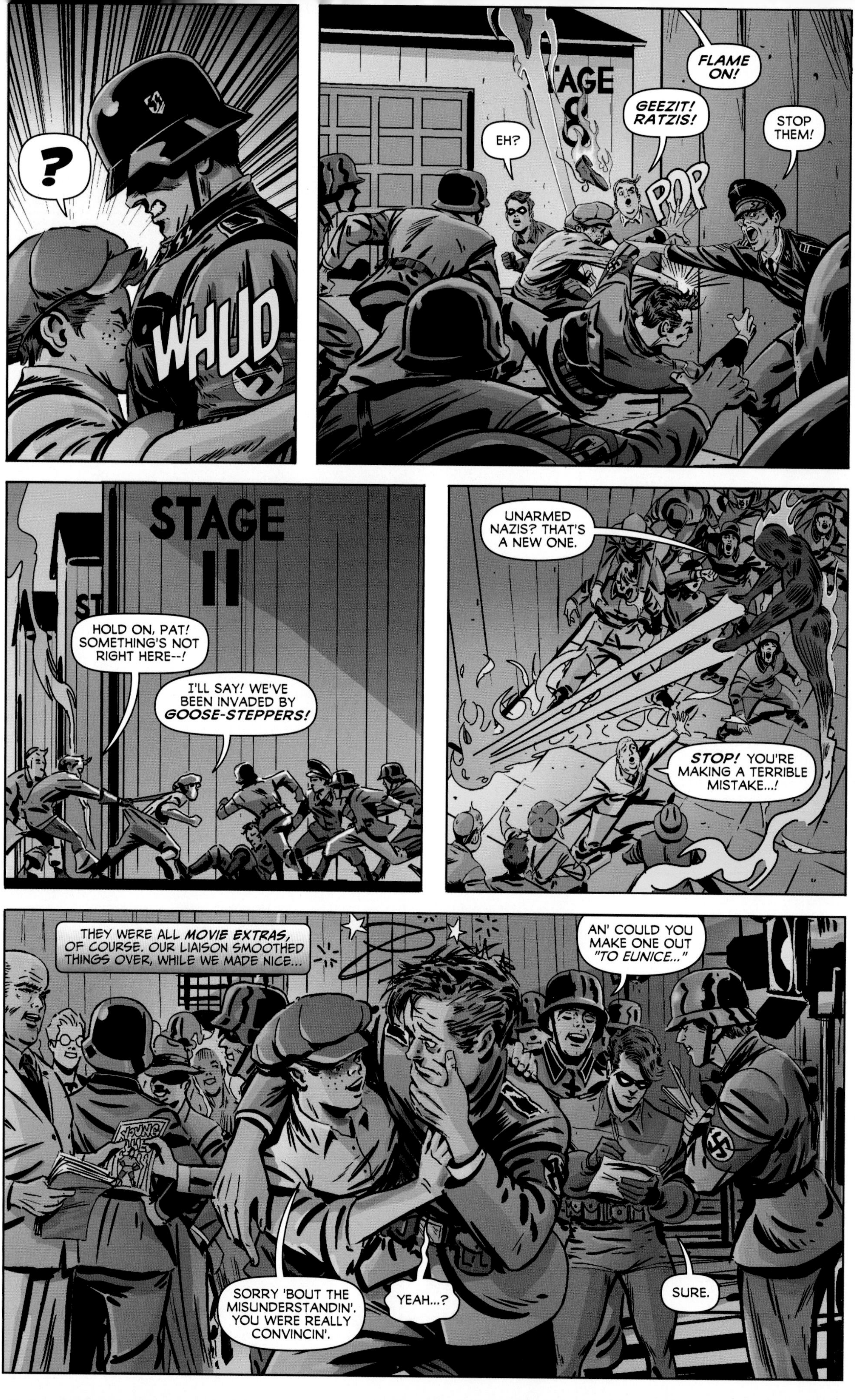
?
WHUD
FLAME ON!
EH?
GEEZIT! RATZIS!
POP
STOP THEM!
STAGE
HOLD ON, PAT! SOMETHING'S NOT RIGHT HERE--!
I'LL SAY! WE'VE BEEN INVADED BY GOOSE-STEPPERS!
UNARMED NAZIS? THAT'S A NEW ONE.
STOP! YOU'RE MAKING A TERRIBLE MISTAKE...!
THEY WERE ALL MOVIE EXTRAS, OF COURSE. OUR LIAISON SMOOTHED THINGS OVER, WHILE WE MADE NICE...
AN' COULD YOU MAKE ONE OUT "TO EUNICE..."
SORRY 'BOUT THE MISUNDERSTANDIN'. YOU WERE REALLY CONVINCIN'.
YEAH...?
SURE.

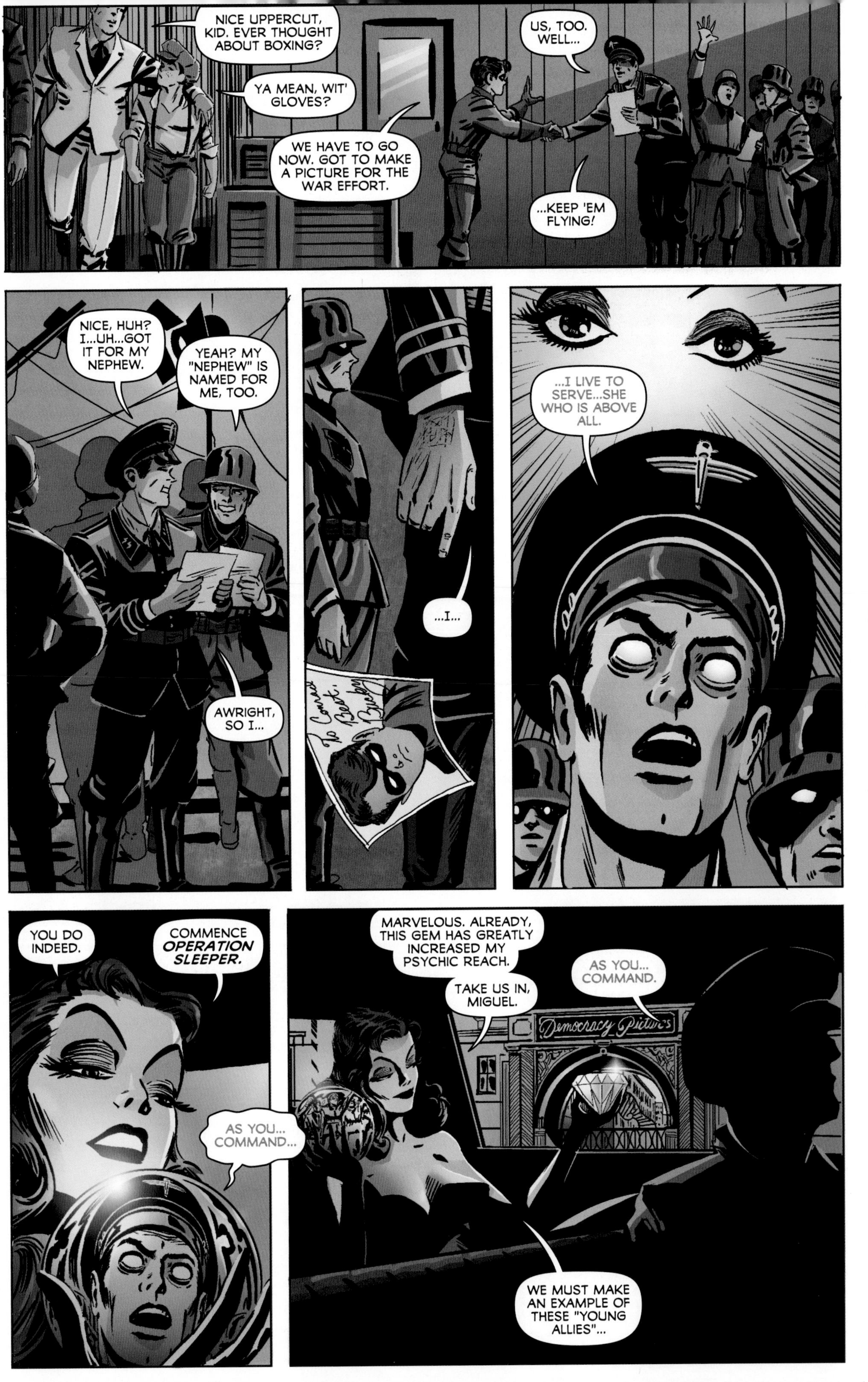
NICE UPPERCUT, KID. EVER THOUGHT ABOUT BOXING?
YA MEAN, WIT' GLOVES?
WE HAVE TO GO NOW. GOT TO MAKE A PICTURE FOR THE WAR EFFORT.
US, TOO. WELL...
...KEEP 'EM FLYING!
NICE, HUH? I...UH...GOT IT FOR MY NEPHEW.
YEAH? MY "NEPHEW" IS NAMED FOR ME, TOO.
AWRIGHT, SO I...
...I...
...I LIVE TO SERVE...SHE WHO IS ABOVE ALL.
YOU DO INDEED.
COMMENCE *OPERATION SLEEPER.*
AS YOU... COMMAND...
MARVELOUS. ALREADY, THIS GEM HAS GREATLY INCREASED MY PSYCHIC REACH.
TAKE US IN, MIGUEL.
AS YOU... COMMAND.
Democracy Pictures
WE MUST MAKE AN EXAMPLE OF THESE "YOUNG ALLIES"...

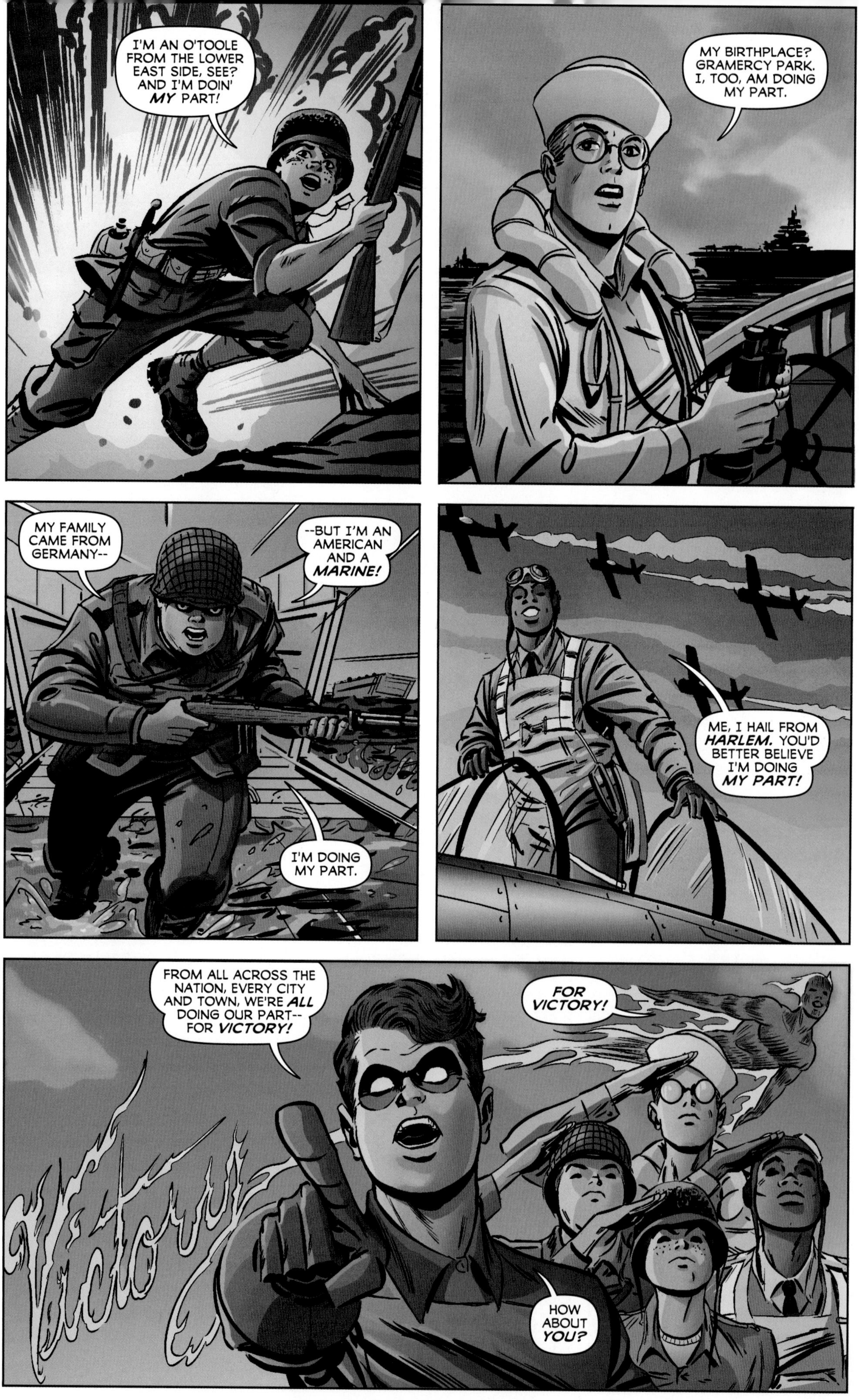

I'M AN O'TOOLE FROM THE LOWER EAST SIDE, SEE? AND I'M DOIN' *MY* PART!
MY BIRTHPLACE? GRAMERCY PARK. I, TOO, AM DOING MY PART.
MY FAMILY CAME FROM GERMANY--
--BUT I'M AN AMERICAN AND A *MARINE!*
I'M DOING MY PART.
ME, I HAIL FROM *HARLEM.* YOU'D BETTER BELIEVE I'M DOING *MY PART!*
FROM ALL ACROSS THE NATION, EVERY CITY AND TOWN, WE'RE *ALL* DOING OUR PART-- FOR *VICTORY!*
FOR VICTORY!
Victory
HOW ABOUT *YOU?*

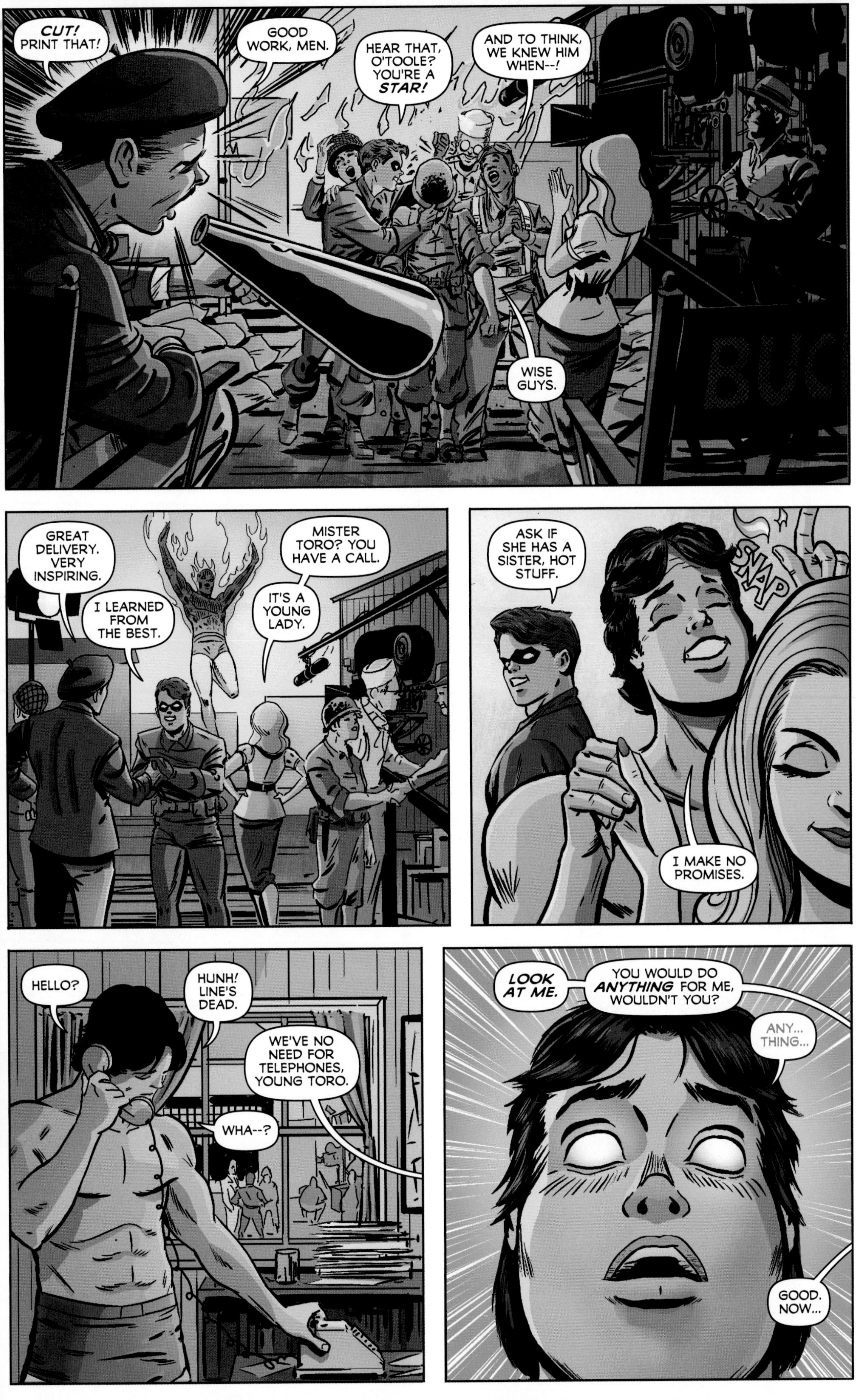
CUT! PRINT THAT!
GOOD WORK, MEN.
HEAR THAT, O'TOOLE? YOU'RE A STAR!
AND TO THINK, WE KNEW HIM WHEN--!
WISE GUYS.
BUC
GREAT DELIVERY. VERY INSPIRING.
I LEARNED FROM THE BEST.
MISTER TORO? YOU HAVE A CALL.
IT'S A YOUNG LADY.
ASK IF SHE HAS A SISTER, HOT STUFF.
SNAP
I MAKE NO PROMISES.
HELLO?
HUNH! LINE'S DEAD.
WE'VE NO NEED FOR TELEPHONES, YOUNG TORO.
WHA--?
LOOK AT ME.
YOU WOULD DO ANYTHING FOR ME, WOULDN'T YOU?
ANY... THING...
GOOD. NOW...

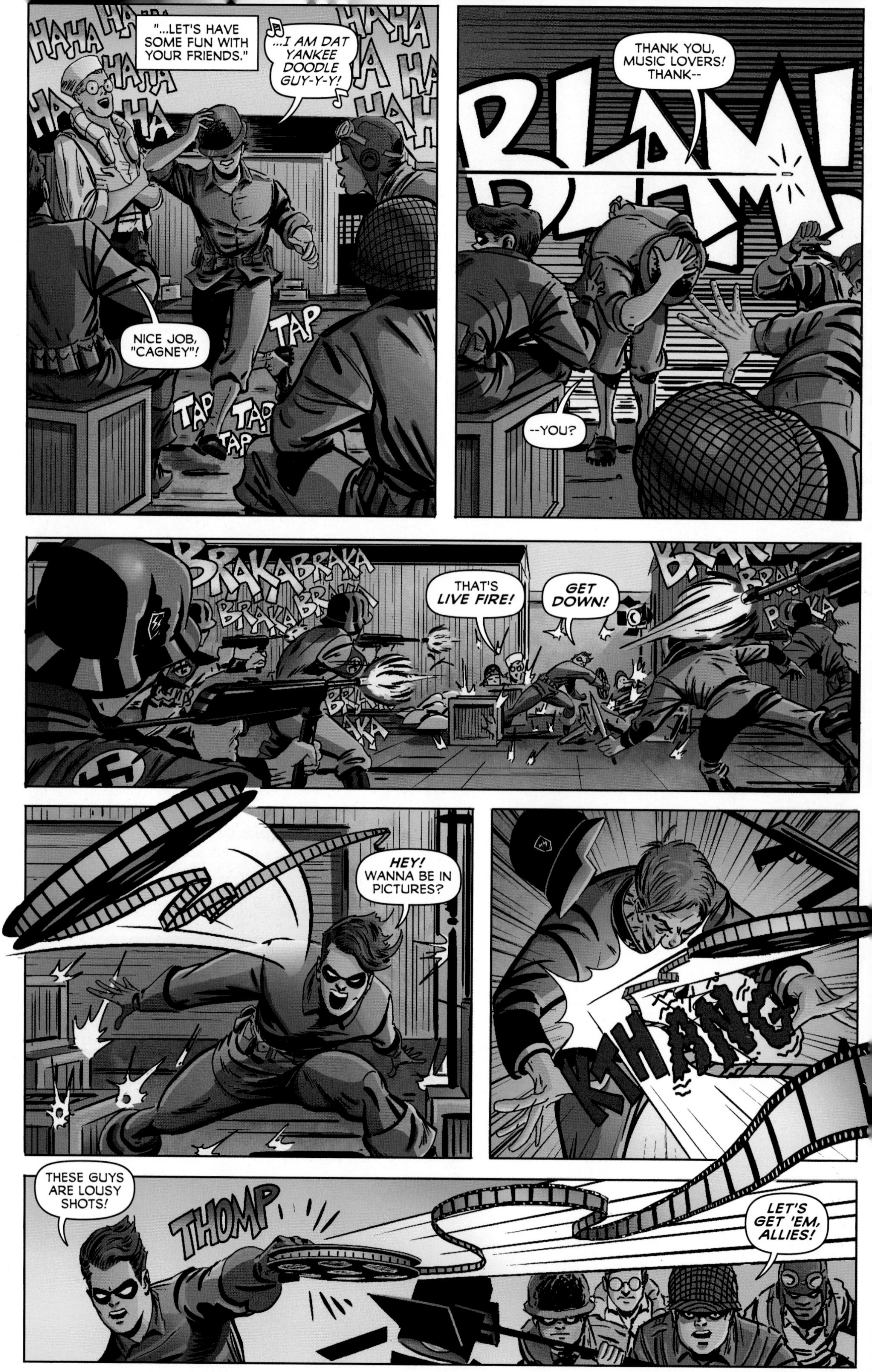
HAHA HAHA HAHA HAHA HAHA
"...LET'S HAVE SOME FUN WITH YOUR FRIENDS."
...I AM DAT YANKEE DOODLE GUY-Y-Y!
HAHA HAHA HAHA
NICE JOB, "CAGNEY"!
TAP
TAP TAP TAP
THANK YOU, MUSIC LOVERS! THANK--
BLAM! BLAM!
--YOU?
BRAKABRAKA
BRAKABRAKA
THAT'S LIVE FIRE!
GET DOWN!
HEY! WANNA BE IN PICTURES?
KTHANG
THESE GUYS ARE LOUSY SHOTS!
THOMP
LET'S GET 'EM, ALLIES!

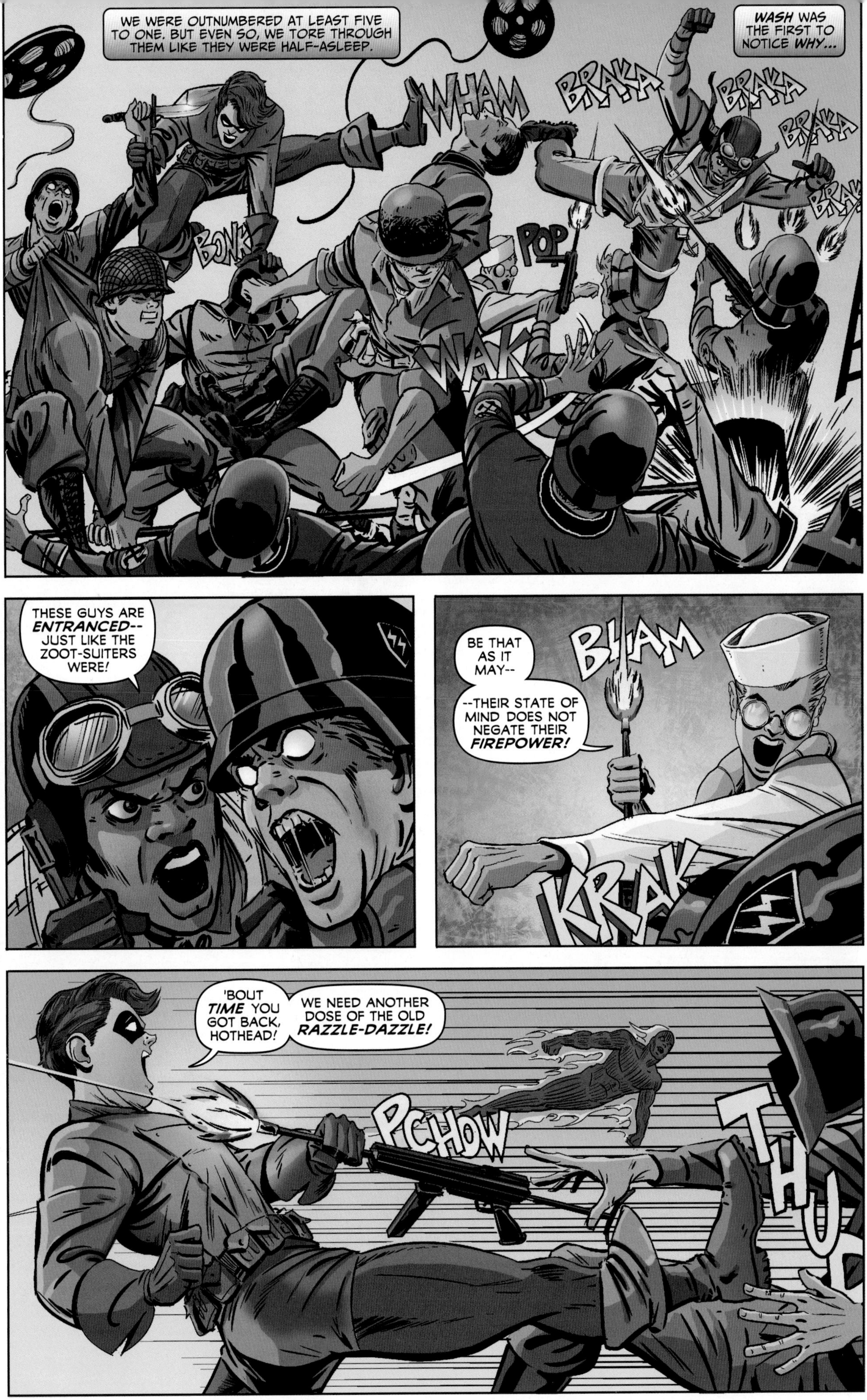
WE WERE OUTNUMBERED AT LEAST FIVE TO ONE. BUT EVEN SO, WE TORE THROUGH THEM LIKE THEY WERE HALF-ASLEEP.
WASH WAS THE FIRST TO NOTICE WHY...
WHAM
BRAKA
BRAKA
BRAKA
BONK
POP
WAK
THESE GUYS ARE ENTRANCED-- JUST LIKE THE ZOOT-SUITERS WERE!
BE THAT AS IT MAY--
--THEIR STATE OF MIND DOES NOT NEGATE THEIR FIREPOWER!
BLAM
KRAK
'BOUT TIME YOU GOT BACK, HOTHEAD!
WE NEED ANOTHER DOSE OF THE OLD RAZZLE-DAZZLE!
PCHOW
THUD

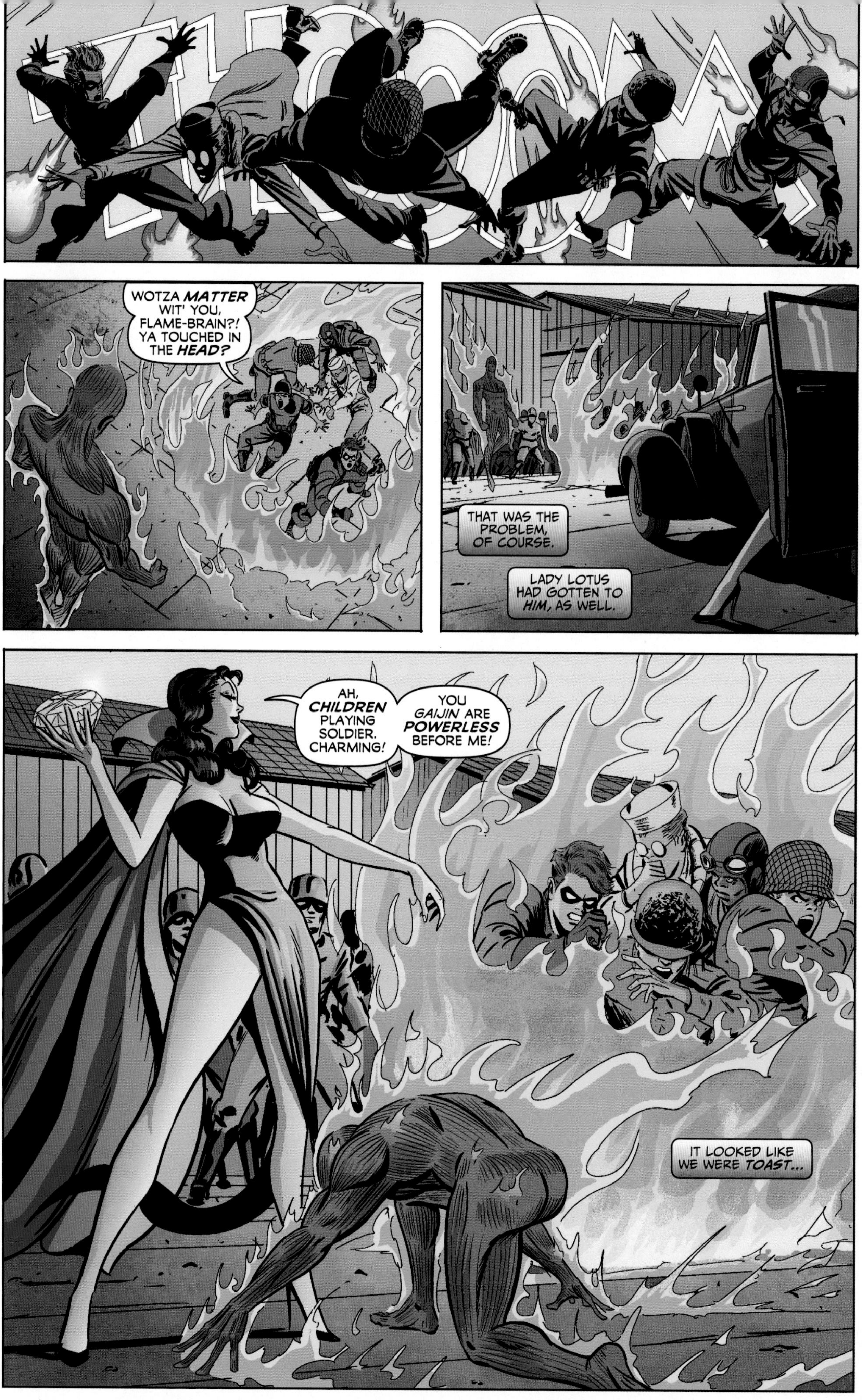
ZHOOOOM
WOTZA MATTER WIT' YOU, FLAME-BRAIN?! YA TOUCHED IN THE HEAD?
THAT WAS THE PROBLEM, OF COURSE.
LADY LOTUS HAD GOTTEN TO HIM, AS WELL.
AH, CHILDREN PLAYING SOLDIER. CHARMING!
YOU GAIJIN ARE POWERLESS BEFORE ME!
IT LOOKED LIKE WE WERE TOAST...

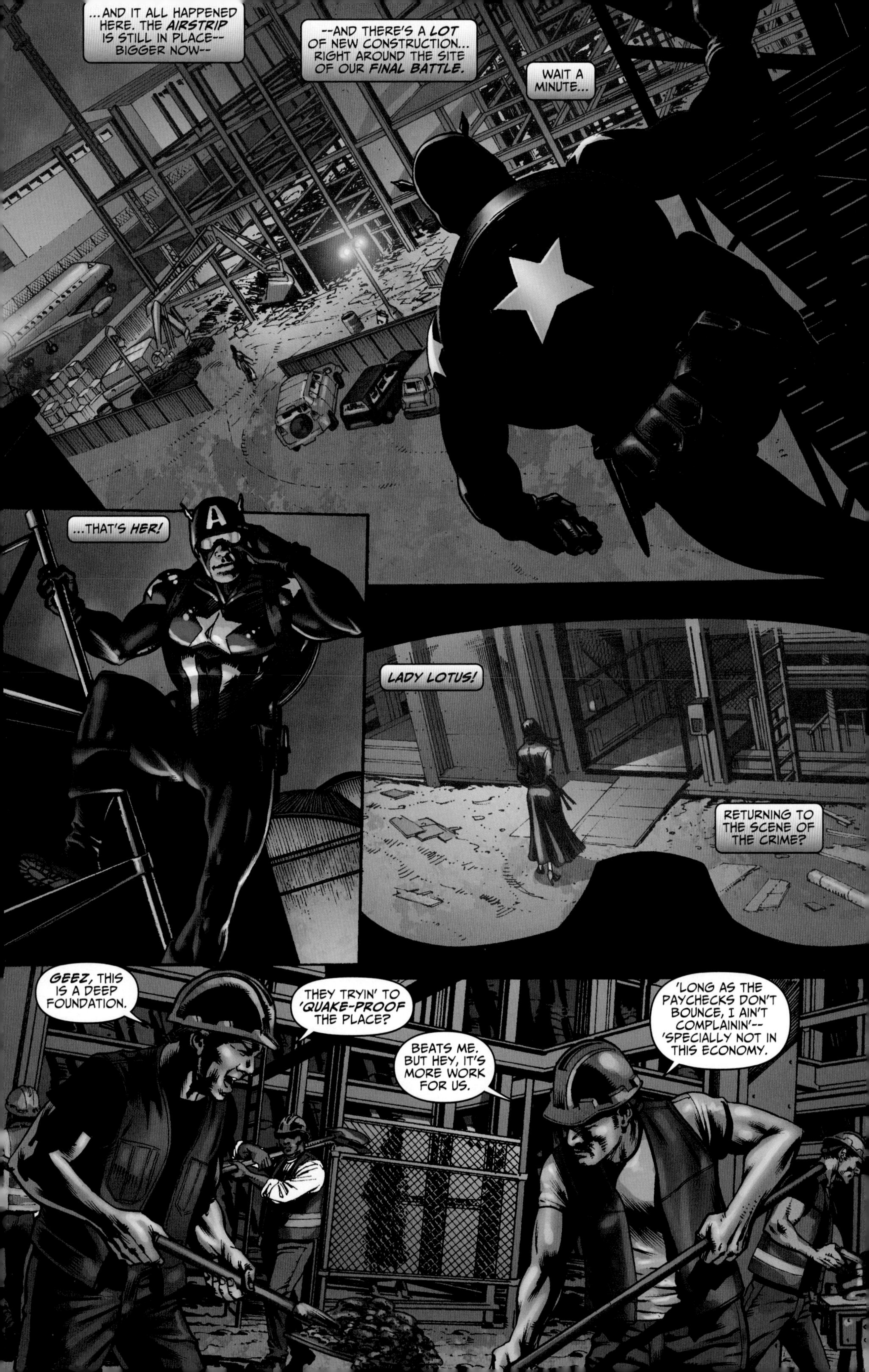
...AND IT ALL HAPPENED HERE. THE AIRSTRIP IS STILL IN PLACE-- BIGGER NOW--
--AND THERE'S A LOT OF NEW CONSTRUCTION... RIGHT AROUND THE SITE OF OUR FINAL BATTLE.
WAIT A MINUTE...
...THAT'S HER!
LADY LOTUS!
RETURNING TO THE SCENE OF THE CRIME?
GEEZ, THIS IS A DEEP FOUNDATION.
THEY TRYIN' TO 'QUAKE-PROOF THE PLACE?
BEATS ME. BUT HEY, IT'S MORE WORK FOR US.
'LONG AS THE PAYCHECKS DON'T BOUNCE, I AIN'T COMPLAININ'-- 'SPECIALLY NOT IN THIS ECONOMY.

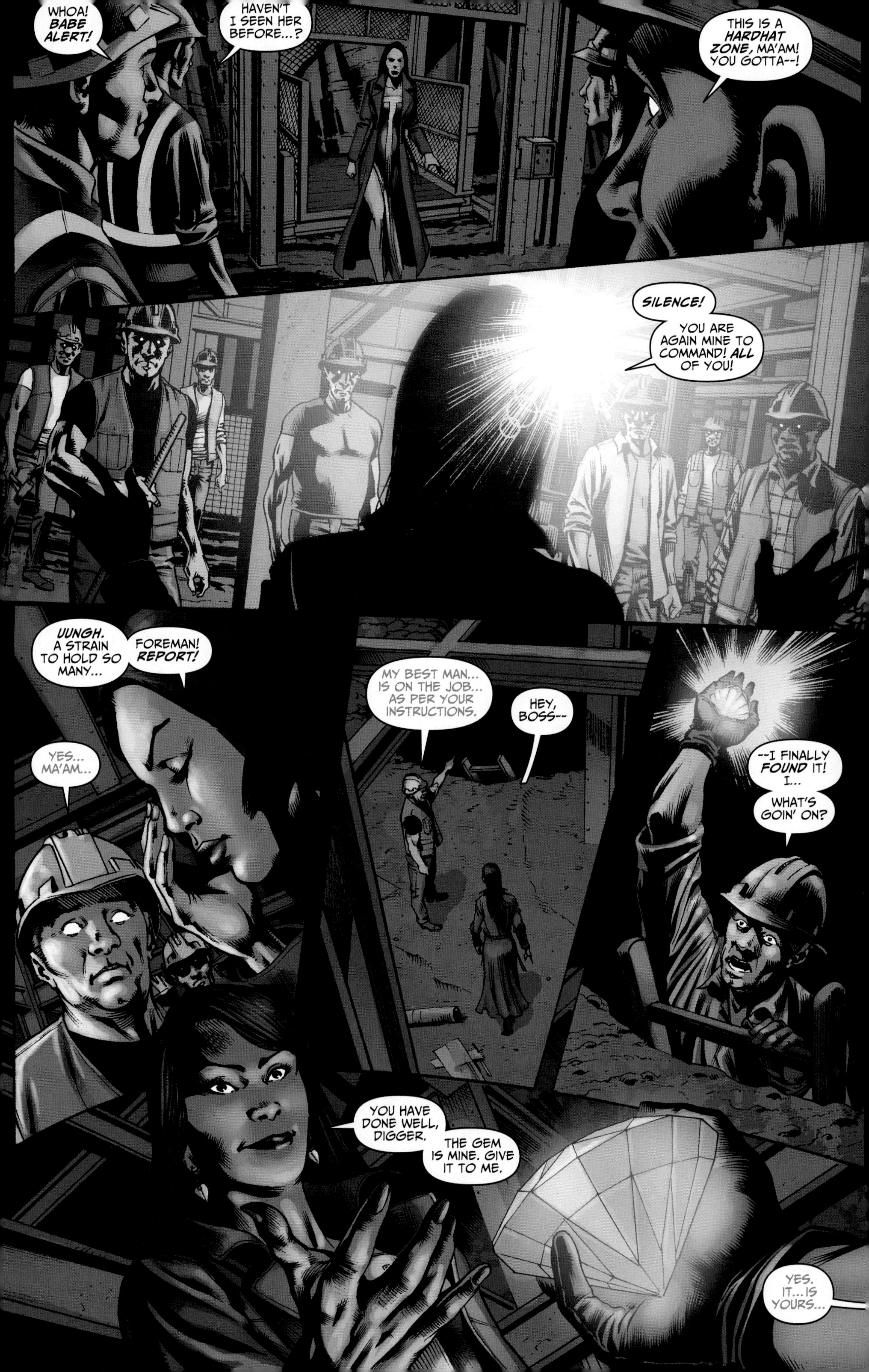
WHOA! BABE ALERT!
HAVEN'T I SEEN HER BEFORE...?
THIS IS A HARDHAT ZONE, MA'AM! YOU GOTTA--!
SILENCE!
YOU ARE AGAIN MINE TO COMMAND! ALL OF YOU!
UUNGH. A STRAIN TO HOLD SO MANY...
FOREMAN! REPORT!
YES... MA'AM...
MY BEST MAN... IS ON THE JOB... AS PER YOUR INSTRUCTIONS.
HEY, BOSS--
--I FINALLY FOUND IT! I...
WHAT'S GOIN' ON?
YOU HAVE DONE WELL, DIGGER.
THE GEM IS MINE. GIVE IT TO ME.
YES. IT...IS YOURS...

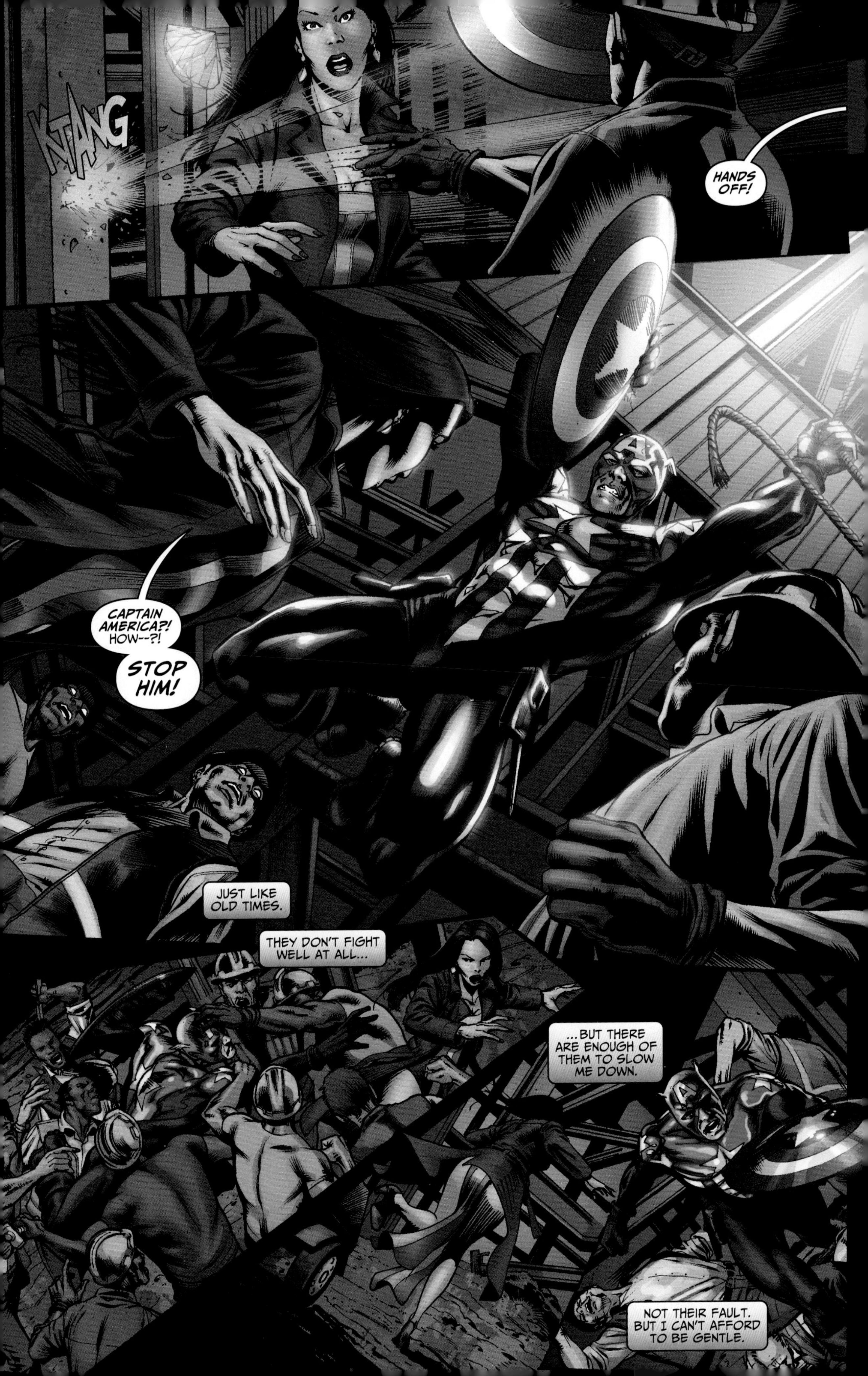
KTANG
HANDS OFF!
CAPTAIN AMERICA?! HOW--?!
STOP HIM!
JUST LIKE OLD TIMES.
THEY DON'T FIGHT WELL AT ALL...
...BUT THERE ARE ENOUGH OF THEM TO SLOW ME DOWN.
NOT THEIR FAULT. BUT I CAN'T AFFORD TO BE GENTLE.

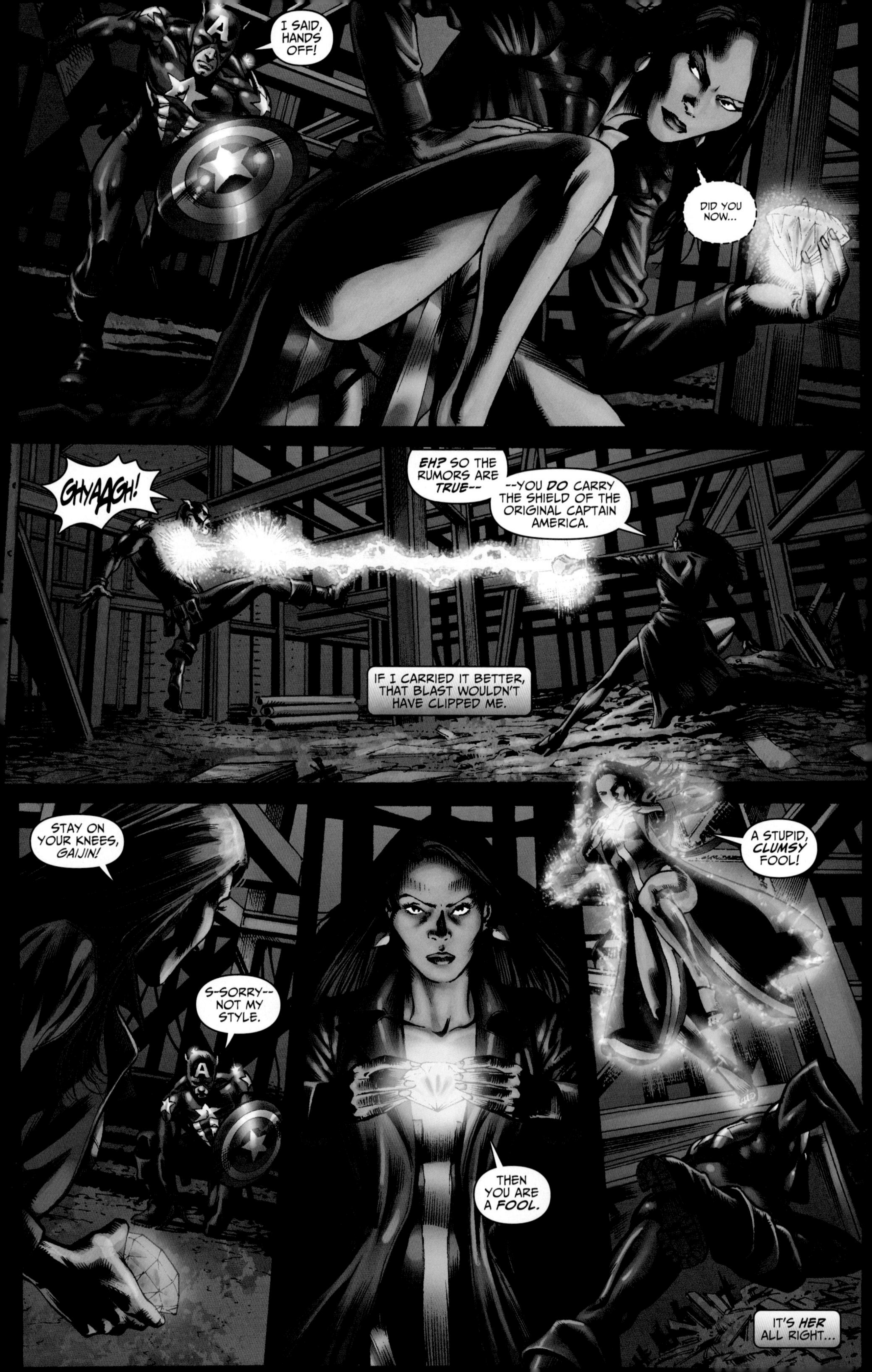
I SAID, HANDS OFF!
DID YOU NOW...
GHYAAGH!
EH? SO THE RUMORS ARE TRUE--
--YOU DO CARRY THE SHIELD OF THE ORIGINAL CAPTAIN AMERICA.
IF I CARRIED IT BETTER, THAT BLAST WOULDN'T HAVE CLIPPED ME.
STAY ON YOUR KNEES, GAIJIN!
S-SORRY-- NOT MY STYLE.
THEN YOU ARE A FOOL.
A STUPID, CLUMSY FOOL!
IT'S HER ALL RIGHT...

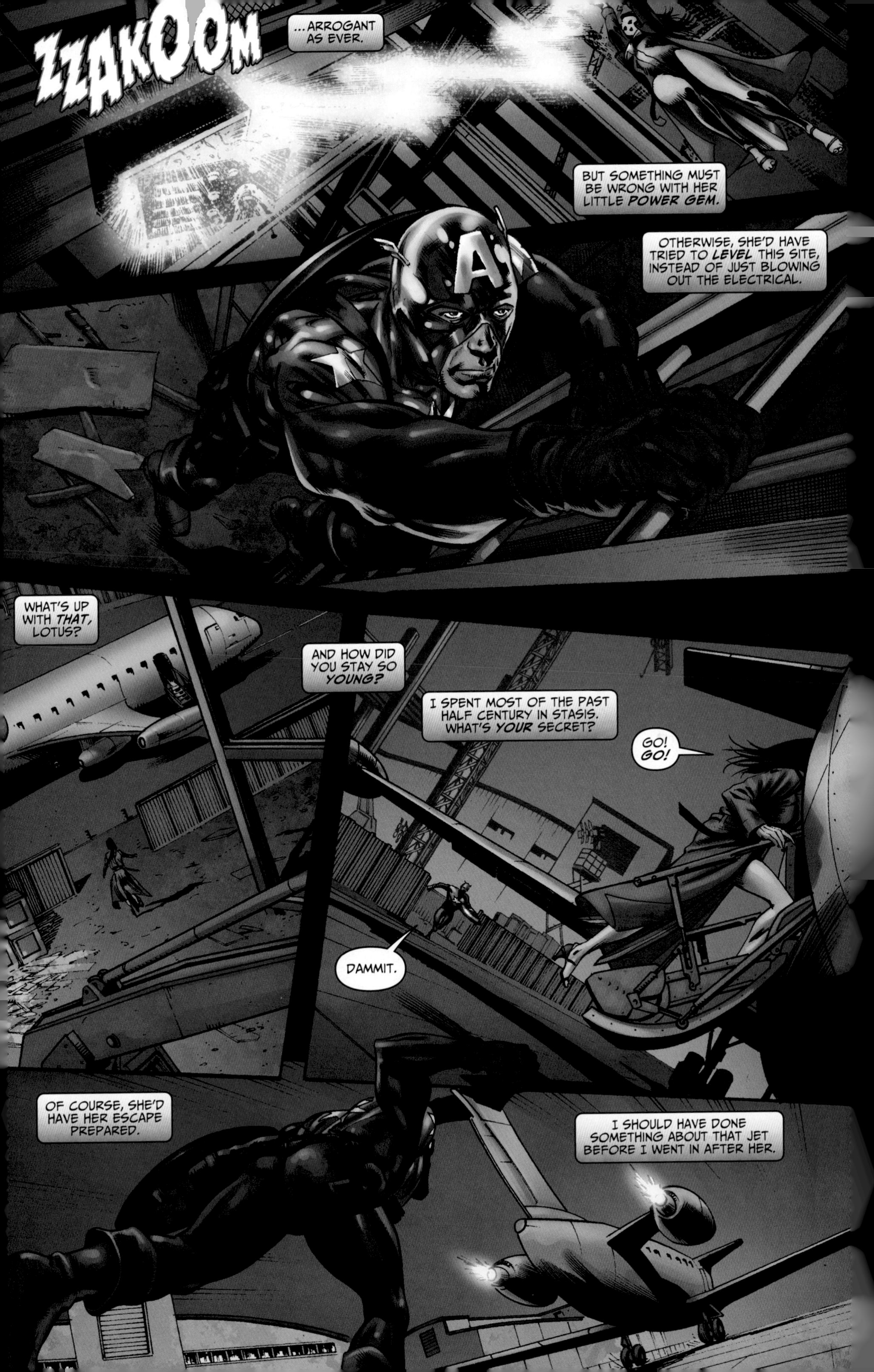
ZZAKOOM
...ARROGANT AS EVER.
BUT SOMETHING MUST BE WRONG WITH HER LITTLE POWER GEM.
OTHERWISE, SHE'D HAVE TRIED TO LEVEL THIS SITE, INSTEAD OF JUST BLOWING OUT THE ELECTRICAL.
WHAT'S UP WITH THAT, LOTUS?
AND HOW DID YOU STAY SO YOUNG?
I SPENT MOST OF THE PAST HALF CENTURY IN STASIS. WHAT'S YOUR SECRET?
GO! GO!
DAMMIT.
OF COURSE, SHE'D HAVE HER ESCAPE PREPARED.
I SHOULD HAVE DONE SOMETHING ABOUT THAT JET BEFORE I WENT IN AFTER HER.

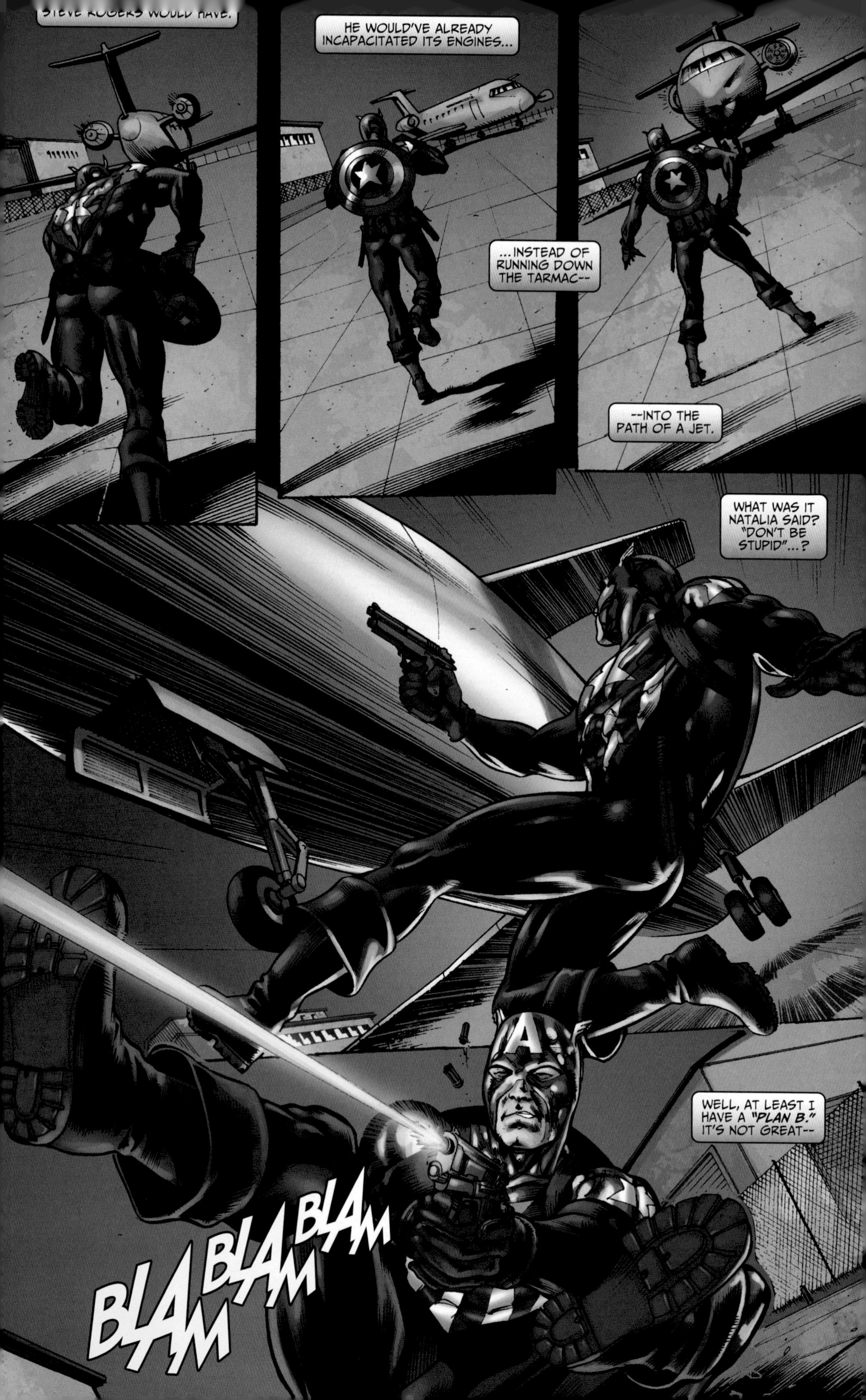
STEVE ROGERS WOULD HAVE.
HE WOULD'VE ALREADY INCAPACITATED ITS ENGINES...
...INSTEAD OF RUNNING DOWN THE TARMAC--
--INTO THE PATH OF A JET.
WHAT WAS IT NATALIA SAID? "DON'T BE STUPID"...?
WELL, AT LEAST I HAVE A "PLAN B." IT'S NOT GREAT--
BLAM BLAM BLAM

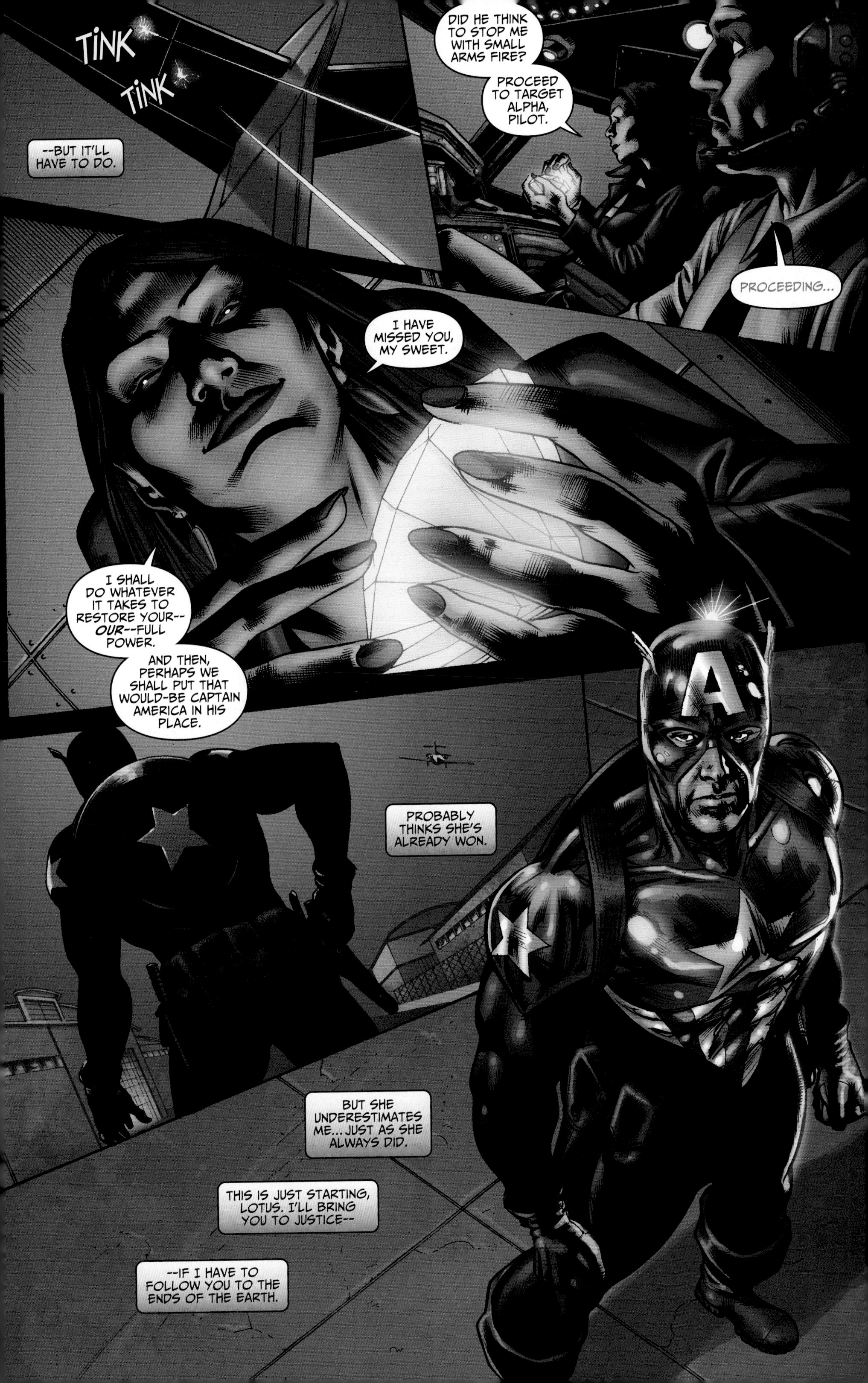
TINK
TINK
--BUT IT'LL HAVE TO DO.
DID HE THINK TO STOP ME WITH SMALL ARMS FIRE?
PROCEED TO TARGET ALPHA, PILOT.
PROCEEDING...
I HAVE MISSED YOU, MY SWEET.
I SHALL DO WHATEVER IT TAKES TO RESTORE YOUR-- OUR--FULL POWER.
AND THEN, PERHAPS WE SHALL PUT THAT WOULD-BE CAPTAIN AMERICA IN HIS PLACE.
PROBABLY THINKS SHE'S ALREADY WON.
BUT SHE UNDERESTIMATES ME... JUST AS SHE ALWAYS DID.
THIS IS JUST STARTING, LOTUS. I'LL BRING YOU TO JUSTICE--
--IF I HAVE TO FOLLOW YOU TO THE ENDS OF THE EARTH.

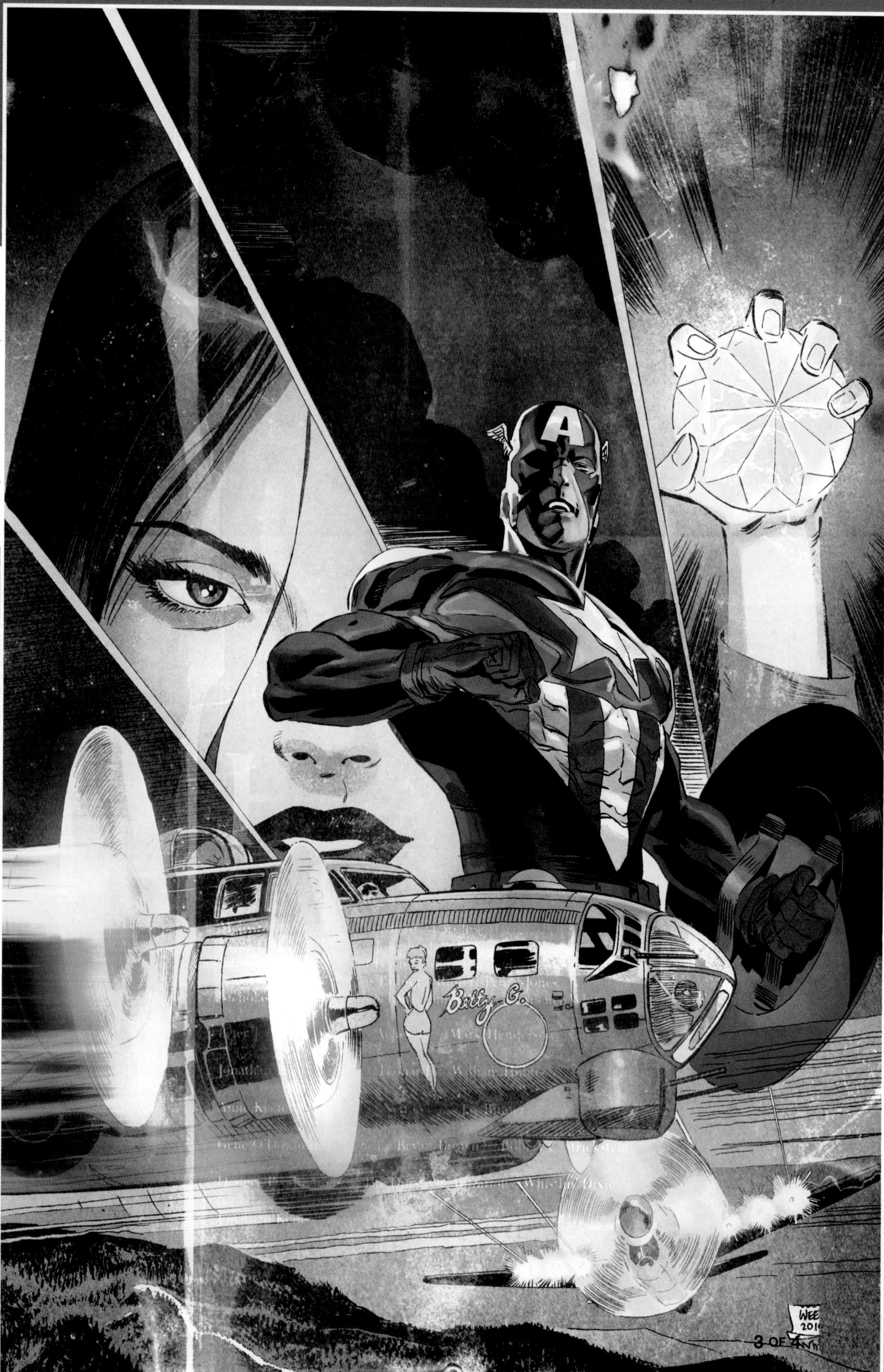
3 OF 4

CAPTAIN AMERICA: FOREVER ALLIES #3

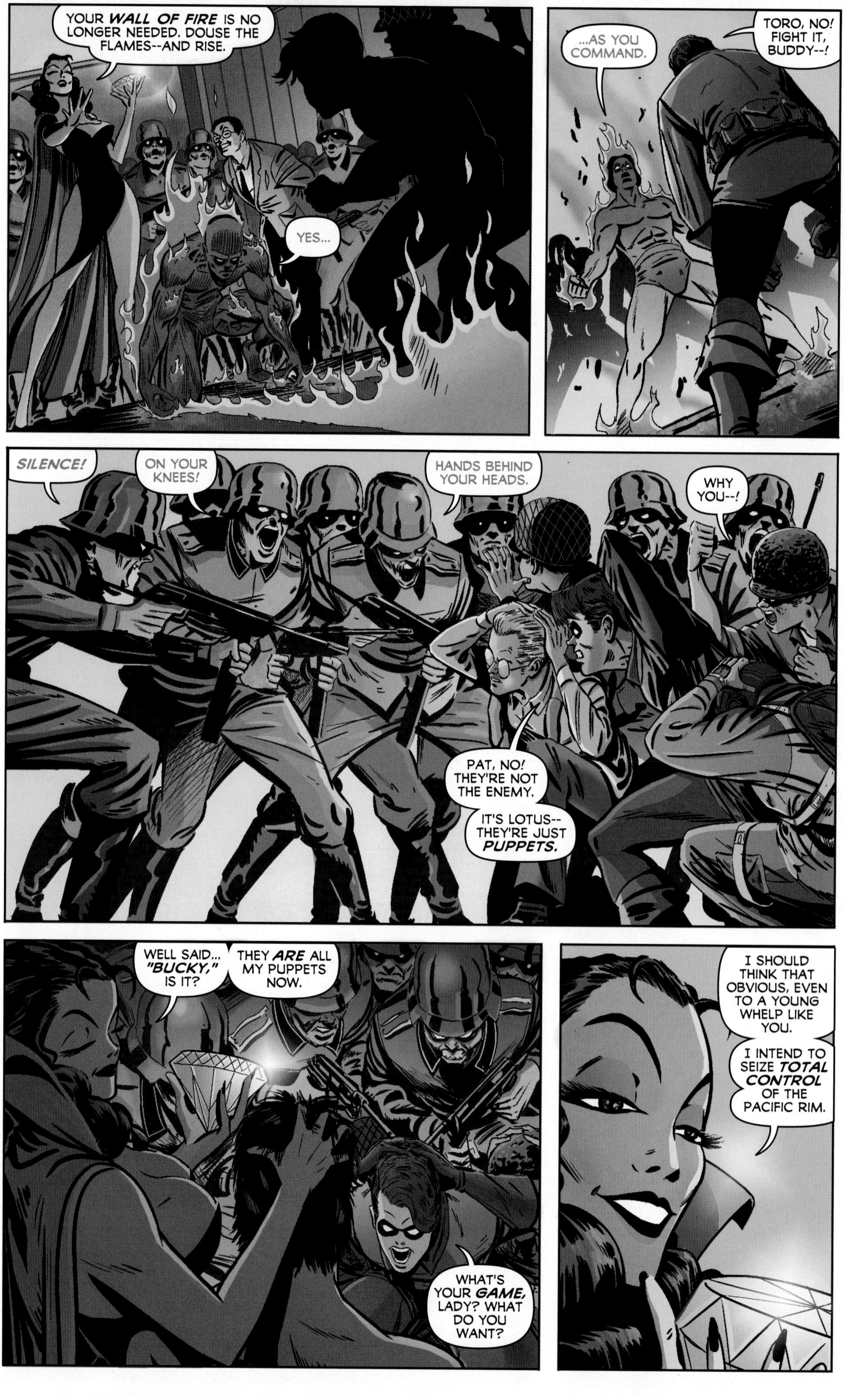
YOUR **WALL OF FIRE** IS NO LONGER NEEDED. DOUSE THE FLAMES--AND RISE.
YES...
...AS YOU COMMAND.
TORO, NO! FIGHT IT, BUDDY--!
SILENCE!
ON YOUR KNEES!
HANDS BEHIND YOUR HEADS.
WHY YOU--!
PAT, NO! THEY'RE NOT THE ENEMY.
IT'S LOTUS-- THEY'RE JUST ***PUPPETS.***
WELL SAID... ***"BUCKY,"*** IS IT?
THEY ***ARE*** ALL MY PUPPETS NOW.
WHAT'S YOUR ***GAME,*** LADY? WHAT DO YOU WANT?
I SHOULD THINK THAT OBVIOUS, EVEN TO A YOUNG WHELP LIKE YOU.
I INTEND TO SEIZE ***TOTAL CONTROL*** OF THE PACIFIC RIM.

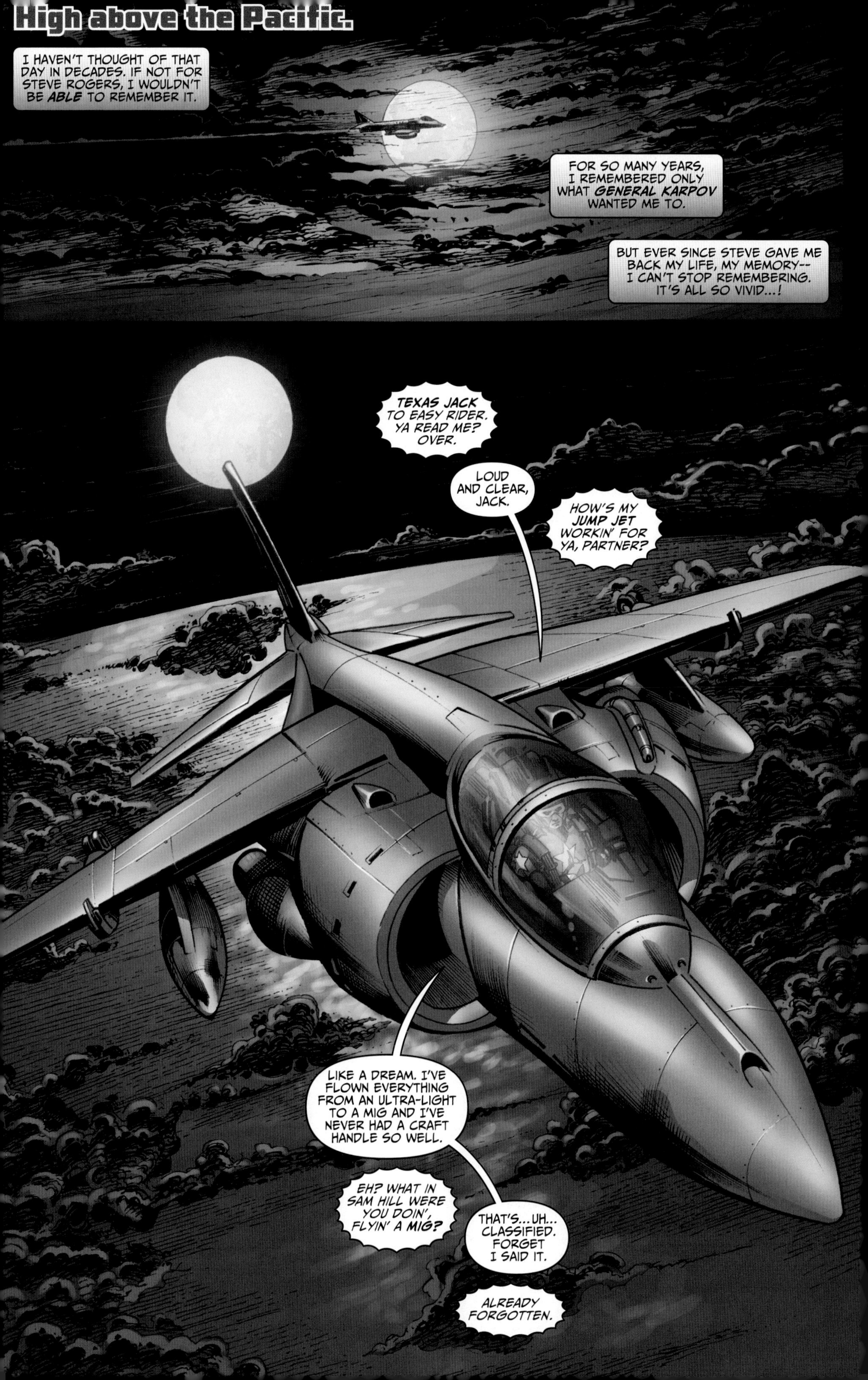
High above the Pacific.
I HAVEN'T THOUGHT OF THAT DAY IN DECADES. IF NOT FOR STEVE ROGERS, I WOULDN'T BE *ABLE* TO REMEMBER IT.
FOR SO MANY YEARS, I REMEMBERED ONLY WHAT *GENERAL KARPOV* WANTED ME TO.
BUT EVER SINCE STEVE GAVE ME BACK MY LIFE, MY MEMORY-- I CAN'T STOP REMEMBERING. IT'S ALL SO VIVID...!
TEXAS JACK TO EASY RIDER. YA READ ME? OVER.
LOUD AND CLEAR, JACK.
HOW'S MY *JUMP JET* WORKIN' FOR YA, PARTNER?
LIKE A DREAM. I'VE FLOWN EVERYTHING FROM AN ULTRA-LIGHT TO A MIG AND I'VE NEVER HAD A CRAFT HANDLE SO WELL.
EH? WHAT IN SAM HILL WERE YOU DOIN', FLYIN' A *MIG?*
THAT'S...UH... CLASSIFIED. FORGET I SAID IT.
ALREADY FORGOTTEN.

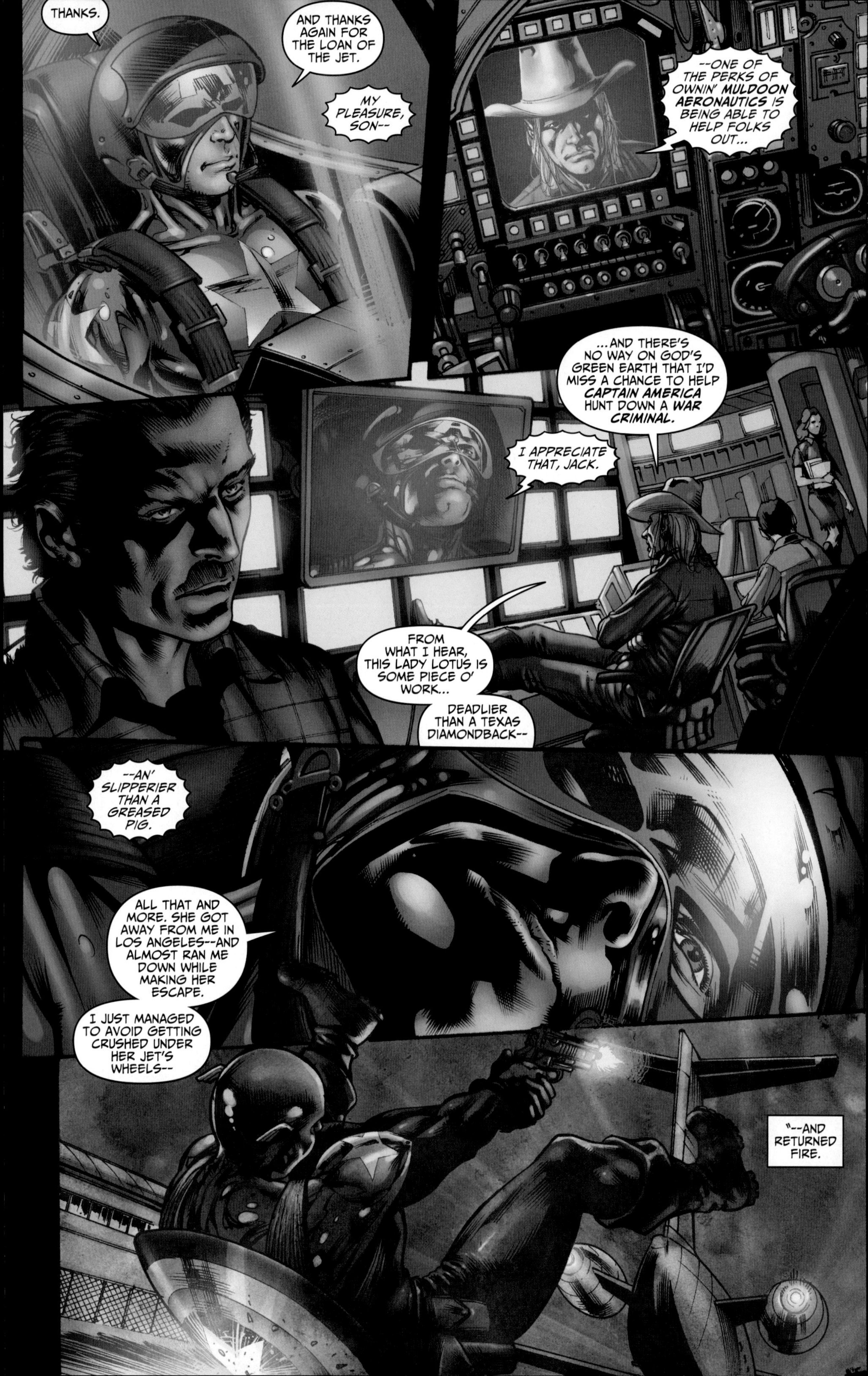
THANKS.
AND THANKS AGAIN FOR THE LOAN OF THE JET.
MY PLEASURE, SON--
--ONE OF THE PERKS OF OWNIN' MULDOON AERONAUTICS IS BEING ABLE TO HELP FOLKS OUT...
...AND THERE'S NO WAY ON GOD'S GREEN EARTH THAT I'D MISS A CHANCE TO HELP CAPTAIN AMERICA HUNT DOWN A WAR CRIMINAL.
I APPRECIATE THAT, JACK.
FROM WHAT I HEAR, THIS LADY LOTUS IS SOME PIECE O' WORK...
DEADLIER THAN A TEXAS DIAMONDBACK--
--AN' SLIPPERIER THAN A GREASED PIG.
ALL THAT AND MORE. SHE GOT AWAY FROM ME IN LOS ANGELES--AND ALMOST RAN ME DOWN WHILE MAKING HER ESCAPE.
I JUST MANAGED TO AVOID GETTING CRUSHED UNDER HER JET'S WHEELS--
"--AND RETURNED FIRE.

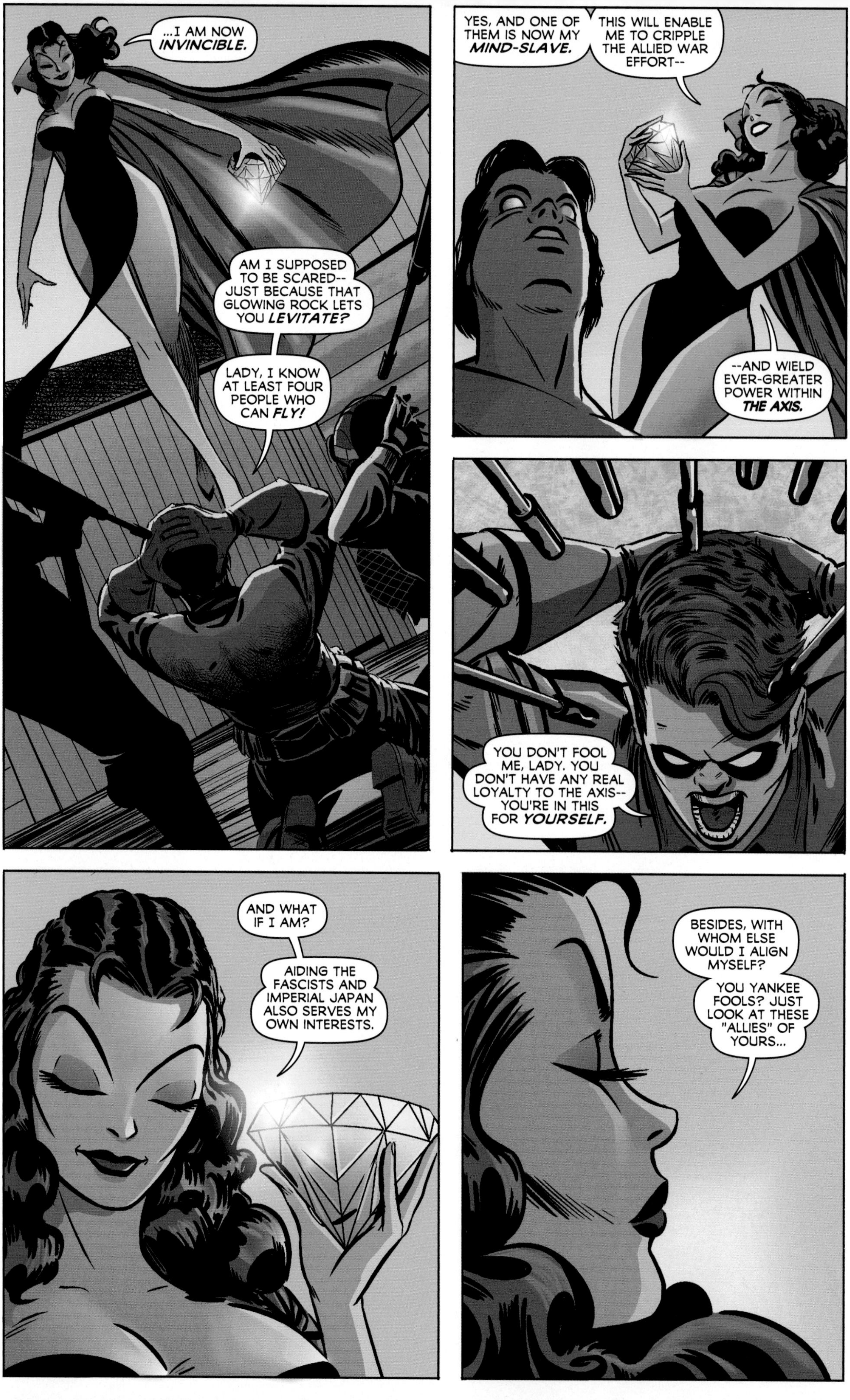

...I AM NOW INVINCIBLE.
AM I SUPPOSED TO BE SCARED-- JUST BECAUSE THAT GLOWING ROCK LETS YOU LEVITATE?
LADY, I KNOW AT LEAST FOUR PEOPLE WHO CAN FLY!
YES, AND ONE OF THEM IS NOW MY MIND-SLAVE.
THIS WILL ENABLE ME TO CRIPPLE THE ALLIED WAR EFFORT--
--AND WIELD EVER-GREATER POWER WITHIN THE AXIS.
YOU DON'T FOOL ME, LADY. YOU DON'T HAVE ANY REAL LOYALTY TO THE AXIS-- YOU'RE IN THIS FOR YOURSELF.
AND WHAT IF I AM?
AIDING THE FASCISTS AND IMPERIAL JAPAN ALSO SERVES MY OWN INTERESTS.
BESIDES, WITH WHOM ELSE WOULD I ALIGN MYSELF?
YOU YANKEE FOOLS? JUST LOOK AT THESE "ALLIES" OF YOURS...

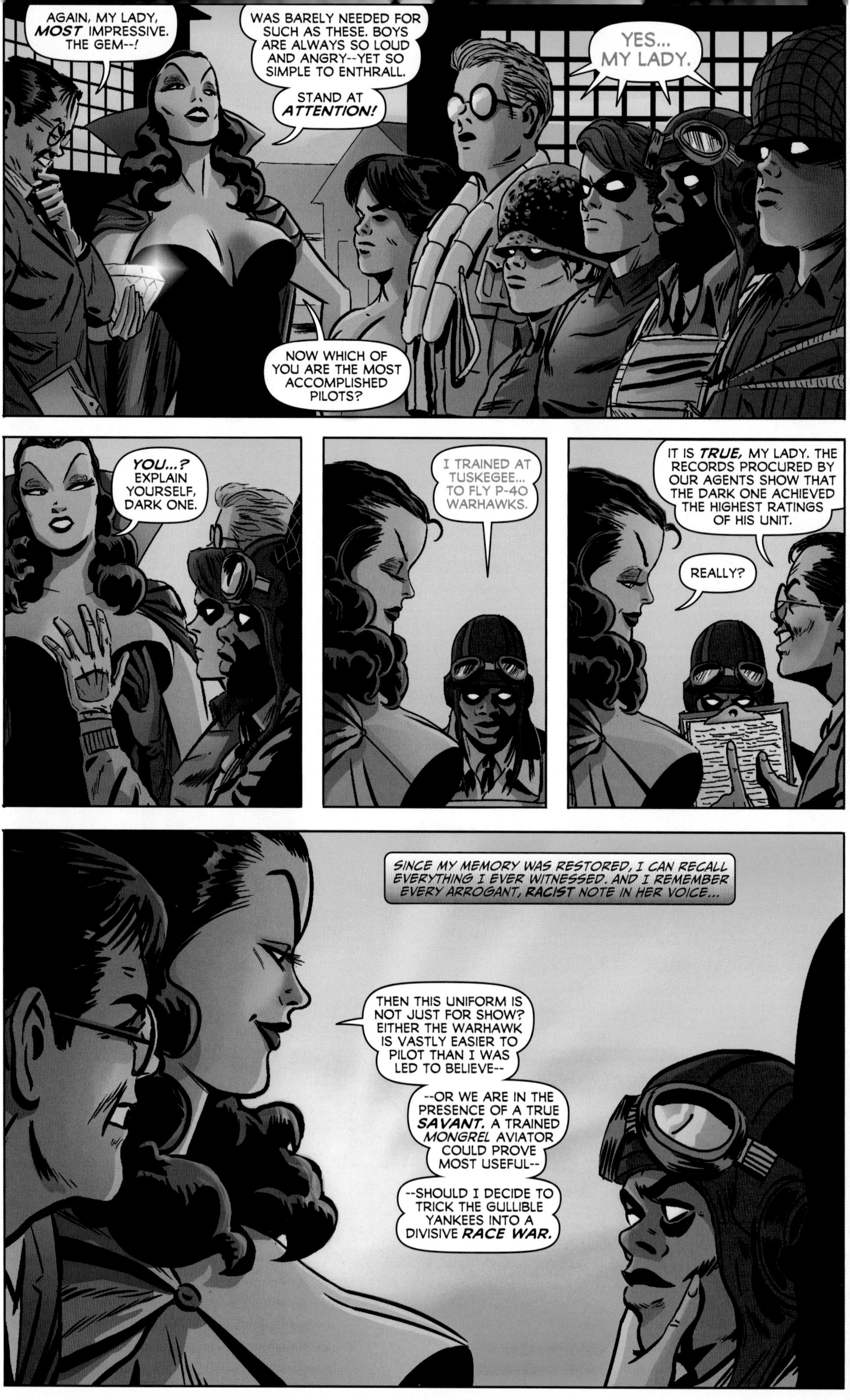
AGAIN, MY LADY, MOST IMPRESSIVE. THE GEM--!
WAS BARELY NEEDED FOR SUCH AS THESE. BOYS ARE ALWAYS SO LOUD AND ANGRY--YET SO SIMPLE TO ENTHRALL.
STAND AT ATTENTION!
YES... MY LADY.
NOW WHICH OF YOU ARE THE MOST ACCOMPLISHED PILOTS?
YOU...? EXPLAIN YOURSELF, DARK ONE.
I TRAINED AT TUSKEGEE... TO FLY P-40 WARHAWKS.
IT IS TRUE, MY LADY. THE RECORDS PROCURED BY OUR AGENTS SHOW THAT THE DARK ONE ACHIEVED THE HIGHEST RATINGS OF HIS UNIT.
REALLY?
SINCE MY MEMORY WAS RESTORED, I CAN RECALL EVERYTHING I EVER WITNESSED. AND I REMEMBER EVERY ARROGANT, RACIST NOTE IN HER VOICE...
THEN THIS UNIFORM IS NOT JUST FOR SHOW? EITHER THE WARHAWK IS VASTLY EASIER TO PILOT THAN I WAS LED TO BELIEVE--
--OR WE ARE IN THE PRESENCE OF A TRUE SAVANT. A TRAINED MONGREL AVIATOR COULD PROVE MOST USEFUL--
--SHOULD I DECIDE TO TRICK THE GULLIBLE YANKEES INTO A DIVISIVE RACE WAR.

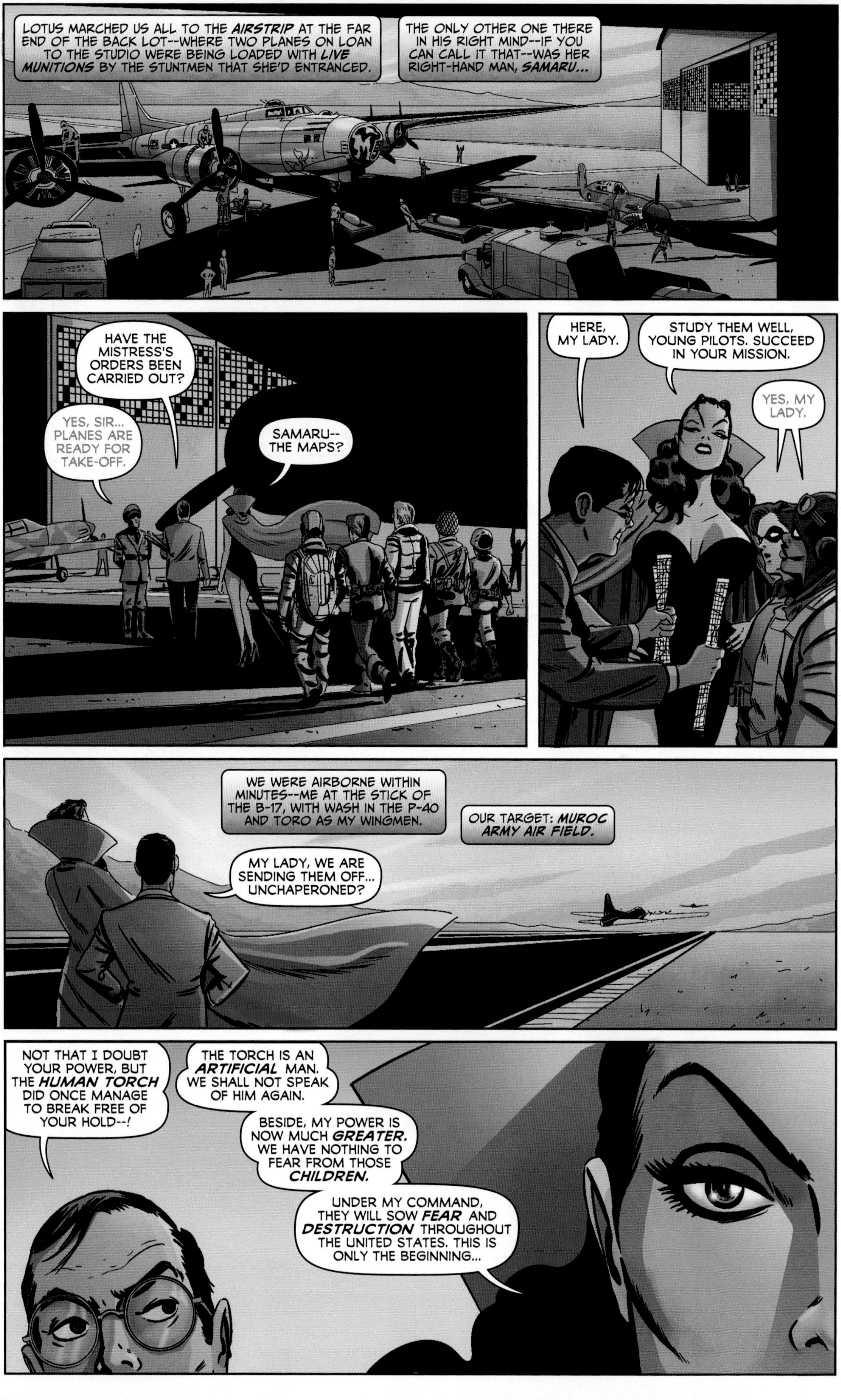
LOTUS MARCHED US ALL TO THE AIRSTRIP AT THE FAR END OF THE BACK LOT--WHERE TWO PLANES ON LOAN TO THE STUDIO WERE BEING LOADED WITH LIVE MUNITIONS BY THE STUNTMEN THAT SHE'D ENTRANCED.
THE ONLY OTHER ONE THERE IN HIS RIGHT MIND--IF YOU CAN CALL IT THAT--WAS HER RIGHT-HAND MAN, SAMARU...
HAVE THE MISTRESS'S ORDERS BEEN CARRIED OUT?
YES, SIR... PLANES ARE READY FOR TAKE-OFF.
SAMARU-- THE MAPS?
HERE, MY LADY.
STUDY THEM WELL, YOUNG PILOTS. SUCCEED IN YOUR MISSION.
YES, MY LADY.
WE WERE AIRBORNE WITHIN MINUTES--ME AT THE STICK OF THE B-17, WITH WASH IN THE P-40 AND TORO AS MY WINGMEN.
OUR TARGET: MUROC ARMY AIR FIELD.
MY LADY, WE ARE SENDING THEM OFF... UNCHAPERONED?
NOT THAT I DOUBT YOUR POWER, BUT THE HUMAN TORCH DID ONCE MANAGE TO BREAK FREE OF YOUR HOLD--!
THE TORCH IS AN ARTIFICIAL MAN. WE SHALL NOT SPEAK OF HIM AGAIN.
BESIDE, MY POWER IS NOW MUCH GREATER. WE HAVE NOTHING TO FEAR FROM THOSE CHILDREN.
UNDER MY COMMAND, THEY WILL SOW FEAR AND DESTRUCTION THROUGHOUT THE UNITED STATES. THIS IS ONLY THE BEGINNING...

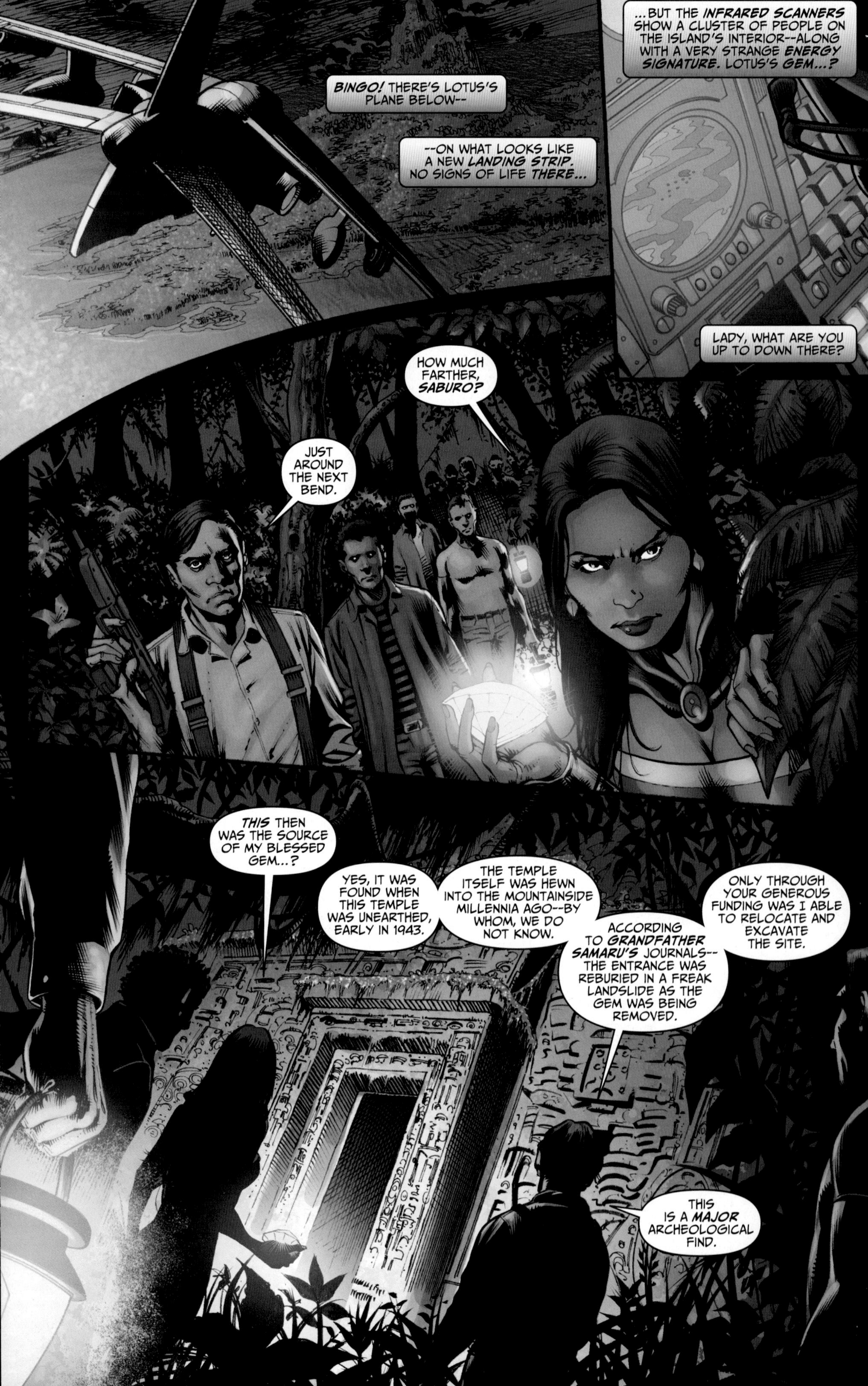
BINGO! THERE'S LOTUS'S PLANE BELOW--
--ON WHAT LOOKS LIKE A NEW LANDING STRIP. NO SIGNS OF LIFE THERE...
...BUT THE INFRARED SCANNERS SHOW A CLUSTER OF PEOPLE ON THE ISLAND'S INTERIOR--ALONG WITH A VERY STRANGE ENERGY SIGNATURE. LOTUS'S GEM...?
LADY, WHAT ARE YOU UP TO DOWN THERE?
HOW MUCH FARTHER, SABURO?
JUST AROUND THE NEXT BEND.
THIS THEN WAS THE SOURCE OF MY BLESSED GEM...?
YES, IT WAS FOUND WHEN THIS TEMPLE WAS UNEARTHED, EARLY IN 1943.
THE TEMPLE ITSELF WAS HEWN INTO THE MOUNTAINSIDE MILLENNIA AGO--BY WHOM, WE DO NOT KNOW.
ACCORDING TO GRANDFATHER SAMARU'S JOURNALS--THE ENTRANCE WAS REBURIED IN A FREAK LANDSLIDE AS THE GEM WAS BEING REMOVED.
ONLY THROUGH YOUR GENEROUS FUNDING WAS I ABLE TO RELOCATE AND EXCAVATE THE SITE.
THIS IS A MAJOR ARCHEOLOGICAL FIND.

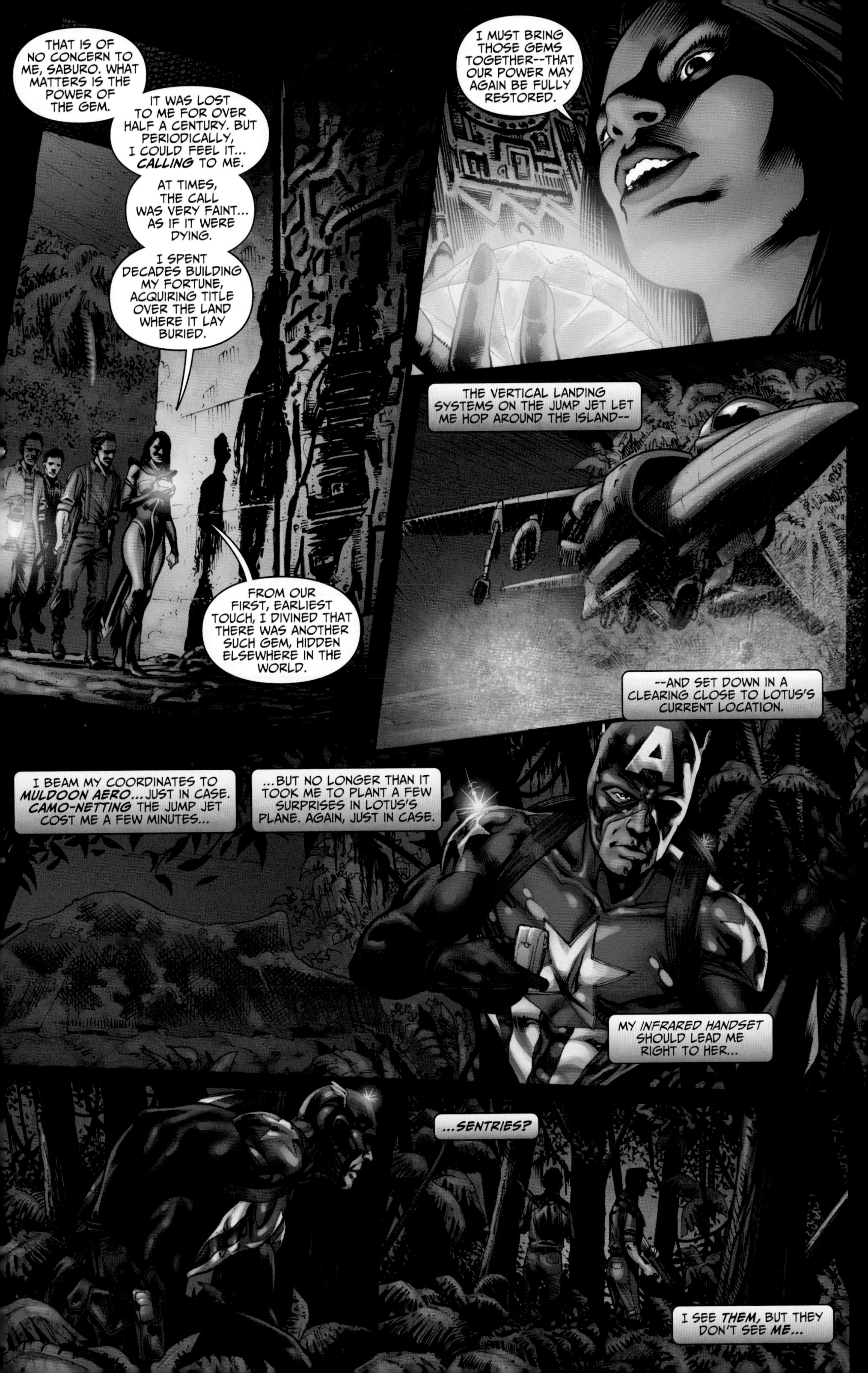
THAT IS OF NO CONCERN TO ME, SABURO. WHAT MATTERS IS THE POWER OF THE GEM.
IT WAS LOST TO ME FOR OVER HALF A CENTURY. BUT PERIODICALLY, I COULD FEEL IT... CALLING TO ME.
AT TIMES, THE CALL WAS VERY FAINT... AS IF IT WERE DYING.
I SPENT DECADES BUILDING MY FORTUNE, ACQUIRING TITLE OVER THE LAND WHERE IT LAY BURIED.
FROM OUR FIRST, EARLIEST TOUCH, I DIVINED THAT THERE WAS ANOTHER SUCH GEM, HIDDEN ELSEWHERE IN THE WORLD.
I MUST BRING THOSE GEMS TOGETHER--THAT OUR POWER MAY AGAIN BE FULLY RESTORED.
THE VERTICAL LANDING SYSTEMS ON THE JUMP JET LET ME HOP AROUND THE ISLAND--
--AND SET DOWN IN A CLEARING CLOSE TO LOTUS'S CURRENT LOCATION.
I BEAM MY COORDINATES TO MULDOON AERO... JUST IN CASE. CAMO-NETTING THE JUMP JET COST ME A FEW MINUTES...
...BUT NO LONGER THAN IT TOOK ME TO PLANT A FEW SURPRISES IN LOTUS'S PLANE. AGAIN, JUST IN CASE.
MY INFRARED HANDSET SHOULD LEAD ME RIGHT TO HER...
...SENTRIES?
I SEE THEM, BUT THEY DON'T SEE ME...

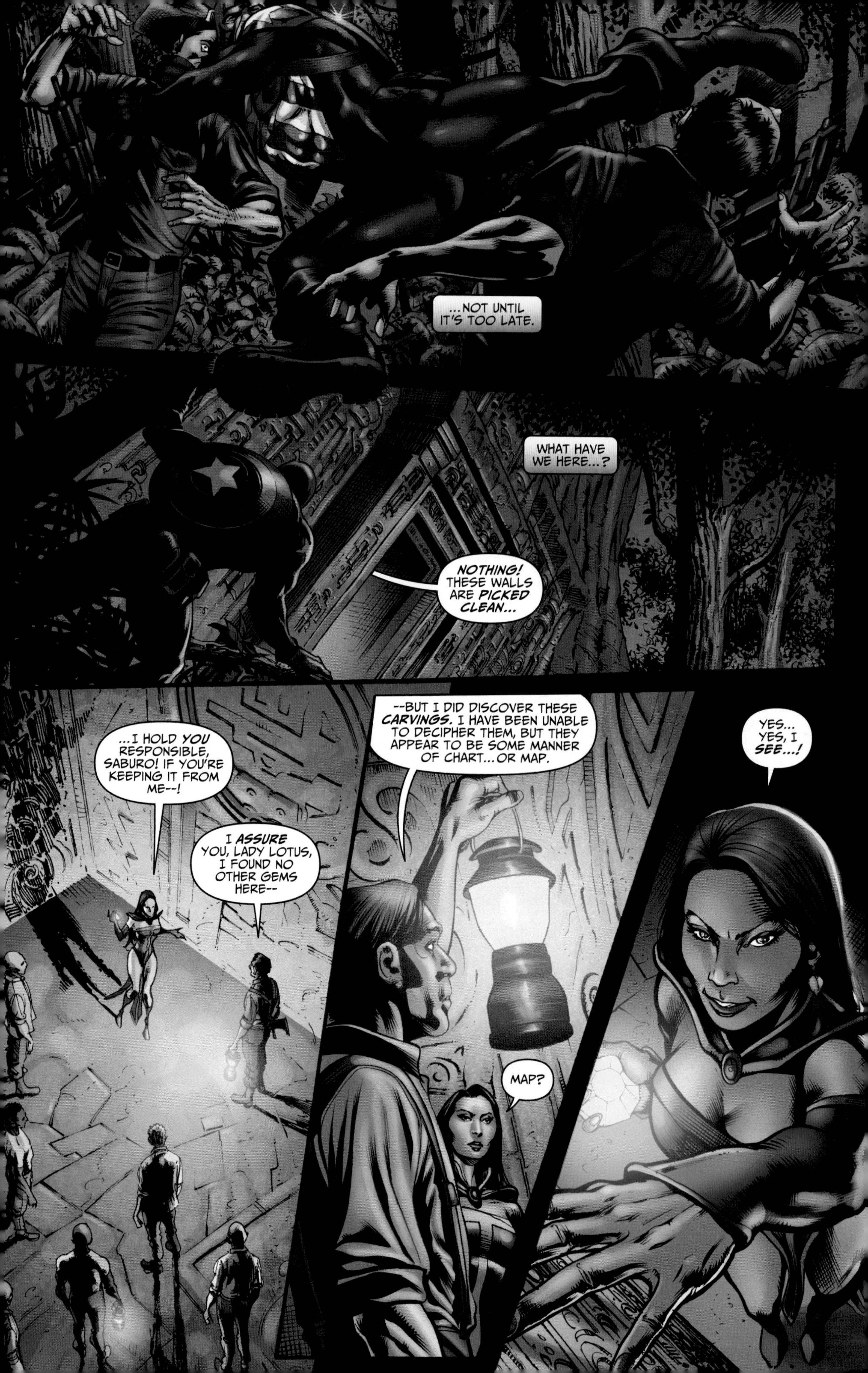
...NOT UNTIL IT'S TOO LATE.
WHAT HAVE WE HERE...?
NOTHING! THESE WALLS ARE PICKED CLEAN...
...I HOLD YOU RESPONSIBLE, SABURO! IF YOU'RE KEEPING IT FROM ME--!
I ASSURE YOU, LADY LOTUS, I FOUND NO OTHER GEMS HERE--
--BUT I DID DISCOVER THESE CARVINGS. I HAVE BEEN UNABLE TO DECIPHER THEM, BUT THEY APPEAR TO BE SOME MANNER OF CHART...OR MAP.
MAP?
YES... YES, I SEE...!

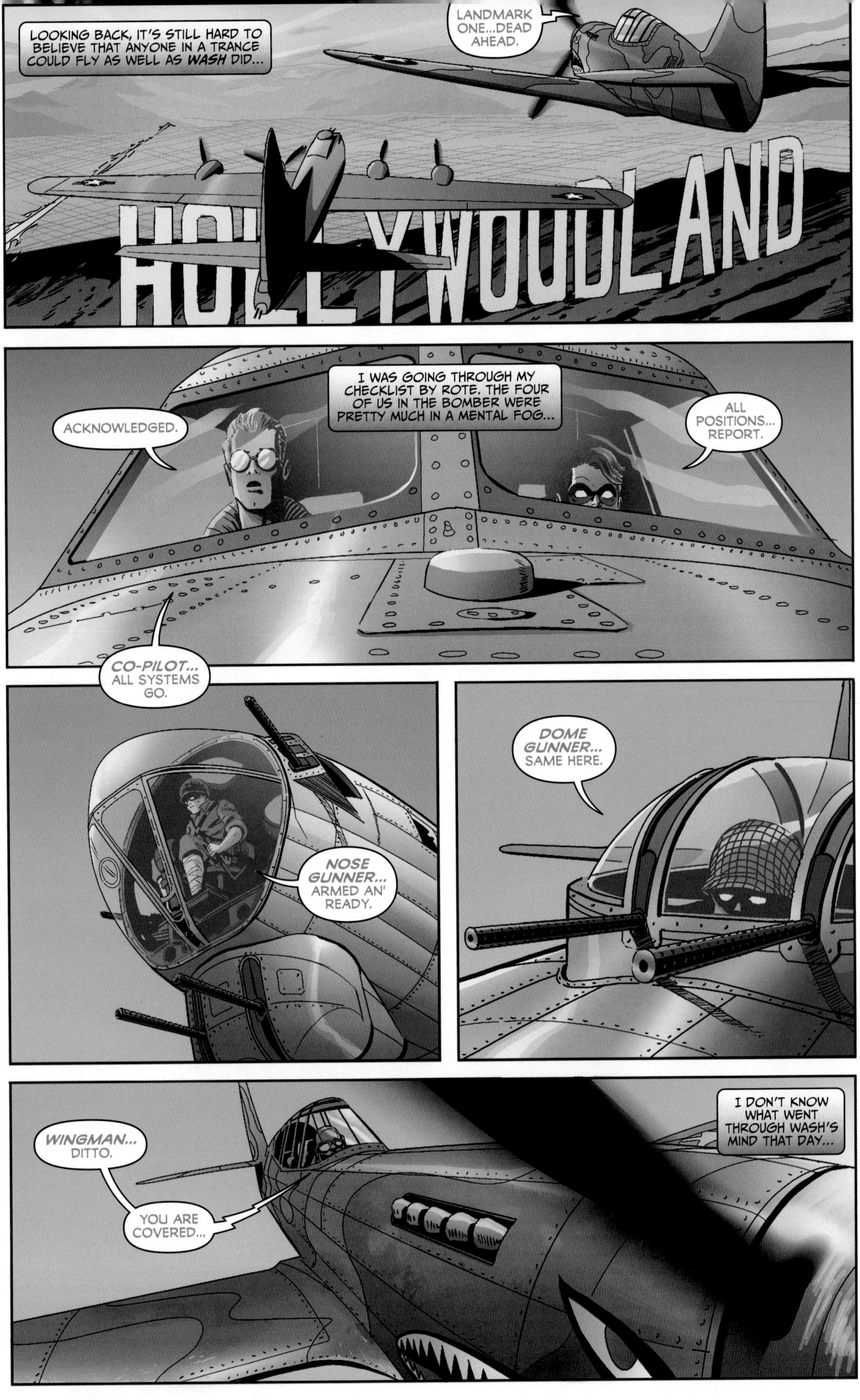
LOOKING BACK, IT'S STILL HARD TO BELIEVE THAT ANYONE IN A TRANCE COULD FLY AS WELL AS WASH DID...
LANDMARK ONE...DEAD AHEAD.
HOLLYWOODLAND
I WAS GOING THROUGH MY CHECKLIST BY ROTE. THE FOUR OF US IN THE BOMBER WERE PRETTY MUCH IN A MENTAL FOG...
ACKNOWLEDGED.
ALL POSITIONS... REPORT.
CO-PILOT... ALL SYSTEMS GO.
NOSE GUNNER... ARMED AN' READY.
DOME GUNNER... SAME HERE.
I DON'T KNOW WHAT WENT THROUGH WASH'S MIND THAT DAY...
WINGMAN... DITTO.
YOU ARE COVERED...

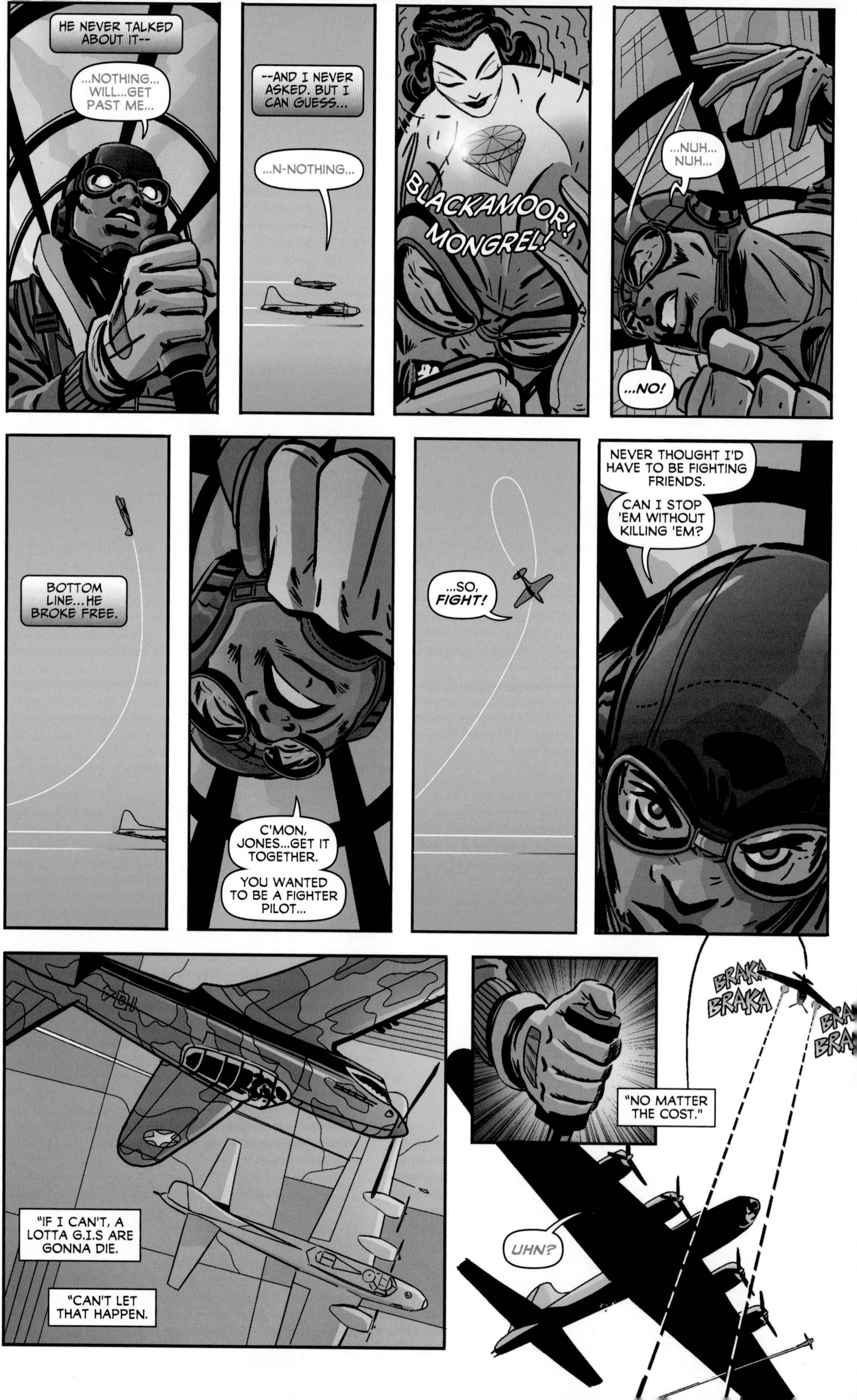
HE NEVER TALKED ABOUT IT--
...NOTHING... WILL...GET PAST ME...
--AND I NEVER ASKED. BUT I CAN GUESS...
...N-NOTHING...
BLACKAMOOR! MONGREL!
...NUH... NUH...
...NO!
BOTTOM LINE...HE BROKE FREE.
C'MON, JONES...GET IT TOGETHER.
YOU WANTED TO BE A FIGHTER PILOT...
...SO, FIGHT!
NEVER THOUGHT I'D HAVE TO BE FIGHTING FRIENDS.
CAN I STOP 'EM WITHOUT KILLING 'EM?
"IF I CAN'T, A LOTTA G.I.S ARE GONNA DIE.
"CAN'T LET THAT HAPPEN.
"NO MATTER THE COST."
BRAKA BRAKA
UHN?

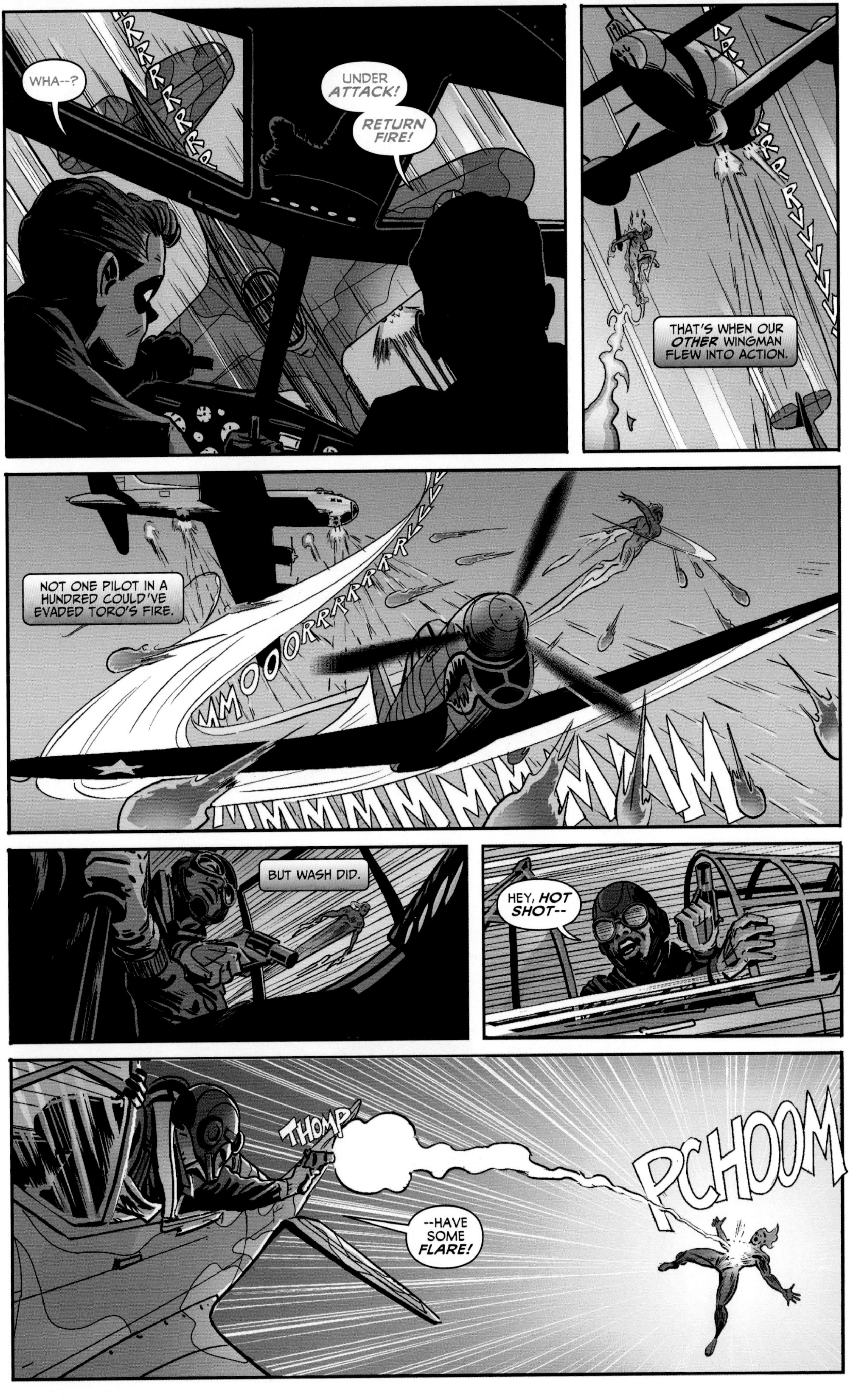

RRRRRRRR
WHA--?
UNDER ATTACK!
RETURN FIRE!
THAT'S WHEN OUR OTHER WINGMAN FLEW INTO ACTION.
NOT ONE PILOT IN A HUNDRED COULD'VE EVADED TORO'S FIRE.
MMOOOORRRRRRRRRVVV
MMMMMMMMMM
BUT WASH DID.
HEY, HOT SHOT--
THOMP
--HAVE SOME FLARE!
PCHOOM

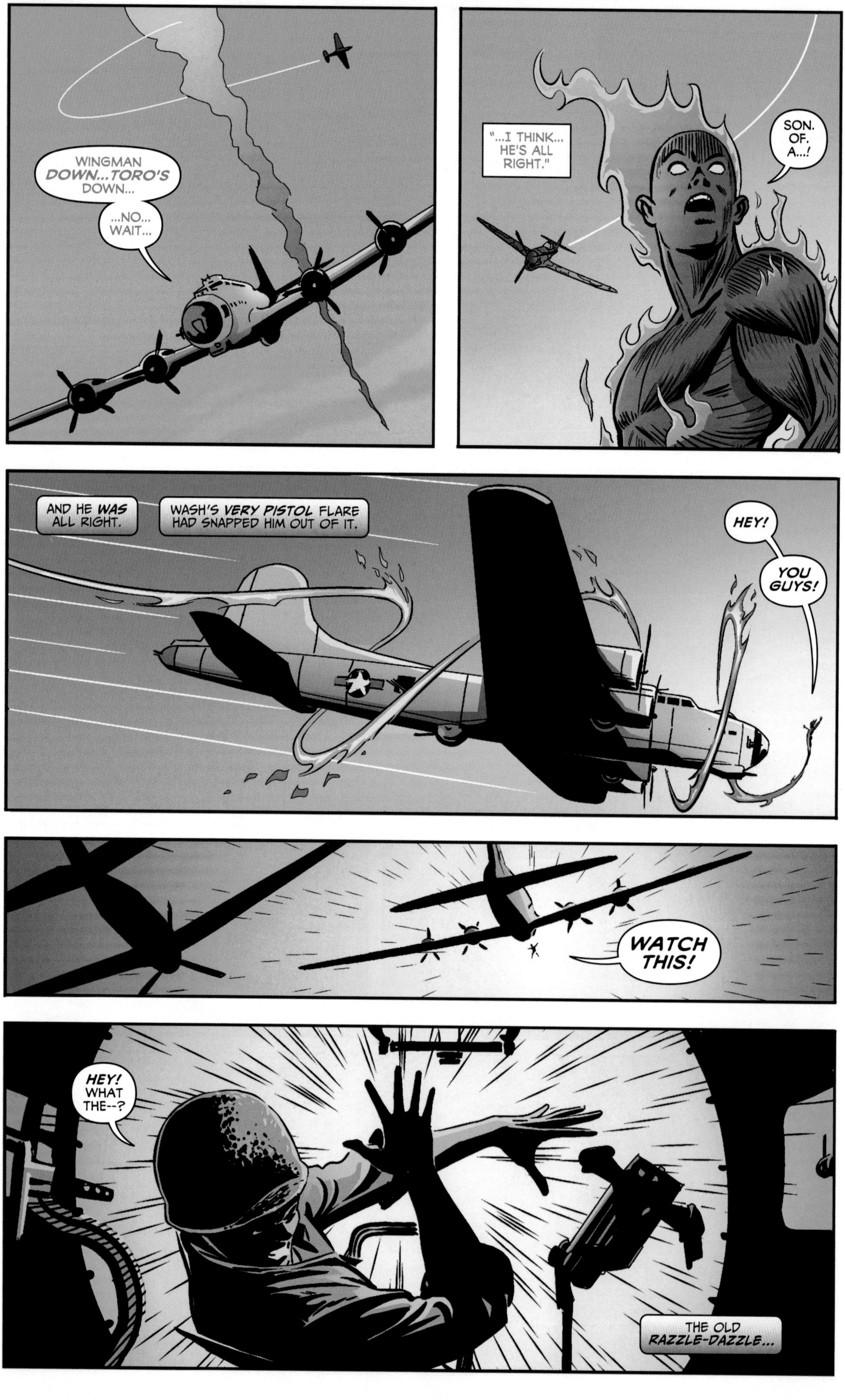
WINGMAN DOWN...TORO'S DOWN...
...NO... WAIT...
"...I THINK... HE'S ALL RIGHT."
SON. OF. A...!
AND HE WAS ALL RIGHT.
WASH'S VERY PISTOL FLARE HAD SNAPPED HIM OUT OF IT.
HEY!
YOU GUYS!
WATCH THIS!
HEY! WHAT THE--?
THE OLD RAZZLE-DAZZLE...

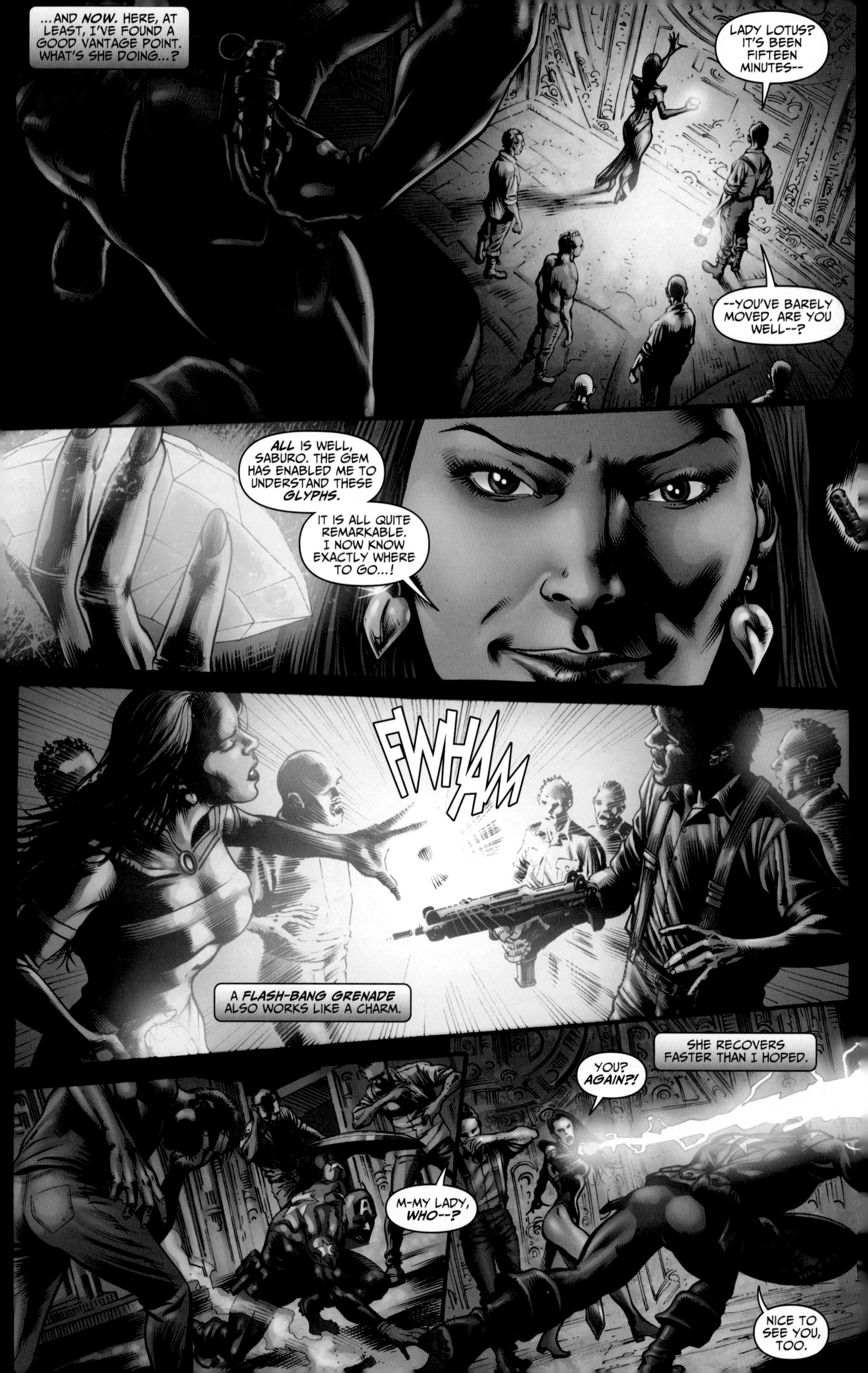
...AND NOW. HERE, AT LEAST, I'VE FOUND A GOOD VANTAGE POINT. WHAT'S SHE DOING...?
LADY LOTUS? IT'S BEEN FIFTEEN MINUTES--
--YOU'VE BARELY MOVED. ARE YOU WELL--?
ALL IS WELL, SABURO. THE GEM HAS ENABLED ME TO UNDERSTAND THESE GLYPHS.
IT IS ALL QUITE REMARKABLE. I NOW KNOW EXACTLY WHERE TO GO...!
FWHAM
A FLASH-BANG GRENADE ALSO WORKS LIKE A CHARM.
SHE RECOVERS FASTER THAN I HOPED.
YOU? AGAIN?!
M-MY LADY, WHO--?
NICE TO SEE YOU, TOO.

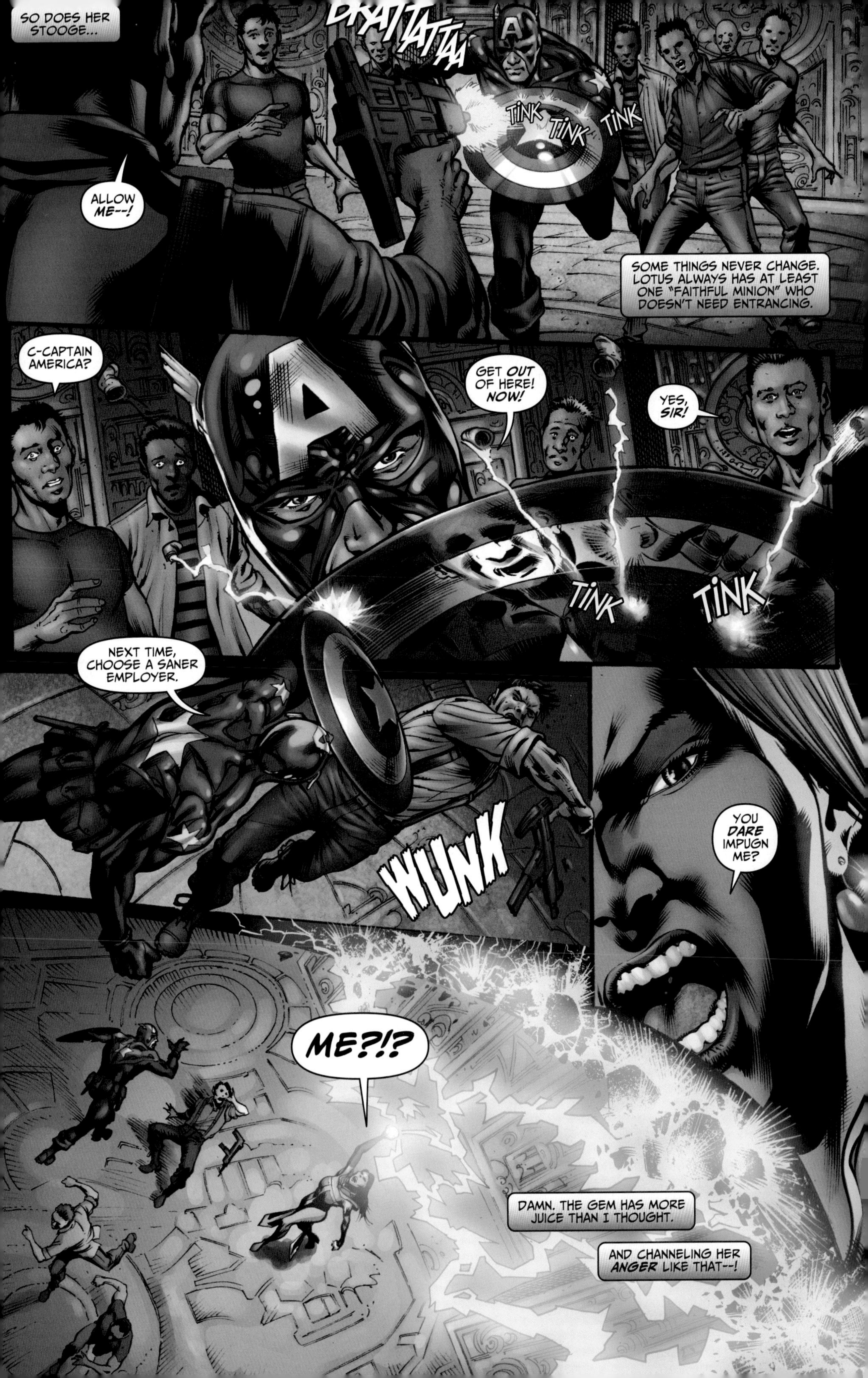
SO DOES HER STOOGE...
DRAT TAT TAA
ALLOW ME--!
TINK TINK TINK
SOME THINGS NEVER CHANGE. LOTUS ALWAYS HAS AT LEAST ONE "FAITHFUL MINION" WHO DOESN'T NEED ENTRANCING.
C-CAPTAIN AMERICA?
GET OUT OF HERE! NOW!
YES, SIR!
TINK
TINK
NEXT TIME, CHOOSE A SANER EMPLOYER.
WUNK
YOU DARE IMPUGN ME?
ME?!?
DAMN. THE GEM HAS MORE JUICE THAN I THOUGHT.
AND CHANNELING HER ANGER LIKE THAT--!

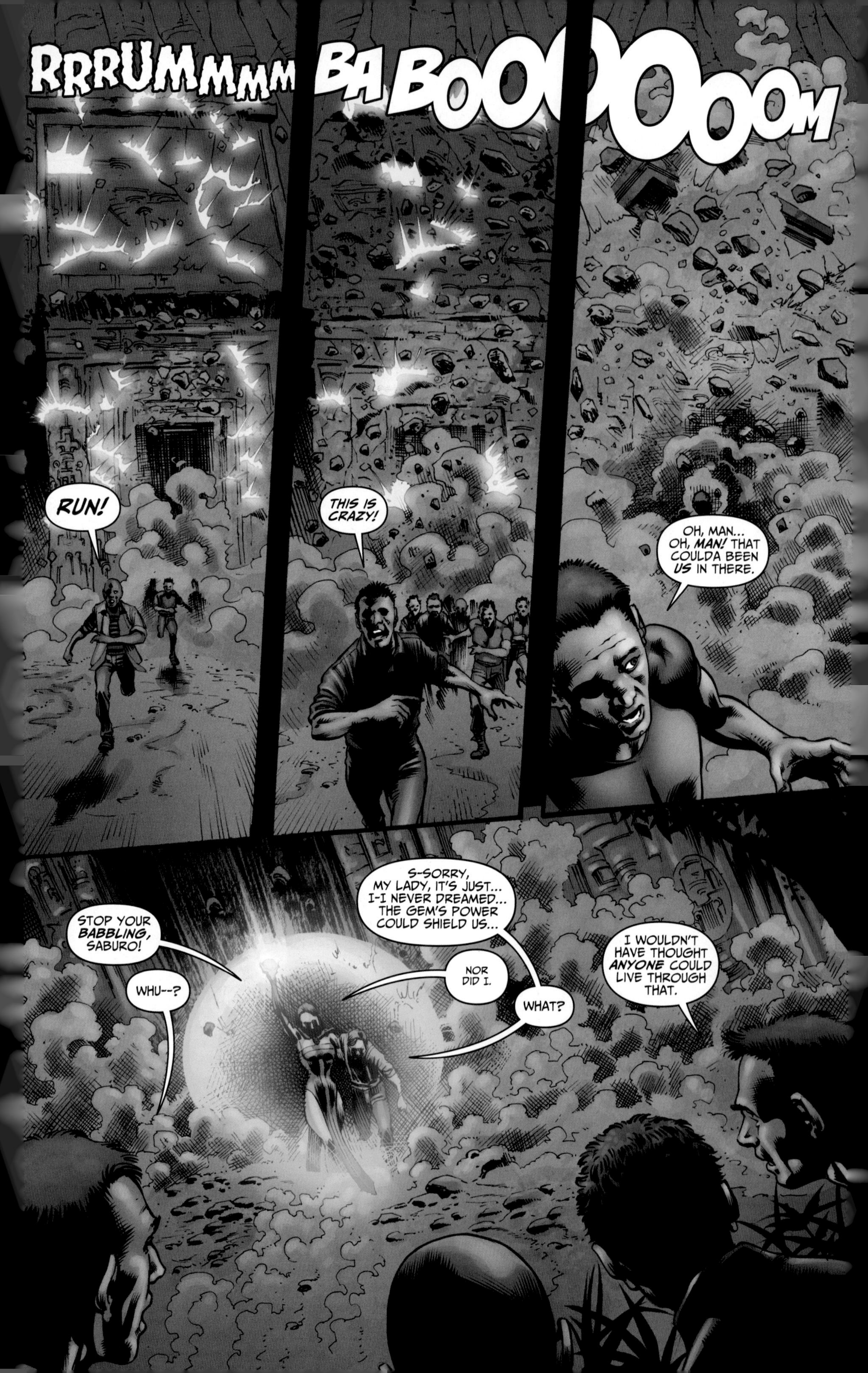
RRRUMMMMM BA BOOOOOOOM
RUN!
THIS IS CRAZY!
OH, MAN... OH, MAN! THAT COULDA BEEN US IN THERE.
STOP YOUR BABBLING, SABURO!
WHU--?
S-SORRY, MY LADY, IT'S JUST... I-I NEVER DREAMED... THE GEM'S POWER COULD SHIELD US...
NOR DID I.
WHAT?
I WOULDN'T HAVE THOUGHT ANYONE COULD LIVE THROUGH THAT.

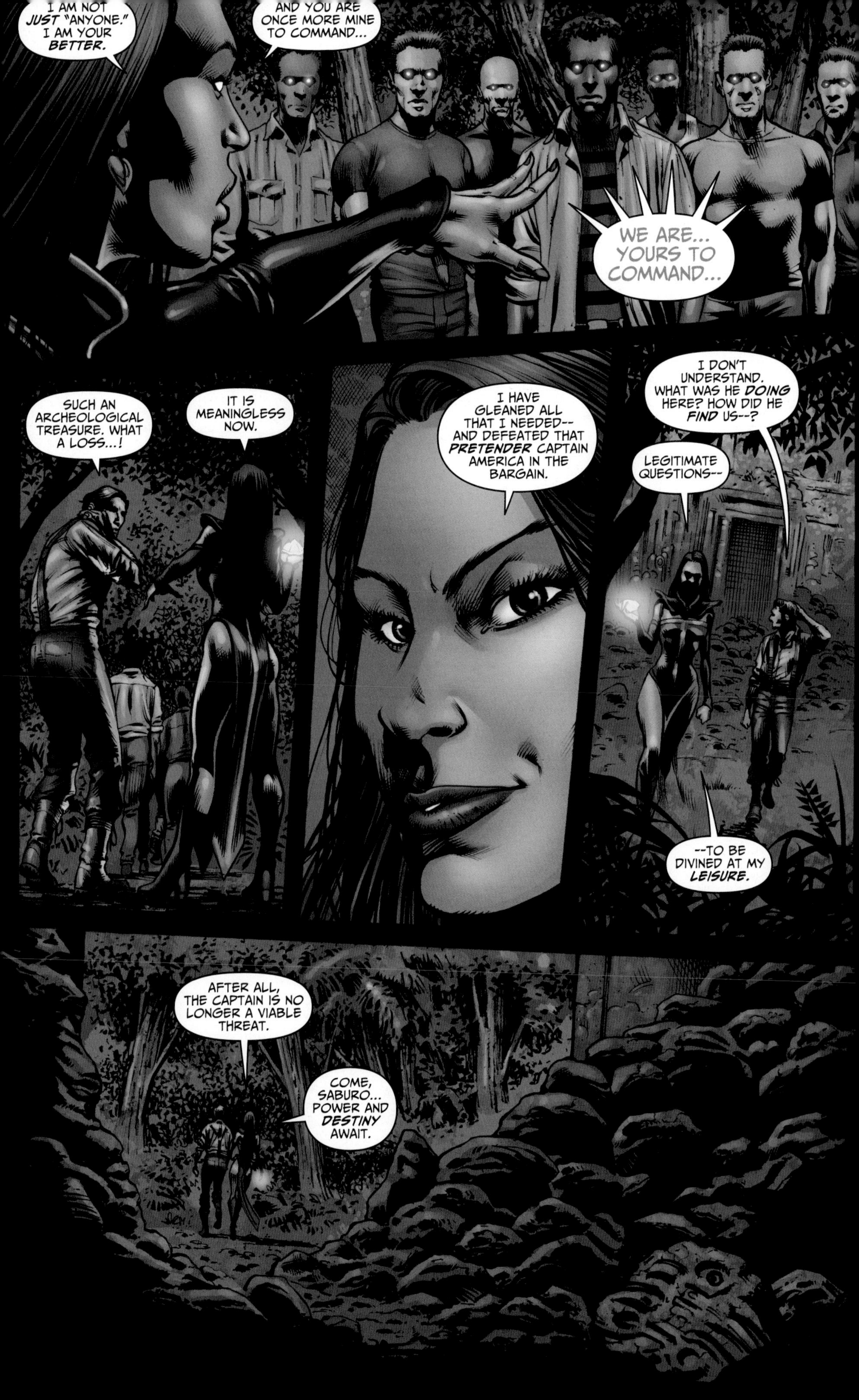
I AM NOT JUST "ANYONE." I AM YOUR BETTER.
AND YOU ARE ONCE MORE MINE TO COMMAND...
WE ARE... YOURS TO COMMAND...
SUCH AN ARCHEOLOGICAL TREASURE. WHAT A LOSS...!
IT IS MEANINGLESS NOW.
I HAVE GLEANED ALL THAT I NEEDED-- AND DEFEATED THAT PRETENDER CAPTAIN AMERICA IN THE BARGAIN.
I DON'T UNDERSTAND. WHAT WAS HE DOING HERE? HOW DID HE FIND US--?
LEGITIMATE QUESTIONS--
--TO BE DIVINED AT MY LEISURE.
AFTER ALL, THE CAPTAIN IS NO LONGER A VIABLE THREAT.
COME, SABURO... POWER AND DESTINY AWAIT.

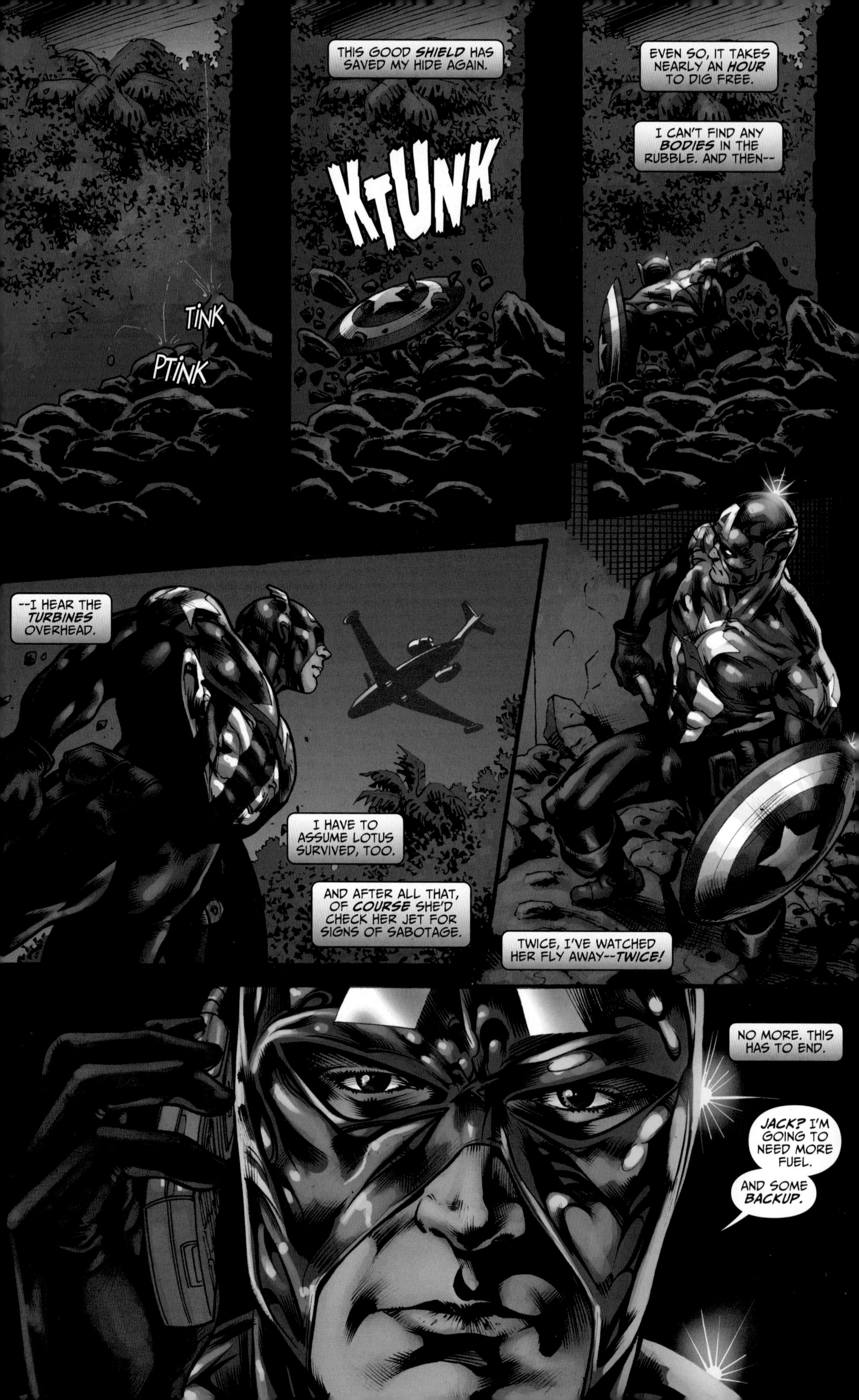
TINK
PTINK
THIS GOOD SHIELD HAS SAVED MY HIDE AGAIN.
KTUNK
EVEN SO, IT TAKES NEARLY AN HOUR TO DIG FREE.
I CAN'T FIND ANY BODIES IN THE RUBBLE. AND THEN--
--I HEAR THE TURBINES OVERHEAD.
I HAVE TO ASSUME LOTUS SURVIVED, TOO.
AND AFTER ALL THAT, OF COURSE SHE'D CHECK HER JET FOR SIGNS OF SABOTAGE.
TWICE, I'VE WATCHED HER FLY AWAY--TWICE!
NO MORE. THIS HAS TO END.
JACK? I'M GOING TO NEED MORE FUEL.
AND SOME BACKUP.

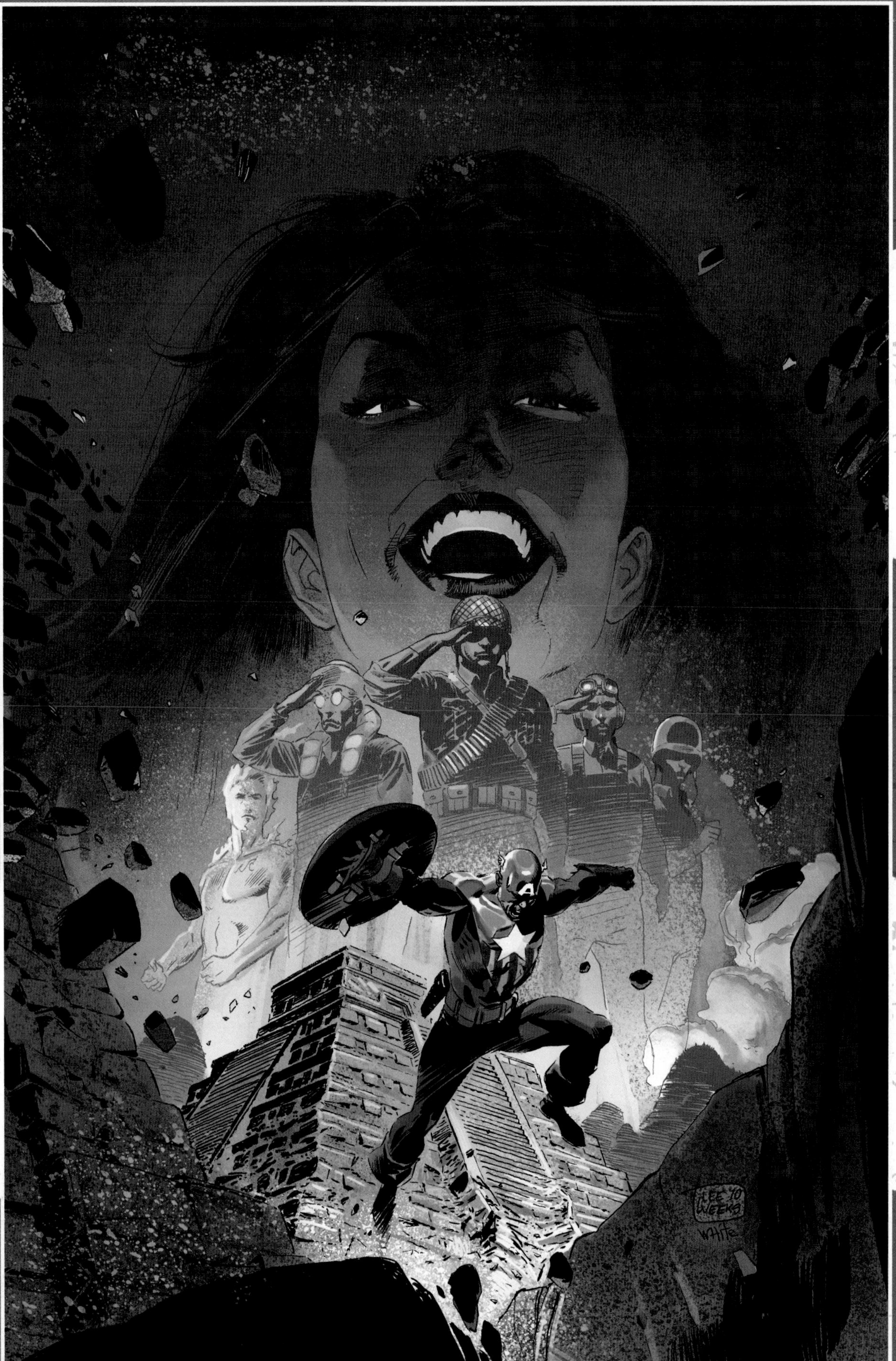

CAPTAIN AMERICA: FOREVER ALLIES #4

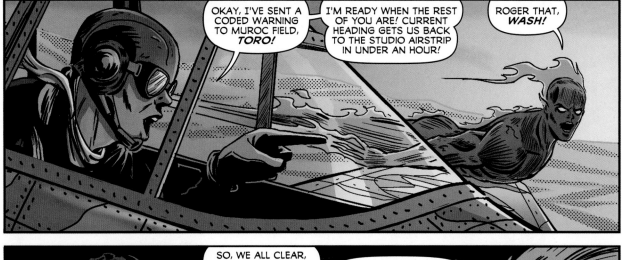

OKAY, I'VE SENT A CODED WARNING TO MUROC FIELD, *TORO!*

I'M READY WHEN THE REST OF YOU ARE! CURRENT HEADING GETS US BACK TO THE STUDIO AIRSTRIP IN UNDER AN HOUR!

ROGER THAT, *WASH!*

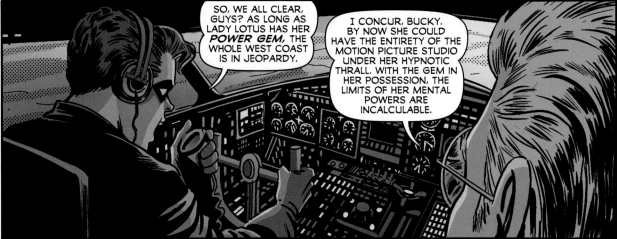

SO, WE ALL CLEAR, GUYS? AS LONG AS LADY LOTUS HAS HER *POWER GEM,* THE WHOLE WEST COAST IS IN JEOPARDY.

I CONCUR, BUCKY. BY NOW SHE COULD HAVE THE ENTIRETY OF THE MOTION PICTURE STUDIO UNDER HER HYPNOTIC THRALL. WITH THE GEM IN HER POSSESSION, THE LIMITS OF HER MENTAL POWERS ARE INCALCULABLE.

AND IF LOTUS FINDS OUT *WE'RE* FREE OF HER CONTROL, THE GAME'S OVER.

WE HAVE TO BE CAREFUL--!

YEAH, BUT--AW, NUTS! I STILL SAY WE OUGHTTA DROP A BOMB RIGHT SMACK ON LADY LOTUS'S--!

I HEAR YA, PAT. BUT IT'S NOT THAT EASY.

TOO MANY INNOCENT PEOPLE WILL GET HURT IF WE GO IN WITH GUNS BLAZING.

LOTUS SENT US OFF TO BOMB A MILITARY TARGET. IF WE'VE ANY HOPE OF STOPPING HER, WE HAVE TO CONVINCE HER THAT WE'VE CARRIED OUT THAT MISSION.

ALL THESE YEARS LATER, I'M STILL LOOKING FOR A WAY TO STOP LADY LOTUS...

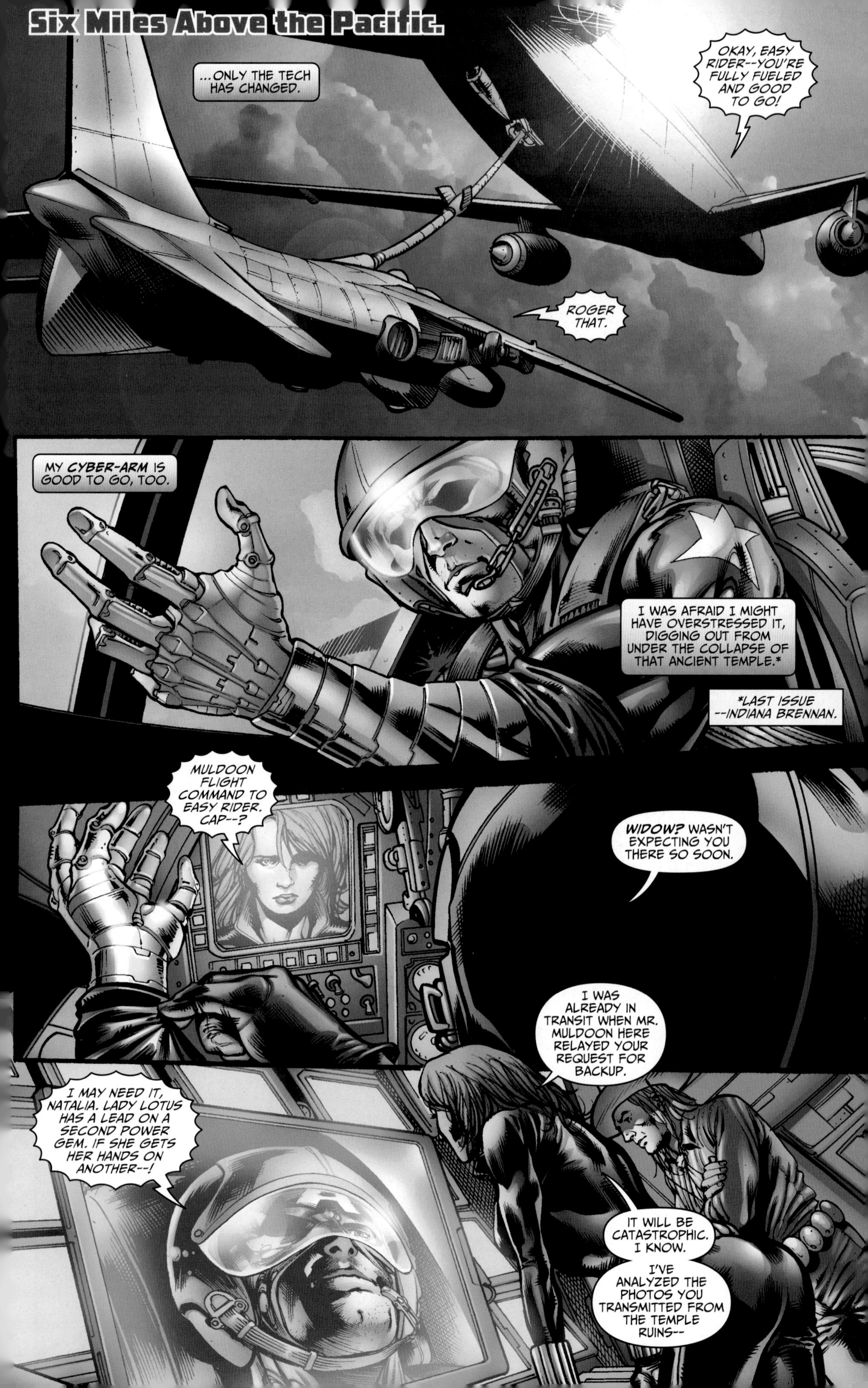
Six Miles Above the Pacific.
...ONLY THE TECH HAS CHANGED.
OKAY, EASY RIDER--YOU'RE FULLY FUELED AND GOOD TO GO!
ROGER THAT.
MY CYBER-ARM IS GOOD TO GO, TOO.
I WAS AFRAID I MIGHT HAVE OVERSTRESSED IT, DIGGING OUT FROM UNDER THE COLLAPSE OF THAT ANCIENT TEMPLE.*
*LAST ISSUE --INDIANA BRENNAN.
MULDOON FLIGHT COMMAND TO EASY RIDER. CAP--?
WIDOW? WASN'T EXPECTING YOU THERE SO SOON.
I WAS ALREADY IN TRANSIT WHEN MR. MULDOON HERE RELAYED YOUR REQUEST FOR BACKUP.
I MAY NEED IT, NATALIA. LADY LOTUS HAS A LEAD ON A SECOND POWER GEM. IF SHE GETS HER HANDS ON ANOTHER--!
IT WILL BE CATASTROPHIC. I KNOW.
I'VE ANALYZED THE PHOTOS YOU TRANSMITTED FROM THE TEMPLE RUINS--

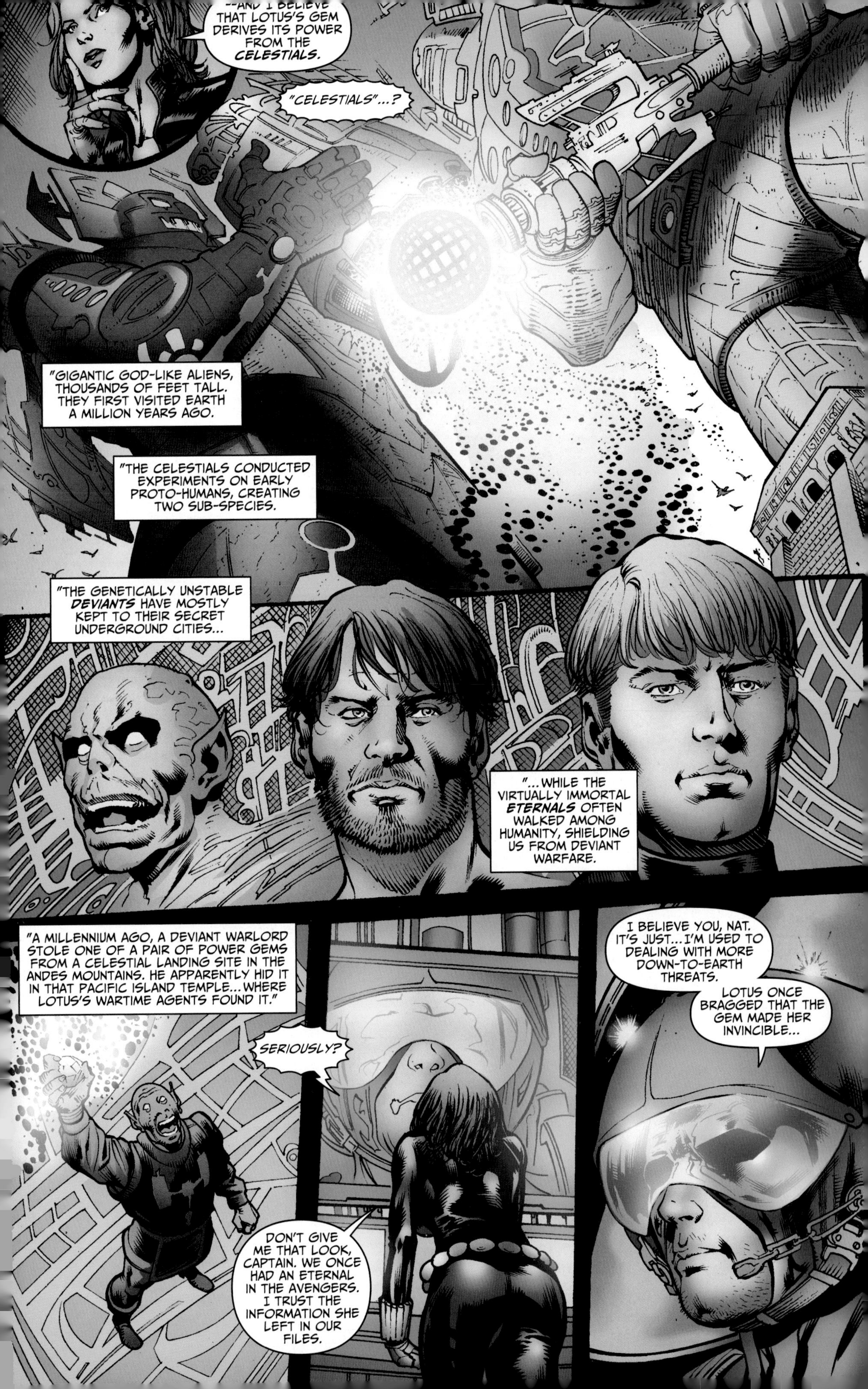
--AND I BELIEVE THAT LOTUS'S GEM DERIVES ITS POWER FROM THE CELESTIALS.
"CELESTIALS"...?
"GIGANTIC GOD-LIKE ALIENS, THOUSANDS OF FEET TALL. THEY FIRST VISITED EARTH A MILLION YEARS AGO.
"THE CELESTIALS CONDUCTED EXPERIMENTS ON EARLY PROTO-HUMANS, CREATING TWO SUB-SPECIES.
"THE GENETICALLY UNSTABLE DEVIANTS HAVE MOSTLY KEPT TO THEIR SECRET UNDERGROUND CITIES...
"...WHILE THE VIRTUALLY IMMORTAL ETERNALS OFTEN WALKED AMONG HUMANITY, SHIELDING US FROM DEVIANT WARFARE.
"A MILLENNIUM AGO, A DEVIANT WARLORD STOLE ONE OF A PAIR OF POWER GEMS FROM A CELESTIAL LANDING SITE IN THE ANDES MOUNTAINS. HE APPARENTLY HID IT IN THAT PACIFIC ISLAND TEMPLE... WHERE LOTUS'S WARTIME AGENTS FOUND IT."
SERIOUSLY?
DON'T GIVE ME THAT LOOK, CAPTAIN. WE ONCE HAD AN ETERNAL IN THE AVENGERS. I TRUST THE INFORMATION SHE LEFT IN OUR FILES.
I BELIEVE YOU, NAT. IT'S JUST... I'M USED TO DEALING WITH MORE DOWN-TO-EARTH THREATS.
LOTUS ONCE BRAGGED THAT THE GEM MADE HER INVINCIBLE...

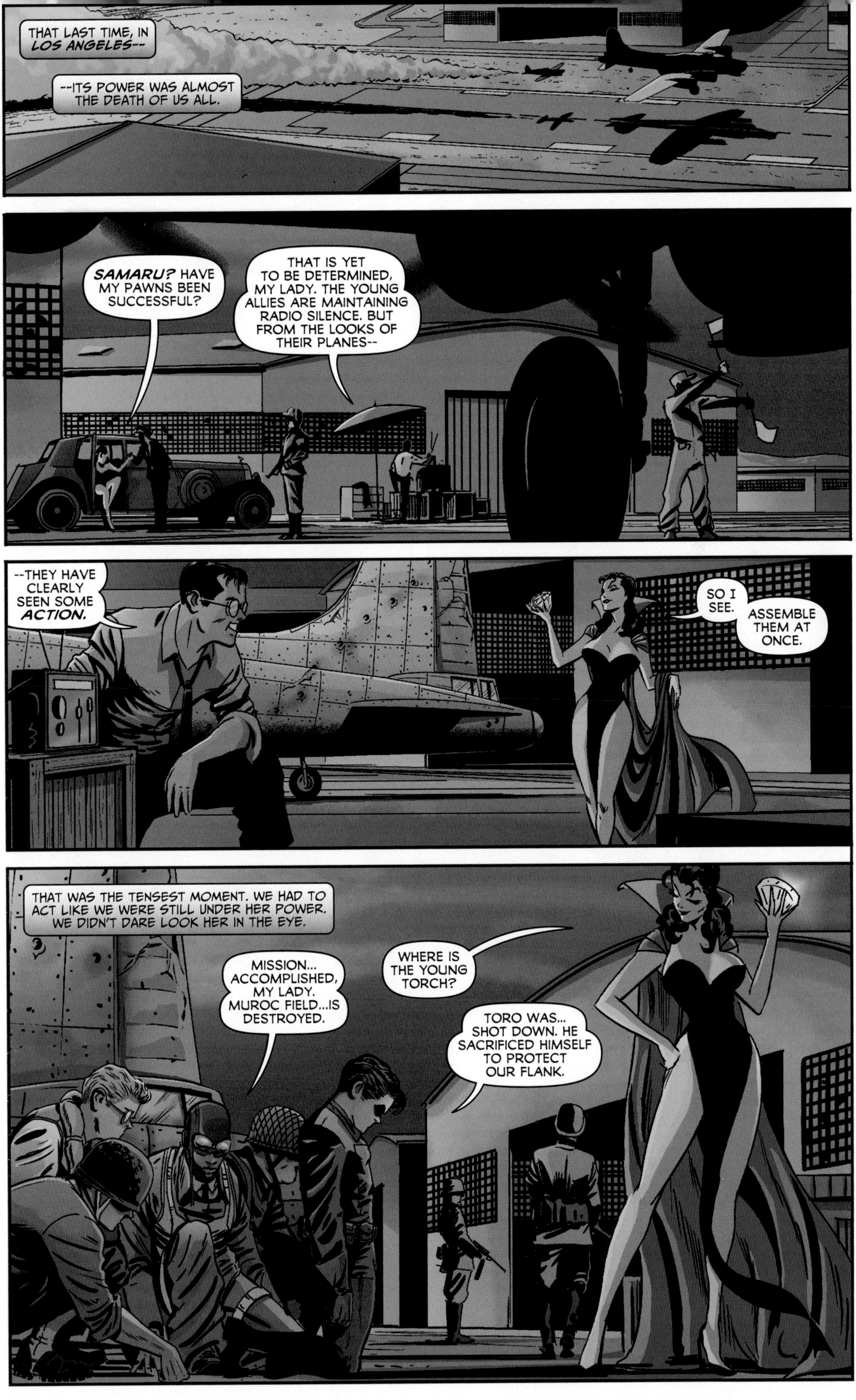
THAT LAST TIME, IN LOS ANGELES--
--ITS POWER WAS ALMOST THE DEATH OF US ALL.
SAMARU? HAVE MY PAWNS BEEN SUCCESSFUL?
THAT IS YET TO BE DETERMINED, MY LADY. THE YOUNG ALLIES ARE MAINTAINING RADIO SILENCE. BUT FROM THE LOOKS OF THEIR PLANES--
--THEY HAVE CLEARLY SEEN SOME ACTION.
SO I SEE.
ASSEMBLE THEM AT ONCE.
THAT WAS THE TENSEST MOMENT. WE HAD TO ACT LIKE WE WERE STILL UNDER HER POWER. WE DIDN'T DARE LOOK HER IN THE EYE.
MISSION... ACCOMPLISHED, MY LADY. MUROC FIELD...IS DESTROYED.
WHERE IS THE YOUNG TORCH?
TORO WAS... SHOT DOWN. HE SACRIFICED HIMSELF TO PROTECT OUR FLANK.

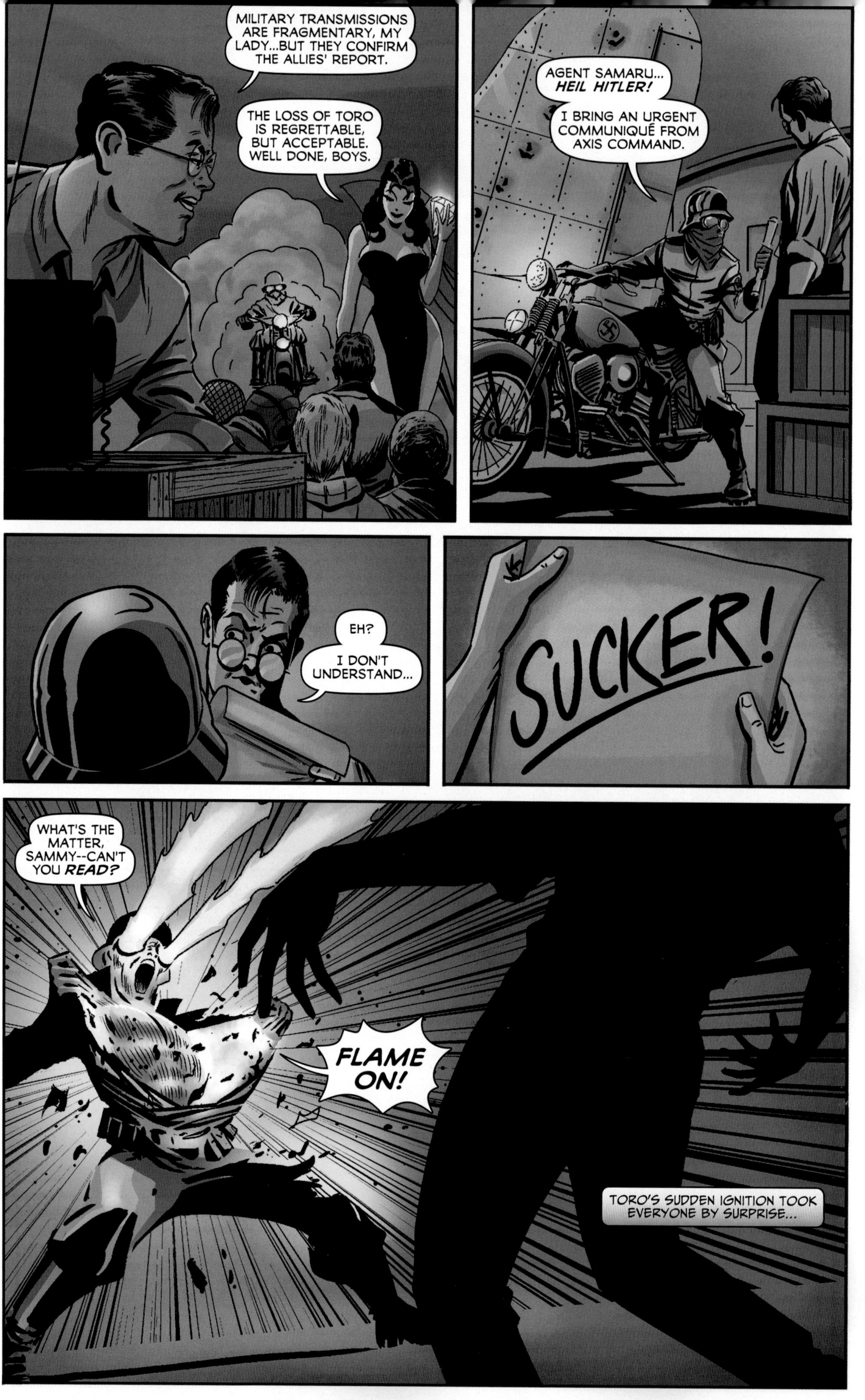
MILITARY TRANSMISSIONS ARE FRAGMENTARY, MY LADY...BUT THEY CONFIRM THE ALLIES' REPORT.
THE LOSS OF TORO IS REGRETTABLE, BUT ACCEPTABLE. WELL DONE, BOYS.
AGENT SAMARU... HEIL HITLER!
I BRING AN URGENT COMMUNIQUÉ FROM AXIS COMMAND.
EH?
I DON'T UNDERSTAND...
SUCKER!
WHAT'S THE MATTER, SAMMY--CAN'T YOU READ?
FLAME ON!
TORO'S SUDDEN IGNITION TOOK EVERYONE BY SURPRISE...

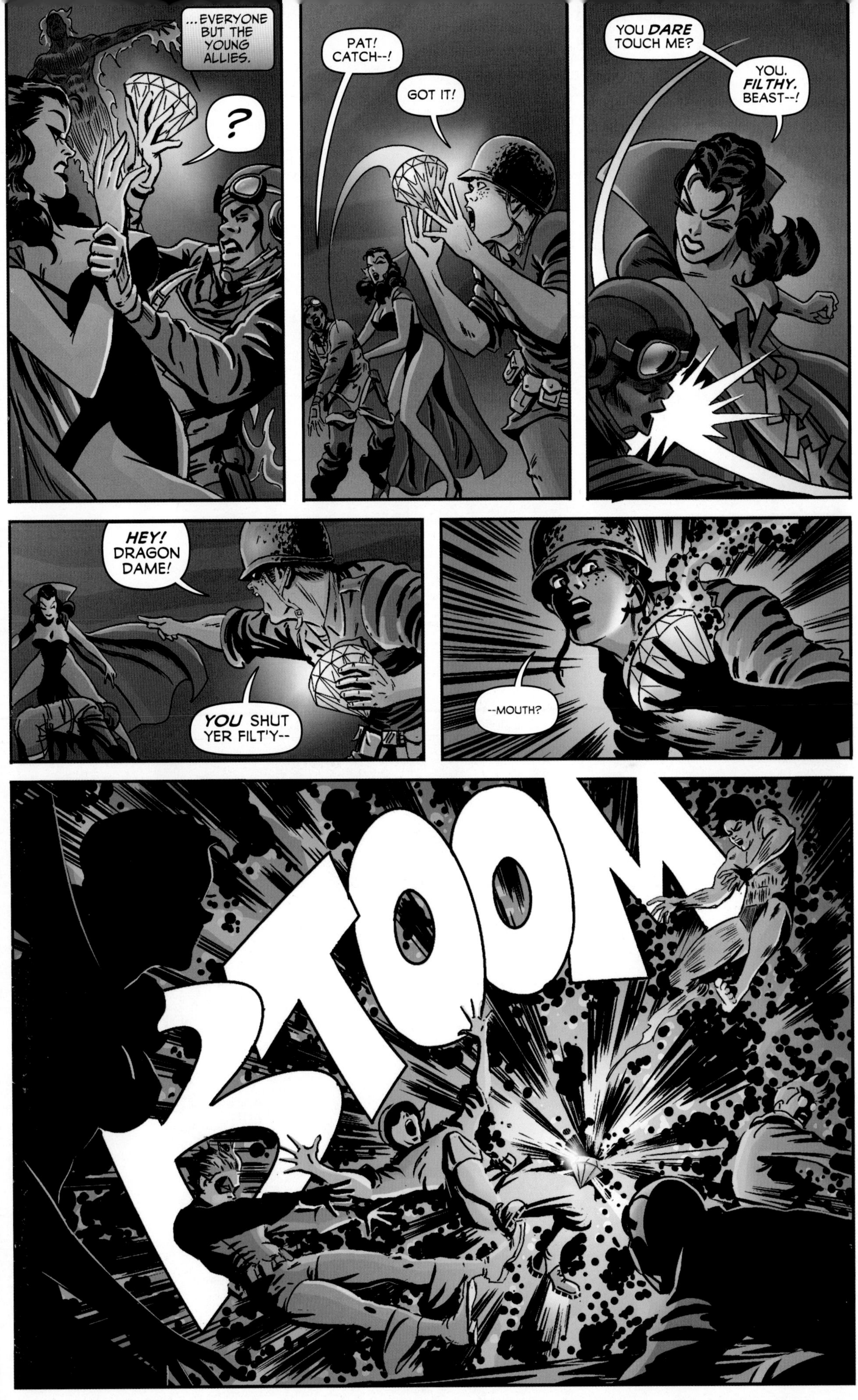
...EVERYONE BUT THE YOUNG ALLIES.
?
PAT! CATCH--!
GOT IT!
YOU DARE TOUCH ME?
YOU. FILTHY. BEAST--!
KRAKK
HEY! DRAGON DAME!
YOU SHUT YER FILT'Y--
--MOUTH?
BTOOM

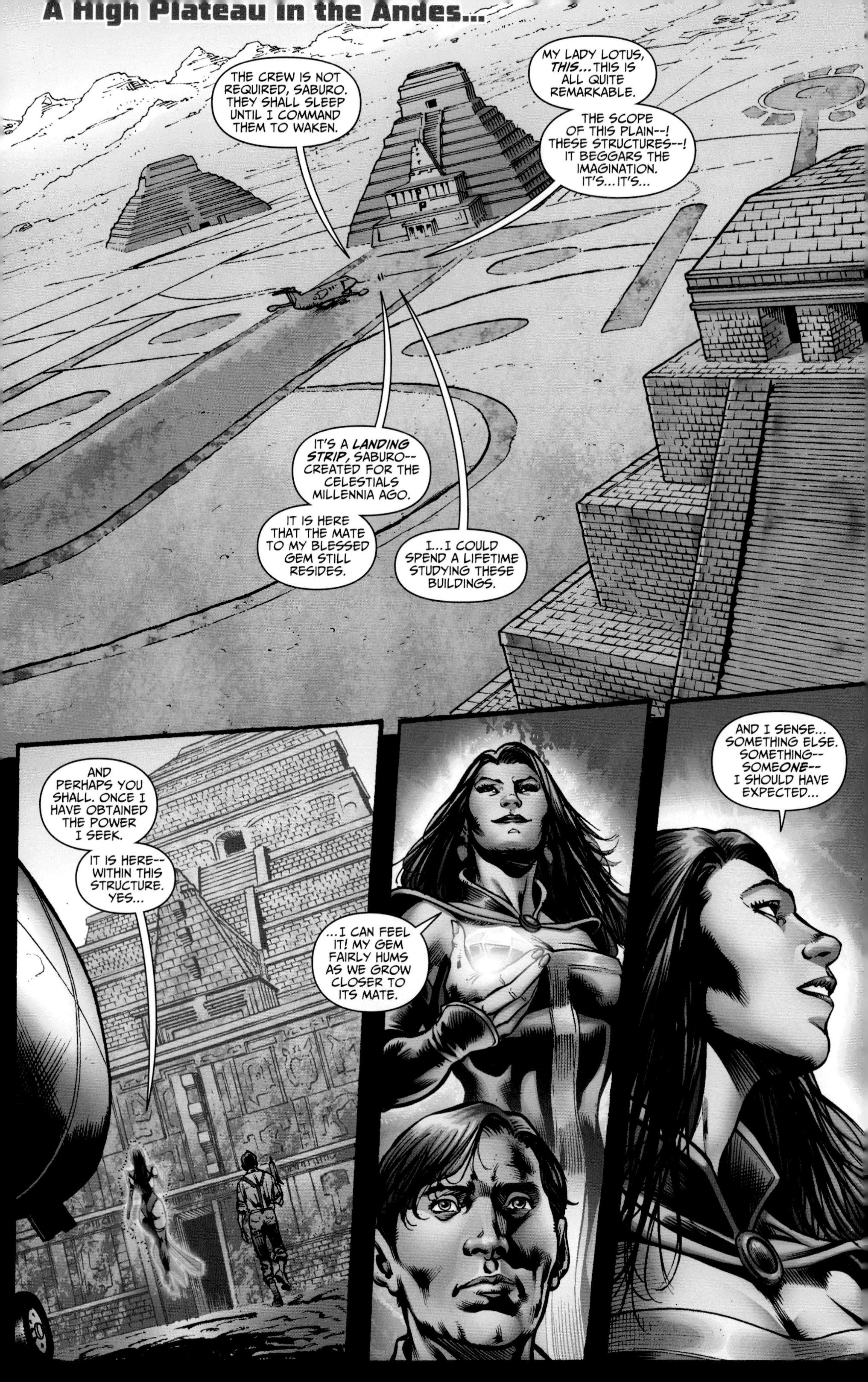
A High Plateau in the Andes...
THE CREW IS NOT REQUIRED, SABURO. THEY SHALL SLEEP UNTIL I COMMAND THEM TO WAKEN.
MY LADY LOTUS, THIS... THIS IS ALL QUITE REMARKABLE.
THE SCOPE OF THIS PLAIN--! THESE STRUCTURES--! IT BEGGARS THE IMAGINATION. IT'S... IT'S...
IT'S A LANDING STRIP, SABURO-- CREATED FOR THE CELESTIALS MILLENNIA AGO.
IT IS HERE THAT THE MATE TO MY BLESSED GEM STILL RESIDES.
I... I COULD SPEND A LIFETIME STUDYING THESE BUILDINGS.
AND PERHAPS YOU SHALL. ONCE I HAVE OBTAINED THE POWER I SEEK.
IT IS HERE-- WITHIN THIS STRUCTURE. YES...
...I CAN FEEL IT! MY GEM FAIRLY HUMS AS WE GROW CLOSER TO ITS MATE.
AND I SENSE... SOMETHING ELSE. SOMETHING-- SOMEONE-- I SHOULD HAVE EXPECTED...

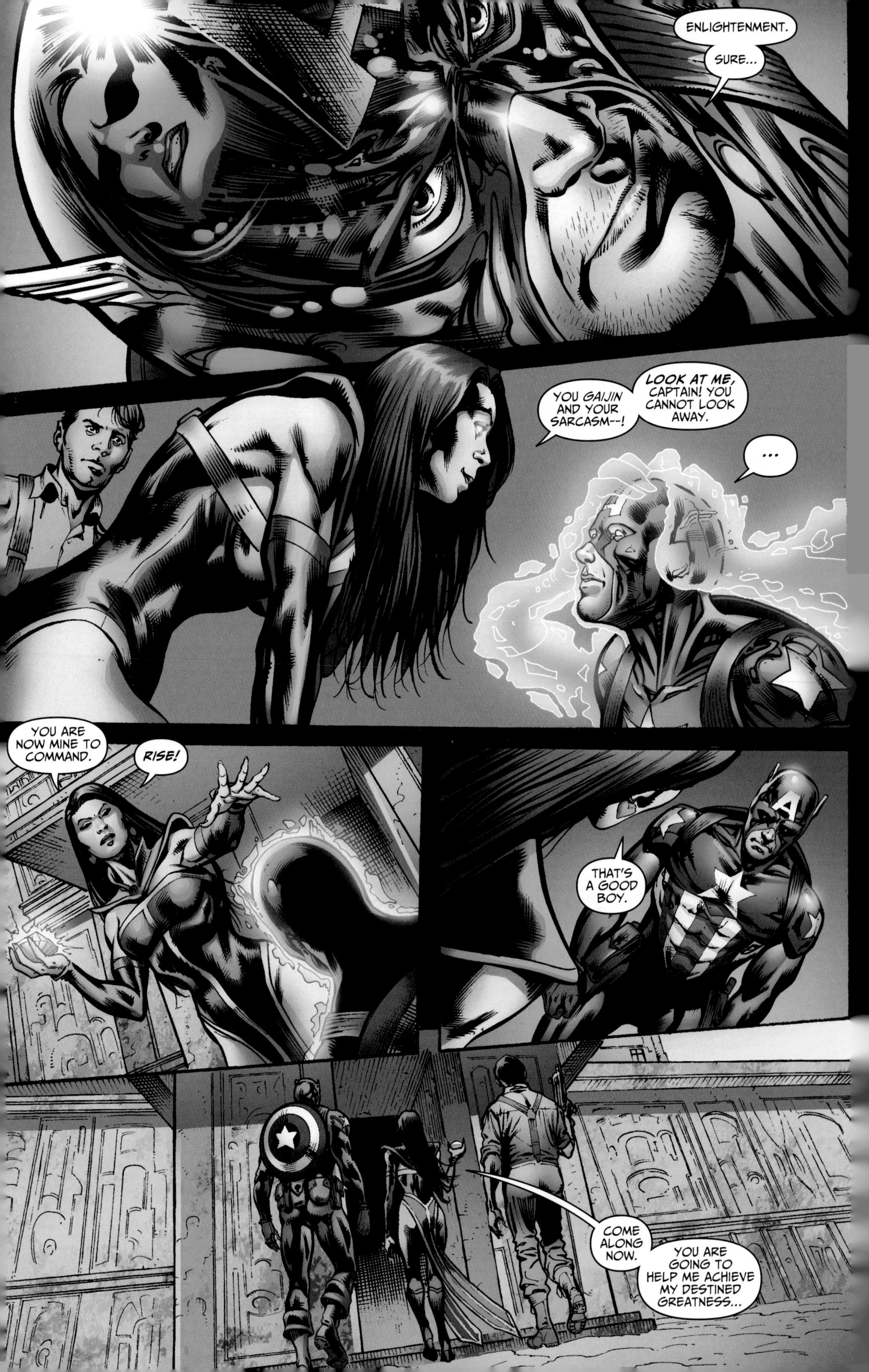

ENLIGHTENMENT.
SURE...
YOU GAIJIN AND YOUR SARCASM--!
LOOK AT ME, CAPTAIN! YOU CANNOT LOOK AWAY.
...
YOU ARE NOW MINE TO COMMAND.
RISE!
THAT'S A GOOD BOY.
COME ALONG NOW.
YOU ARE GOING TO HELP ME ACHIEVE MY DESTINED GREATNESS...

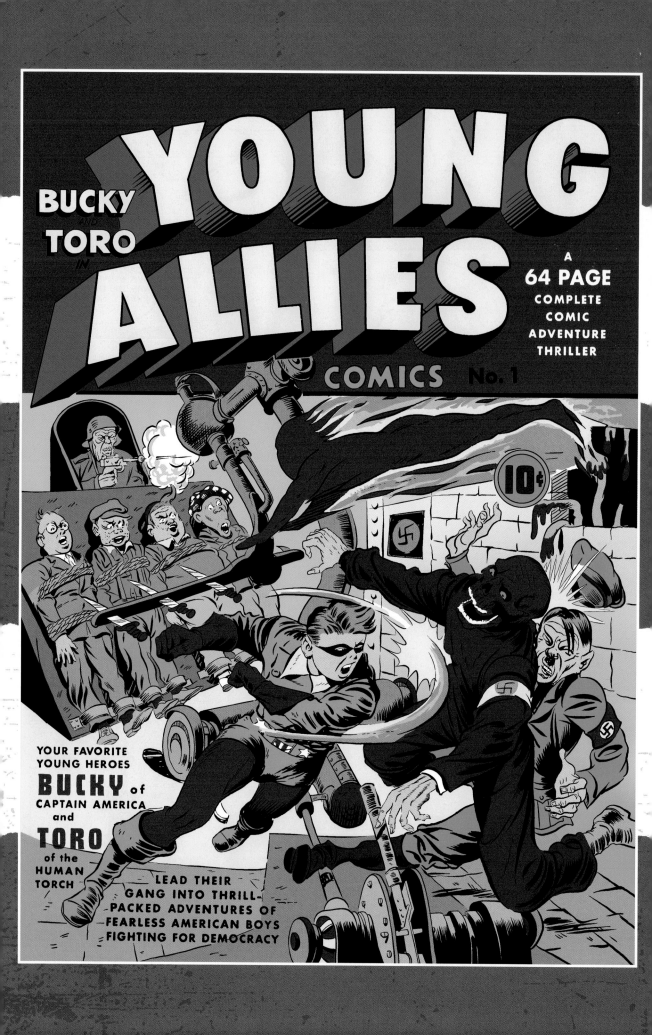

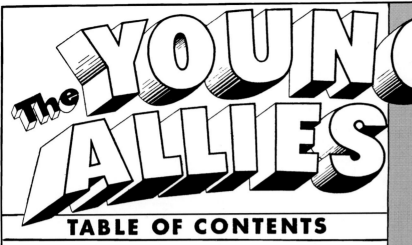

The YOUNG ALLIES

Vol. 1
No. 1
Summer Issue

JOE SIMON
Art editor

JACK KIRBY
Art director

The character TORO is from the Human Torch.

By CARL BURGOS

TABLE OF CONTENTS

CHAPTER I

When the sinister forces of dictator governments reach American shores in pursuit of a secret due to shock the world, a new and powerful group of young patriots spring to the defense of their beloved land.

CHAPTER II

Bucky and his Young Allies have pledged themselves to help Agent Zero of the British Intelligence, for the sake of democracy. But now a sinister menace threatens their very lives, as they come face to face with . . . THE RED SKULL!

CHAPTER III

Determined to keep their promise to dying Agent X, to rescue Agent Zero from the merciless clutches of the insidious RED SKULL, Bucky and his Young Allies make their way to war-torn Europe, into the very heart of Slave-land!

CHAPTER IV

Surrounded by enemies on all sides, the Young Allies now match wits with the relentless, cunning Red Skull, in a daring attempt to steal Agent Zero from under the noses of all Nazidom!

CHAPTER V

The Young Allies and Agent Zero, pursued by the Nazi demons, cross half the world, with death at every turn!

CHAPTER VI

Across the broad Pacific and back to America, after their thrilling odyssey around the world! But again the Red Skull strikes, and only aid can save the Young Allies and Agent Zero . . . aid from THE HUMAN TORCH and CAPTAIN AMERICA!

THE FIRST COWARD: A Short Novelette

Unsolved Mysteries

YOUNG ALLIES is published quarterly by U. S. A. Comic Magazine Corp. at Meriden, Conn. Application for second class entry is pending at the Post Office, at Meriden, Conn., under act of March 3, 1879. Contents copyright 1941 by U. S. A. Comic Magazine Corp., 330 W. 42nd St., New York, N. Y. Single copies 10c. Yearly subscription 40c in the U. S. A. Summer, 1941 issue. Printed in the U.S.A.

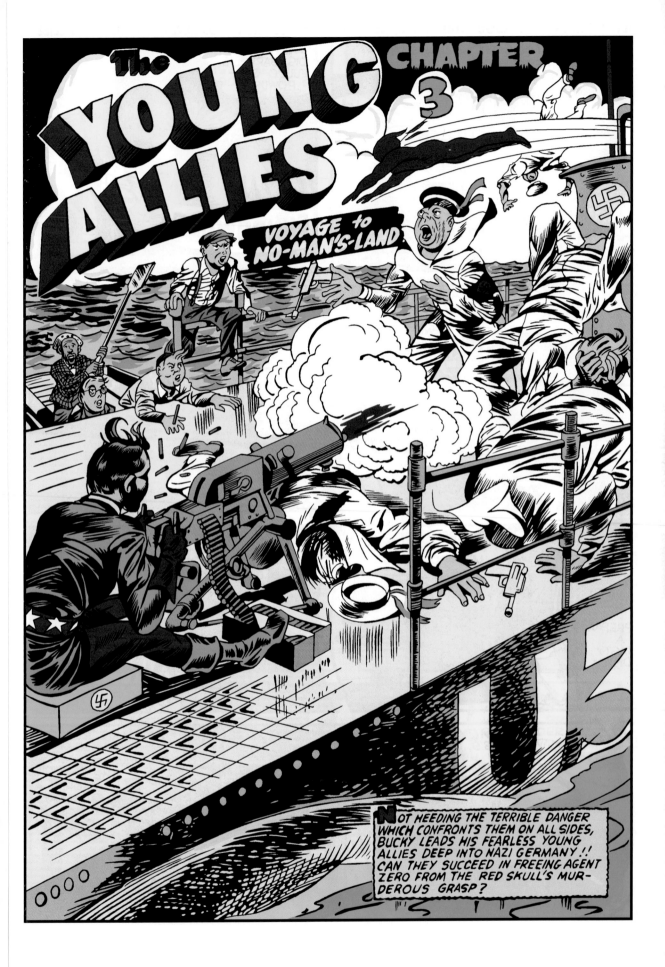

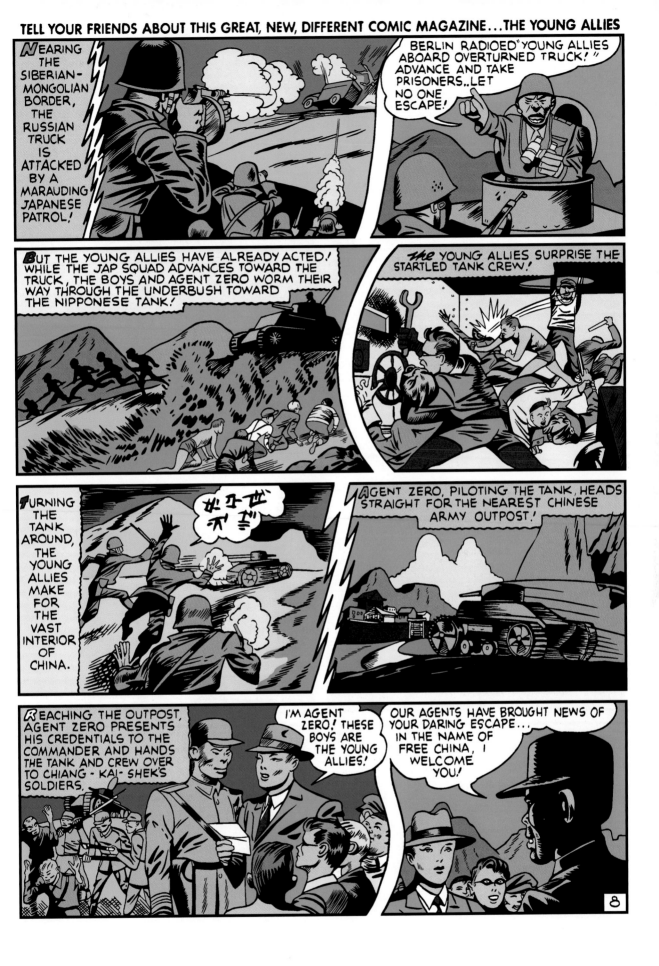

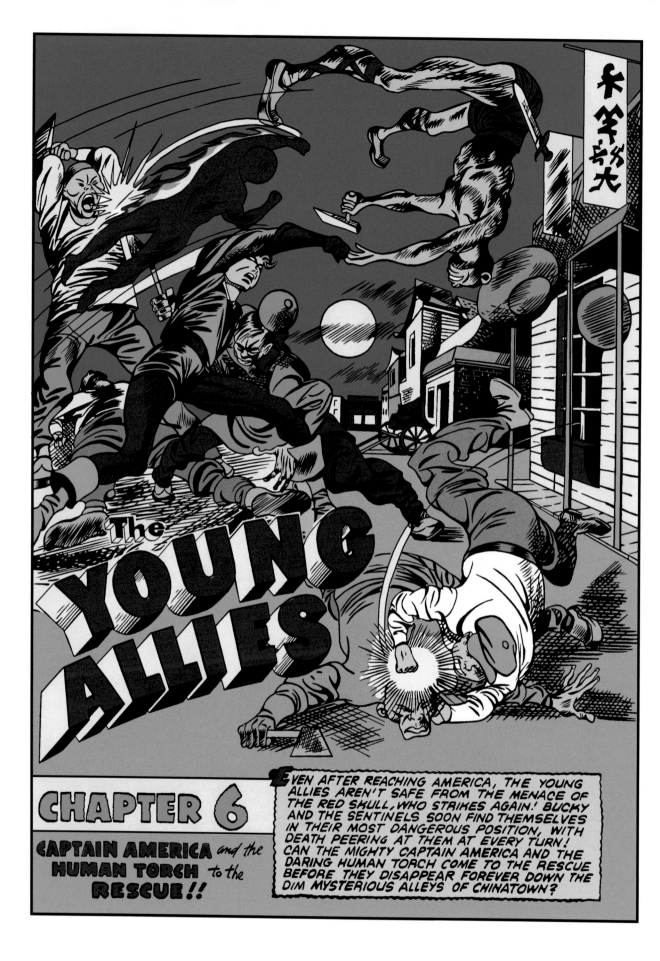

CROOKS ARE COWARDS

"WHAT!" Biff Jenkins cried. "Come again?" Biff was a star reporter for the World Wide Tribune and a bit of a sleuth thrown in.

"I said the Billingslys were just held up for everyrhing they had on them. They were on the way to the yacht hotel from the race track," Burt Higgins told him. "I ran across them on my beat and I'm on my way to call headquarters. Gotta rush. Y'owe me a fiver for this!"

Burt beat it on to the nearest telephone. Biff stood lost in thought for a moment then turned and ran after him. "How much loot did the thugs get?" he asked Burt as they ran side by side.

"Don't know. Didn't take time to question them."

"That's all I want'a know," Biff said, then struck out for the yacht hotel. He had little trouble finding the whereabouts of the frantic couple, although he was afraid at first that they would already be on their yacht, then he probably couldn't have seen them.

"Yes," Mr. Billingsly stated, "You're the first we've released any facts about the robbery to, except to tell the officer that we were robbed."

"Well, listen folks," Biff said, "I have a plan by which the thugs can be brought to justice if you'll work with me."

"Shoot, sonny," the wealthy old man said quickly. "Let's have it."

"D-d-deah me. M-my deah boy," the prostrated Mrs. Billingsly said nervously. "D-do let's have it!"

"Okay," Biff shot. "Listen—"

The Tribune the next morning carried the huge headline: "BILLINGSLYS ROBBED OF 200,000 DOLLARS IN JEWELS".

Biff threw his long legs across his little desk the next morning as he read his own work and a smile wrinkled his freckled nose. "If the executive editor knew what I did," he thought, "he would give me my time and a swift kick!" Now that his little plan was working, Biff didn't feel so bold about having done it. In fact, he was more than a little nervous. But Biff thought he knew who did that job, and if he was right, this was the best way to get them. They were too smart to play the ordinary way. The two Anson brothers were tough, too, and he knew that he was playing with dynamite.

But when the Tribune carried a smaller headline that afternoon: "BILLINGSLY ROBBERS STILL AT LARGE", he smiled again. So far so good.

Biff then went to police headquarters and asked for a couple of men to go with him.

"Ok, Biff," Chief Wells agreed. "But what for?"

"Rather not tell you yet, Chief. I might be wrong, and I wouldn't want to get your hopes aroused."

But Biff didn't admit even to himself that he stood much chance of being wrong. His plans had to work out, because if they didn't, the story would get out and he would lose his job and maybe get into serious trouble. No, he had to be right!

Biff knew John Athey and Bob Robins, the two plain clothes men the chief had let him have. He knew them well; they were two good men and would be right there in case of trouble — which Biff expected — even hoped for. The three of them went through the city that Saturday night in Biff's car, Biff being the only one knowing their destination. And his companions did not ask.

On the outer edge of the business district Biff pulled up in front of a small jewelry store. It was the only jewelry store that wasn't right in the middle of the business district and Biff was certain that if the robbers did as he expected, they would come here. He parked his car and told the plain clothes men

"John, you stroll down one way and you the other, Bob. I expect the two thugs who robbed the Billingslys last night, or more likely just one of them, to come here any minute. If we're careful they won't notice us, it being Saturday night and the streets so crowded. In case of trouble, Bob, you come on in the store right away, and John, you guard the entrance — and don't let anybody out!"

"Wow!" Bob Robins exclaimed. "This *is* something!"

"Boy, oh boy!" John Athey confirmed. "How right you are! And Biff, I hope you're right, too!"

"Not half as much as I do," Biff answered Then suddenly he stiffened — his body tensed. "Oh-oh! Boys, I think we might be late for the party!"

At the same time as his words a shot rang out from the store. A couple of women screamed and people cleared out in front of the place. Biff and his two companions leaped into action. John was the first out of the car and he went bounding into the store.

It was a brave thing to do, but a dangerous one, for a bullet from the thug's gun caught John in the shoulder and knocked him backwards. He fell to the hard marble floor at the entrance to the store and blood spouted from a hole in his vest. You cowards, Bob Robins screamed, as he let go a volley of slugs at the man who had downed John. That man

was disappearing through a door in the back of the jewelry store's front room, and so far as Biff could see he had not been hit. Biff yelled at a couple of pedestrians to take care of John and shot after Bob Robins, his pet twenty-five automatic in his hand.

By the time Biff caught up with Bob they were both at the door that entered into the front of the jewelry store, and the thug — there was only one — was going out the back door that opened into the alley. Heavy brick buildings lined the alley on each side. Before running into the alley he poured a couple of bullets back at the two men after him. Both bullets went wild, the closest crashing through the door Biff had just come through.

Biff was the first to the back door and when he raced through it and into the alley the robber was already far down the alley. Biff took careful aim and fired. But the short little automatic was made only for close range and the thug kept running. Soon he would be at the end of the alley and lost in the Saturday night crowds. This was one time Biff felt like swearing. There was only one thing to do; run after the fellow.

But just as Biff started to run there was a blast at his shoulder that felt as though it would break his eardrums. The report of Bob Robin's service revolver.

The hands of the man at the end of the alley reached frantically toward the skies for something that wasn't there. He careened crazily, then fell flat on his face. Biff reached around and grabbed Bob's hand, shook it. "Nice work," he complimented.

"But Biff," Chief Wells asked later. "How did you happen to

know the thug would be at that jewelry store?"

They were standing beside John Athey's bed at the hospital. Will, smiling, said: "Yeah, I think I deserve to know that, too." The doctor had said John would be OK in a few weeks.

"You certainly do!" Biff admitted. "Well, you see, I asked the Billingslys to let me state in my story that the jewels the thugs took from them were worth two hundred thousand, when in reality they were worth only a thousand bucks. I knew when the thugs read that in the paper they would think they got more than they expected, thus demand more of their fence. But their fence would tell them the stuff wasn't worth what they wanted, and naturally the thugs wouldn't believe him. They'd rather take a chance on going to some small jewelry store and getting the stuff evaluated. To play safe they'd pick a place as far out from town as possible, so if the jeweler became suspicious and called the law, or they had to quiet him they'd be on their way out of town. The little place where we nabbed the thief was the only logical one I could figure, the only one not in the middle of town. Need I say more?"

"Well I'll be darned," Chief Wells exclaimed.

"All thieves are cowards and all cowards get caught in the end," Biff Jenkins explained. "So with the other thug in irons from the confession of his buddy and John here getting better every day, and the little jeweler the same way, I'd better go do a little explaining to the executive editor!"

THE END

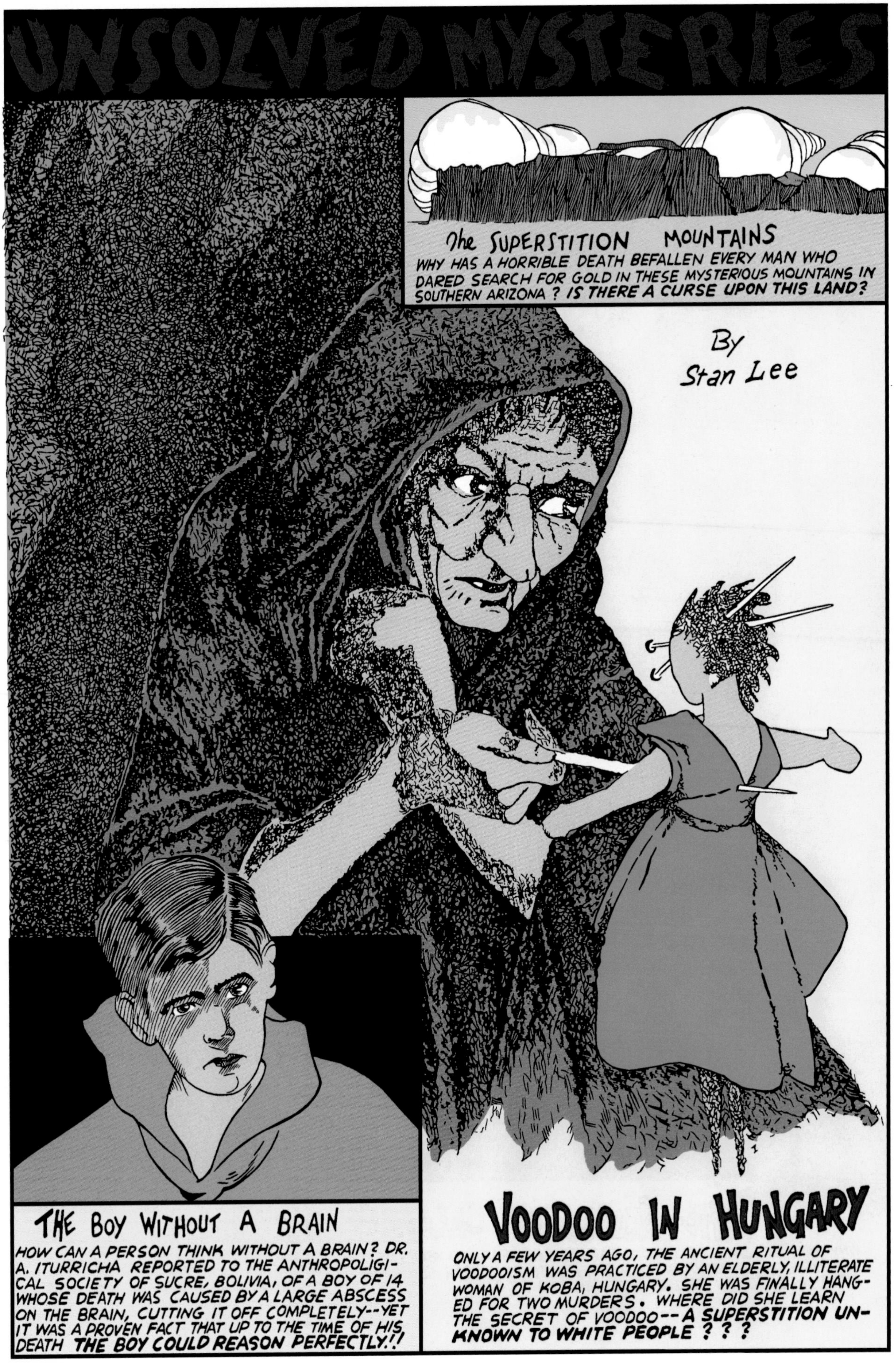

UNSOLVED MYSTERIES
The SUPERSTITION MOUNTAINS
WHY HAS A HORRIBLE DEATH BEFALLEN EVERY MAN WHO DARED SEARCH FOR GOLD IN THESE MYSTERIOUS MOUNTAINS IN SOUTHERN ARIZONA ? IS THERE A CURSE UPON THIS LAND?
By Stan Lee
THE BOY WITHOUT A BRAIN
HOW CAN A PERSON THINK WITHOUT A BRAIN? DR. A. ITURRICHA REPORTED TO THE ANTHROPOLIGICAL SOCIETY OF SUCRE, BOLIVIA, OF A BOY OF 14 WHOSE DEATH WAS CAUSED BY A LARGE ABSCESS ON THE BRAIN, CUTTING IT OFF COMPLETELY--YET IT WAS A PROVEN FACT THAT UP TO THE TIME OF HIS DEATH THE BOY COULD REASON PERFECTLY!!
VOODOO IN HUNGARY
ONLY A FEW YEARS AGO, THE ANCIENT RITUAL OF VOODOOISM WAS PRACTICED BY AN ELDERLY, ILLITERATE WOMAN OF KOBA, HUNGARY. SHE WAS FINALLY HANGED FOR TWO MURDERS. WHERE DID SHE LEARN THE SECRET OF VOODOO--A SUPERSTITION UNKNOWN TO WHITE PEOPLE ???

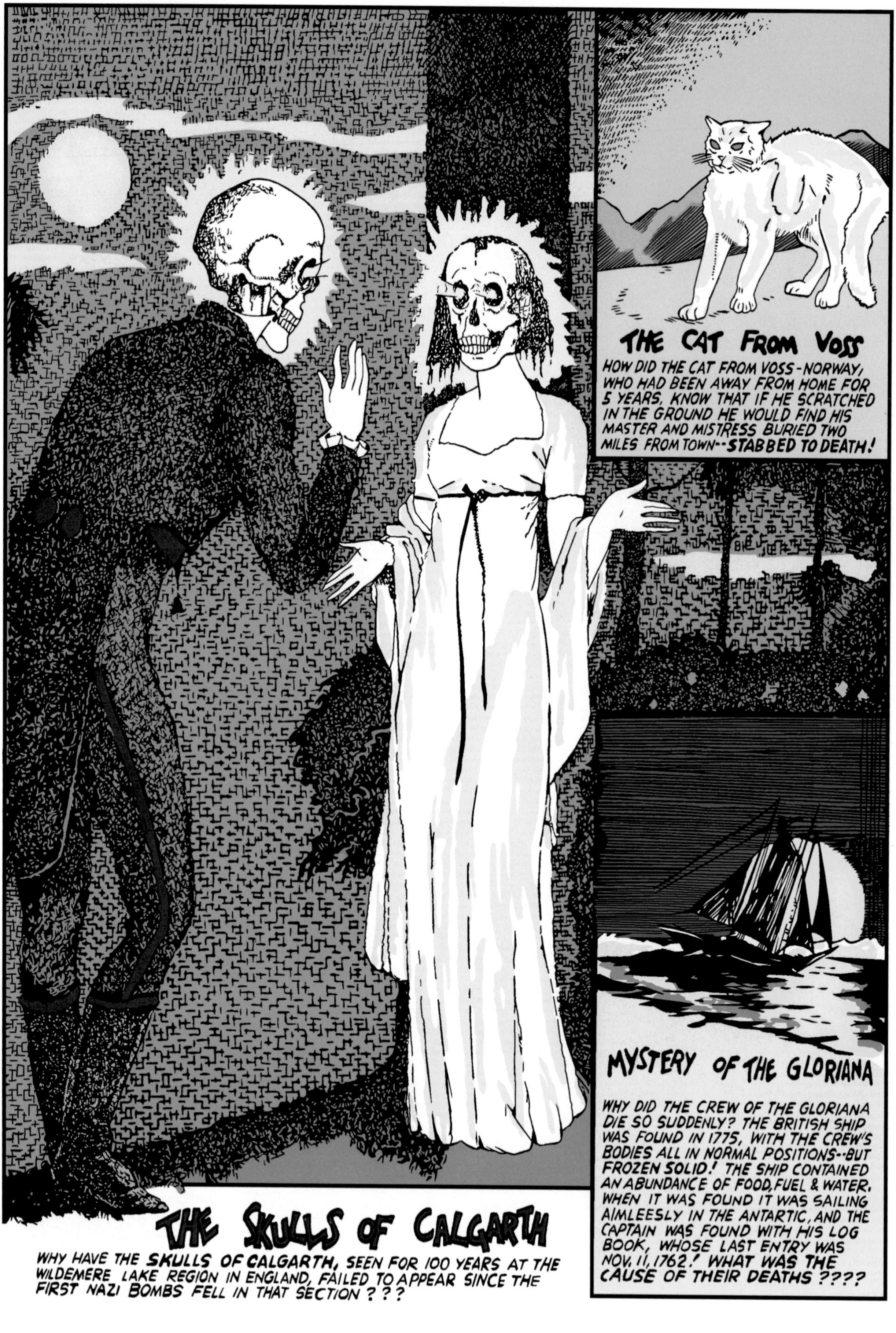
THE CAT FROM VOSS
HOW DID THE CAT FROM VOSS-NORWAY, WHO HAD BEEN AWAY FROM HOME FOR 5 YEARS, KNOW THAT IF HE SCRATCHED IN THE GROUND HE WOULD FIND HIS MASTER AND MISTRESS BURIED TWO MILES FROM TOWN--STABBED TO DEATH!
MYSTERY OF THE GLORIANA
WHY DID THE CREW OF THE GLORIANA DIE SO SUDDENLY? THE BRITISH SHIP WAS FOUND IN 1775, WITH THE CREW'S BODIES ALL IN NORMAL POSITIONS--BUT FROZEN SOLID! THE SHIP CONTAINED AN ABUNDANCE OF FOOD, FUEL & WATER. WHEN IT WAS FOUND IT WAS SAILING AIMLEESLY IN THE ANTARTIC, AND THE CAPTAIN WAS FOUND WITH HIS LOG BOOK, WHOSE LAST ENTRY WAS NOV. 11, 1762! WHAT WAS THE CAUSE OF THEIR DEATHS????
THE SKULLS OF CALGARTH
WHY HAVE THE SKULLS OF CALGARTH, SEEN FOR 100 YEARS AT THE WILDEMERE LAKE REGION IN ENGLAND, FAILED TO APPEAR SINCE THE FIRST NAZI BOMBS FELL IN THAT SECTION???

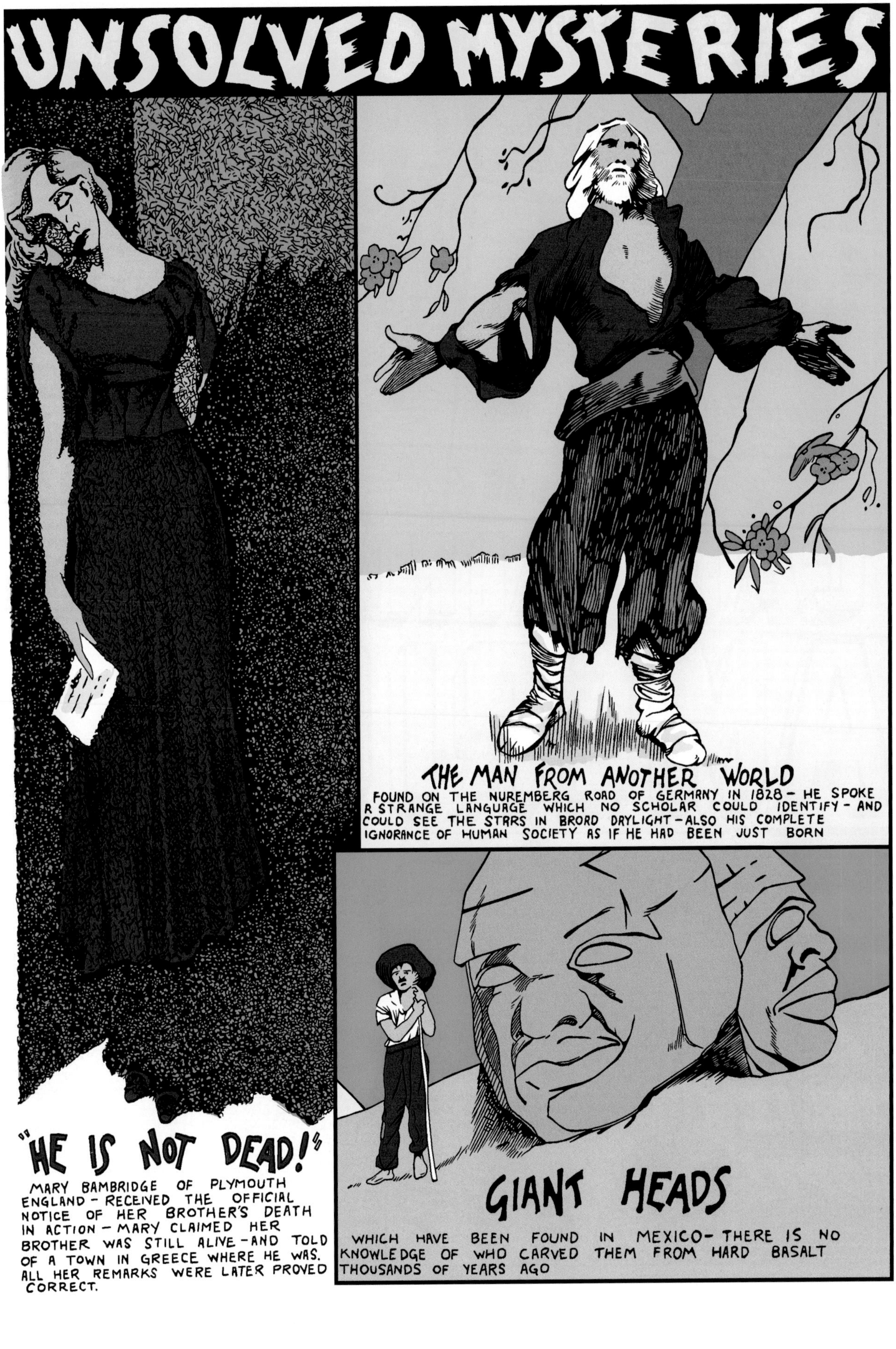
UNSOLVED MYSTERIES
THE MAN FROM ANOTHER WORLD
FOUND ON THE NUREMBERG ROAD OF GERMANY IN 1828 – HE SPOKE A STRANGE LANGUAGE WHICH NO SCHOLAR COULD IDENTIFY – AND COULD SEE THE STARS IN BROAD DAYLIGHT – ALSO HIS COMPLETE IGNORANCE OF HUMAN SOCIETY AS IF HE HAD BEEN JUST BORN
"HE IS NOT DEAD!"
MARY BAMBRIDGE OF PLYMOUTH ENGLAND – RECEIVED THE OFFICIAL NOTICE OF HER BROTHER'S DEATH IN ACTION – MARY CLAIMED HER BROTHER WAS STILL ALIVE – AND TOLD OF A TOWN IN GREECE WHERE HE WAS. ALL HER REMARKS WERE LATER PROVED CORRECT.
GIANT HEADS
WHICH HAVE BEEN FOUND IN MEXICO – THERE IS NO KNOWLEDGE OF WHO CARVED THEM FROM HARD BASALT THOUSANDS OF YEARS AGO

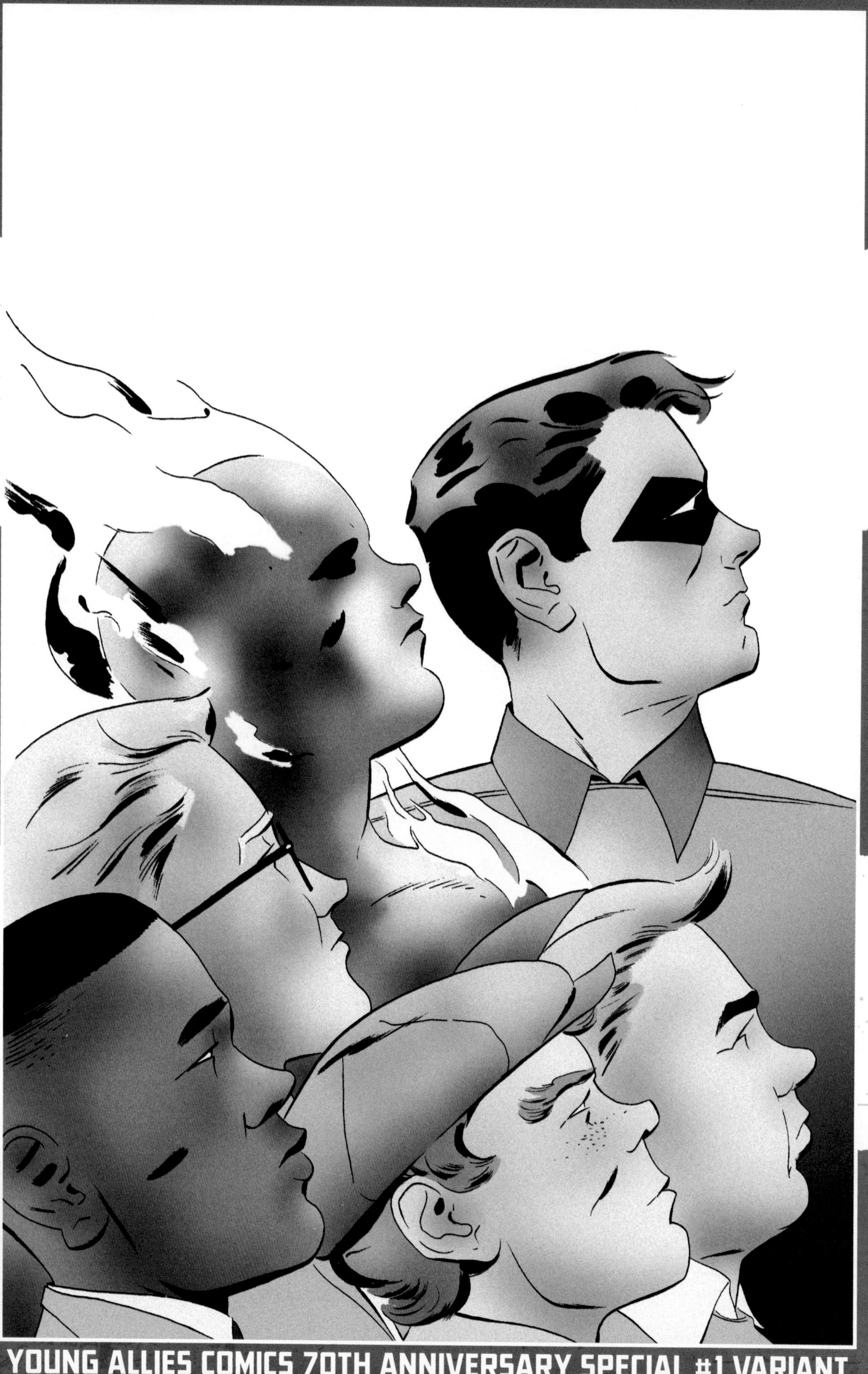

YOUNG ALLIES COMICS 70TH ANNIVERSARY SPECIAL #1 VARIANT
BY MARCOS MARTIN

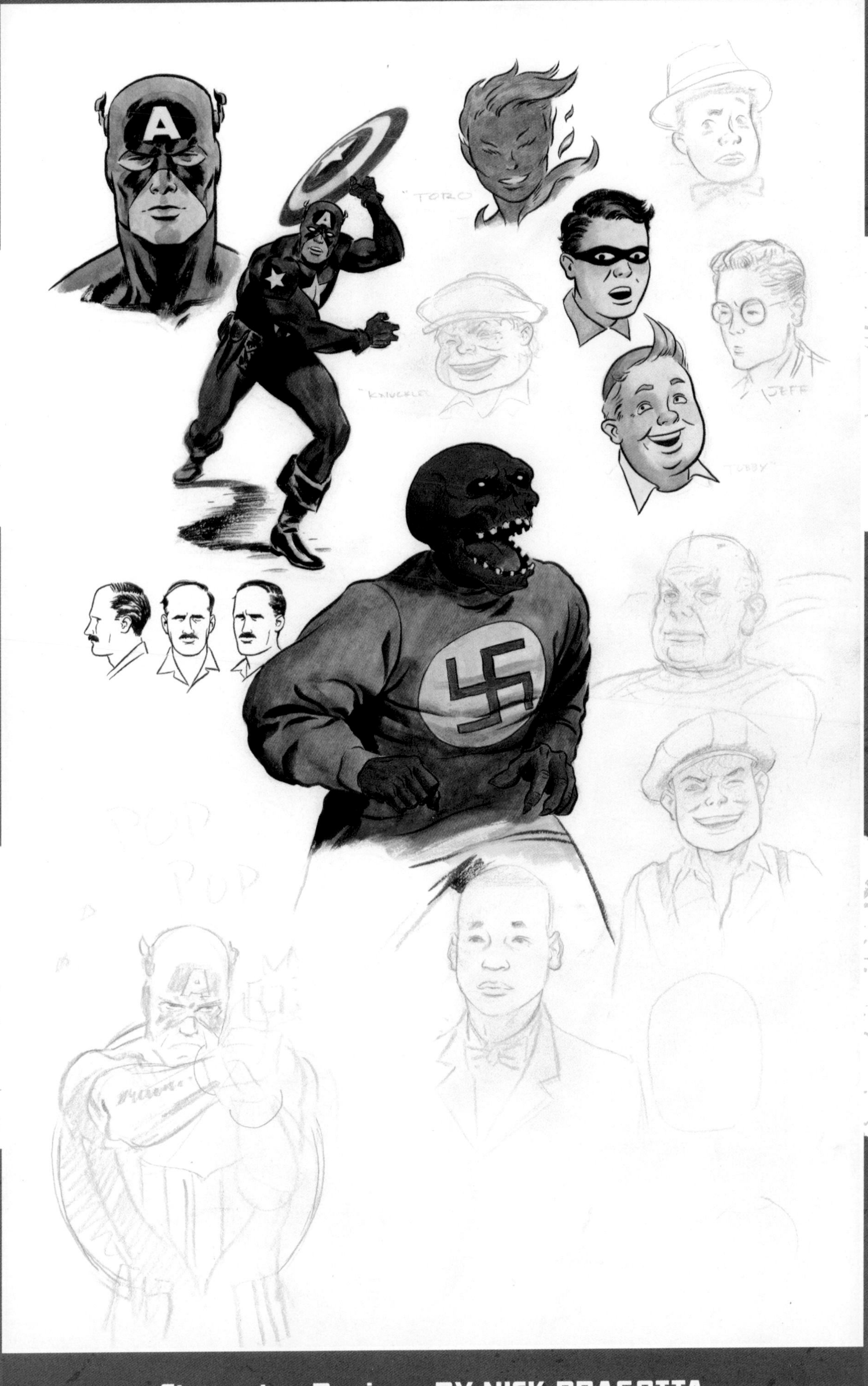
"TORO"
"KNUCKLES"
JEFF
"TUBBY"

Character Designs BY NICK DRAGOTTA

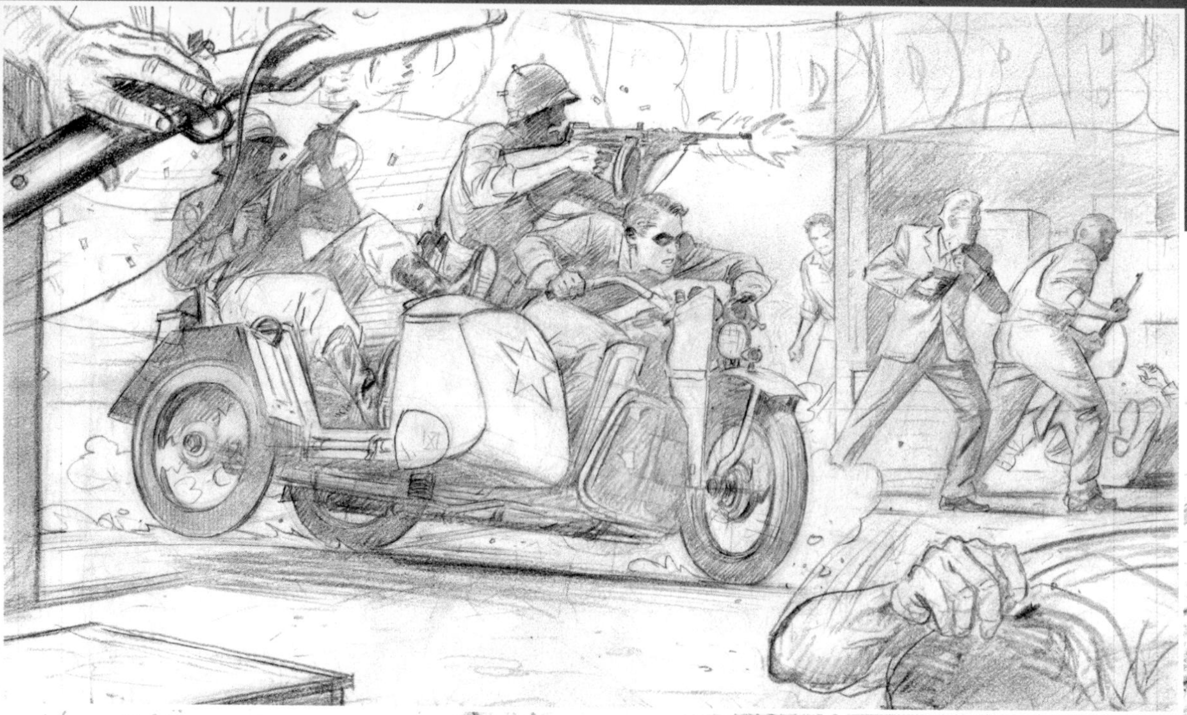

Young Allies Comics #1
70th Anniversary
Special page 13, panel 3
pencils by
NICK DRAGOTTA

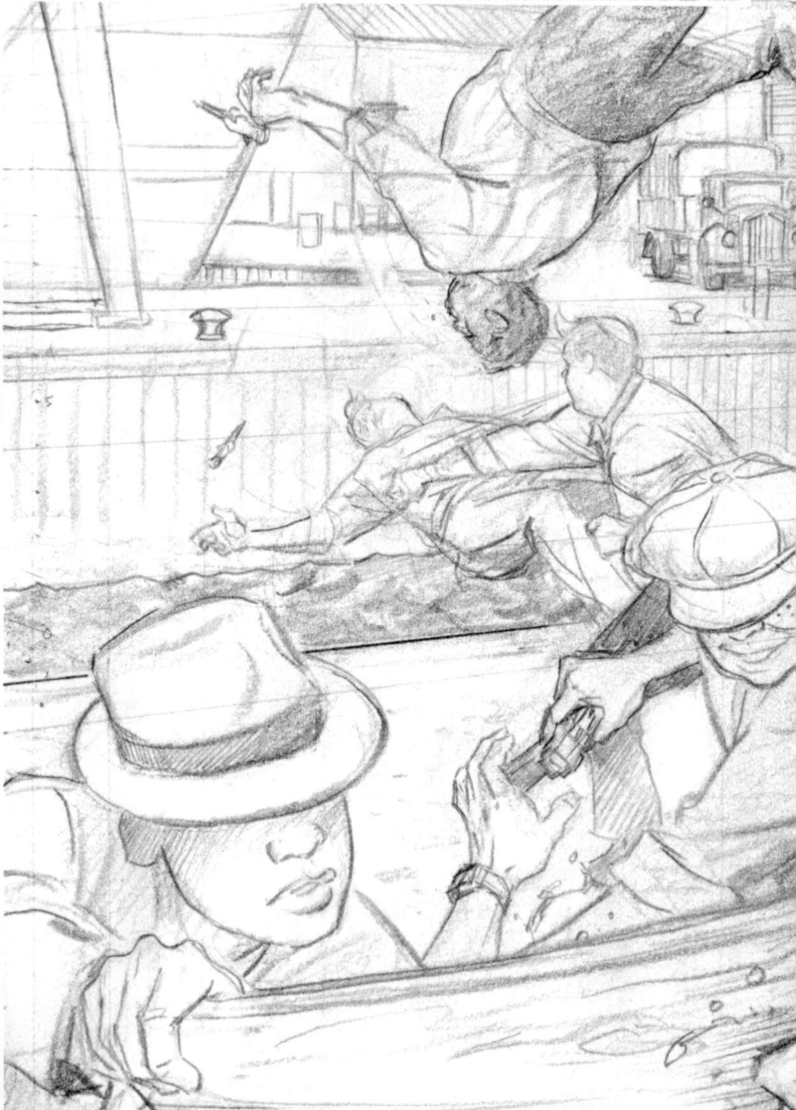

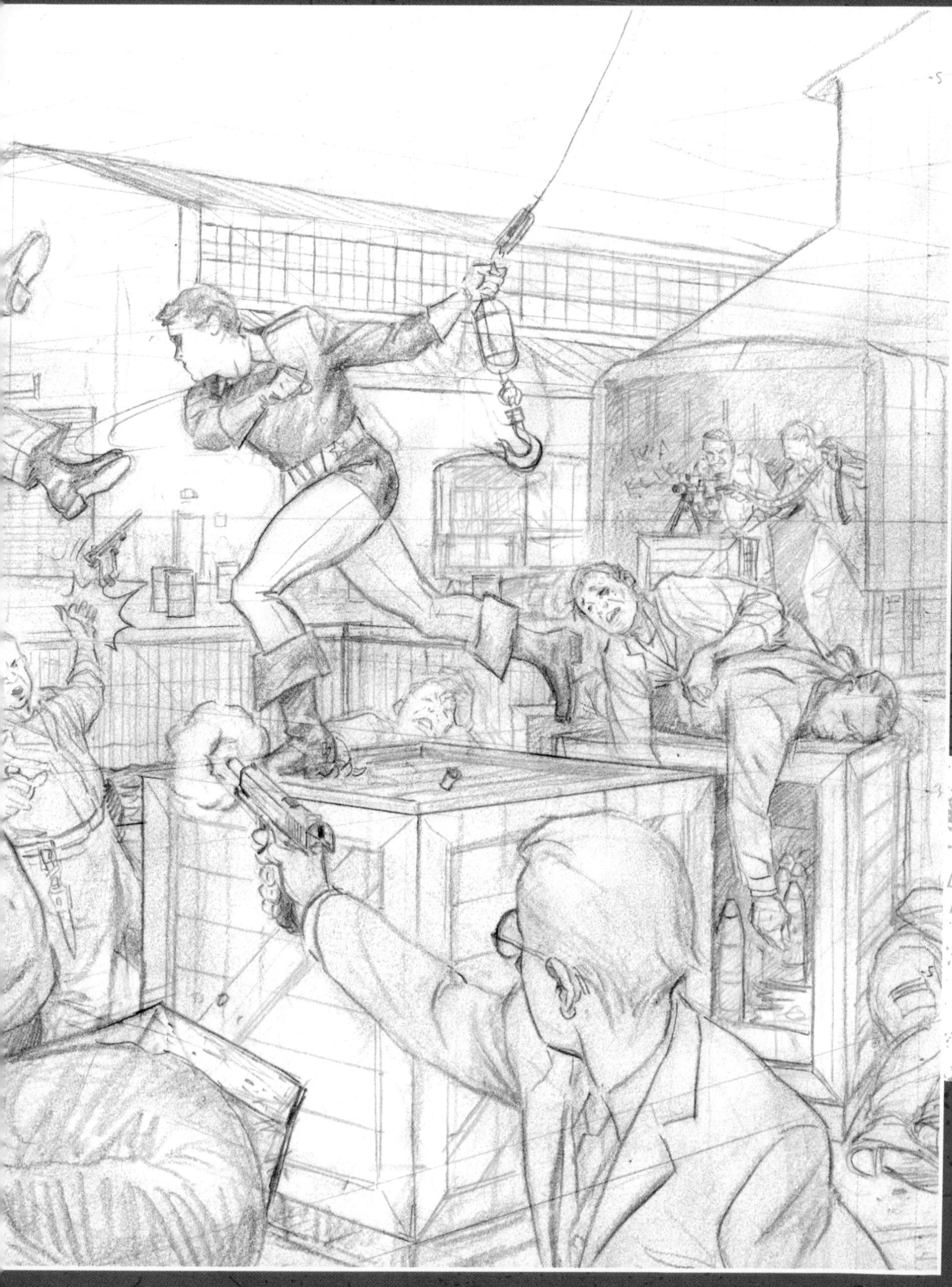

Young Allies Comics #1 70th Anniversary Special
page 4, panel 1 pencils by NICK DRAGOTTA

Captain America: Forever Allies #1 page 1 pencils
BY NICK DRAGOTTA